ILLUSTRATIONS OF INSTINCT.

Καὶ Πνεῦμα ἐν τοῖς πᾶσι.—Ἐκκλησ. C. 3. V. 19.

Nihil agere cum Animus non posset, in his studiis ab initio versatus, existimavi honestissime molestias posse deponi, si me ad Philosophiam retulissem.—CICERO de Officiis. Lib. 1.

ILLUSTRATIONS OF INSTINCT

DEDUCED FROM THE HABITS OF

BRITISH ANIMALS.

BY JONATHAN COUCH, F.L.S.

MEMBER OF THE ROYAL GEOLOGICAL SOCIETY AND OF THE ROYAL
INSTITUTION OF CORNWALL, &c.

———————

LONDON:

JOHN VAN VOORST, PATERNOSTER ROW.

M.DCCC.XLVII.

PREFACE.

Englshort Poets and Philosophers have said, that in his actions Man is governed by Reason, as Animals are by Instinct ; and they represent the latter principle as an unreflecting impulse, which, under all circumstances, "must go right," without consciousness or control in the creature possessing it. It is a consequence of this mode of regarding the subject, that some striking displays of intelligent action among animals have been passed over with little or no attention ; and we have lost the advantage of the lessons they might have taught us in the philosophy of even the human understanding. These creatures also have thus been degraded from the condition they might have occupied, of useful servants or amusing companions, into one of alienation, uselessness, or enmity.

It is one object of the following Work to afford

a different estimate of the animal creation; and while other students of Nature are directing their inquiries to the elucidation of their anatomical structure and the relation of their affinities, the Author's wish is to point out the path by which a better knowledge may be acquired of the conditions of their intellectual existence; the links of the chain that connects insensible with intelligent Being; and the variation which the latter is capable of, when subjected to the influence of disturbing or exciting causes.

Fortified also by the authority of some eminent observers, he has ventured to believe, in the words of Milton, that

They reason not contemptibly;

and that if a higher degree of training were founded on a close study of their individual faculties, the result would be of importance to human interests.

In extending this inquiry into the intellectual dispositions of animals to some of its more minute particulars, preference has been given to examples derived from the creatures of our own country: because these are best known to an ordinary inquirer; and because it is the Author's desire to call into this field of examination a greater number of men capable of useful observations, if their attention were once directed to the pursuit.

Many curious habits remain undescribed, to reward the industry and patience of an observer who will study them abroad in the fields and woods; and the arts by which the wild animals of Britain still maintain their standing among us, in spite of the exterminating endeavours of their great enemy, and amidst so many other opposing influences, form perhaps the most interesting portion of their history.

CONTENTS.

CHAPTER I.

CHAPTER II.

CHAPTER III.

CHAPTER IV.

CHAPTER XII.

CHAPTER XIII.

CHAPTER XIV.

CHAPTER XV.

CHAPTER XVI.

CHAPTER XVII.

CHAPTER XVIII.

ILLUSTRATIONS OF INSTINCT.

CHAPTER I.

To acquire an accurate idea of the intrinsic nature of the faculty termed Instinct, it will be requisite, first, to notice the conditions of living existence below it in the scale of nature; in order that, by tracing the successive manifestations of the increasing faculties, we may understand the precise station which this faculty occupies in the ascending scale, and the means through which its operations are developed. We shall thus be taught that it is not so much an insulated faculty, of which the tissues and organs are no more than instruments — as an accumulation of powers combined together, and occupying a step in the course of a transition from the lowest to a higher condition of natural rank; so that its variation or degree is due to the modification of these inferior powers which together form its constituent parts.

B

It is a modern discovery, that a knowledge of the higher orders of natural beings is best obtained by first studying the structure and functions of those creatures which possess the simplest organization, and which are consequently lowest in the order of existence;—by examining them, in fact, according to the order in which their Author was pleased to call them into being: for thus we reap the advantage of observing functions in action in a simple living being, constituted of no more than a texture or tissue, unmixed with any other organization that might modify or overrule the actions of its living properties.

And in making our primary selection of such a living body for the purposes of this study, it is of little importance whether the object of our choice be vegetable or animal; since, though the higher classes of the former, as well as of the latter, possess great complication of structure and function, in the lower families of each, where these apparently very distinct departments of creation approach near to each other in affinity, the line of demarcation becomes so obscure, and both are in all respects so simple, as to place them much on the same level.

It cannot be affirmed of these, that they have any actions, in the usual sense of that word; and their functions are the simplest results of the composition or structure of their tissue, quickened into independent existence by the endowment of life; by which we mean that ultimate principle that to a living entity is what gravity is to a dead mass, but whose real nature has eluded the researches of the inquirer in both cases.

The whole duty of the existence of these creatures appears to be

"——to draw nutrition, propagate, and rot;"

and the only faculty with which they seem to be endued for this purpose, is what Bichat has denominated *organic* sensibility, and Dr. Fletcher irritation; and which consists in a "perception, by organized beings, of certain stimuli acting upon them otherwise than mechanically or chemically." And yet, in this definition, the word perception is liable to some misapprehension, as the action or function is absolutely without any degree or kind of consciousness. The humble station which they occupy in the scale of being is owing to the nature of the tissue of which they are composed: for, as we shall have occasion to remark when speaking of a higher advance in nature, a more highly-organized tissue will bring us to a class which will display, though still without consciousness, many more of the signs of being a living animal. But when these creatures of the lowest series lay hold of external assistance for the fulfilment of their natural functions, no *animal* sensibility is exercised, no choice manifested; and all that can be called an approach to a semblance of these faculties is, that if a substance be placed near them, for which their tissue or organization has no natural affinity, they do not give it admittance. The endosmodic surface may become corrugated or impervious, or an orifice may close, and so reject what if admitted might have been hurtful;—and yet this is not done because it is known or felt to be hurtful or abhorrent; but it is unconsciously, and while life continues we might almost say mechanically, incapable of admitting this enemy to its existence.

The internal mucous lining of an organ in the higher classes of creatures will detain fluids during life, and assist them in moving along their course; but as soon as the vital powers have left them, it is common to find the same membrane losing this retentive property, and becoming penetrated by its contents; which thus are seen diffused through the neighbouring structures: a circumstance peculiarly liable to happen with the gall bladder and the bile. This remarkable affinity of composition and structure, as regards membrane, may be further instanced in that quality which causes it to give admission and passage to water, in preference to what seems a much more subtle fluid—spirit of wine; and it is the somewhat similar texture of sponge that enables it to admit a large quantity of fluid, which the principle of life within it excites it to propel onward for its own support and nutriment, and, in furtherance of the same power, when it has suffered a change, afterwards enables it to repel. Some species of mosses also, which have not only become dry and shrivelled, but are absolutely dead, will on the application of moisture again expand, and assume the appearance of living growth. The Club Moss of California exhibits an interesting appearance of this; and Linnæus informs us of a skilful adaptation of this property, in another species, to human convenience: "The bountiful provision of nature is evinced in providing mankind with bed and bedding in this savage wilderness. The great Hair moss (*Polytrichum commune*), called by the Laplanders Romsi, grows copiously in their damp forests, and is used for this purpose. They choose the starry-headed plants, out of the tufts of which they cut a surface as large as they please for a bed or bolster, separating it from the earth beneath; and although the shoots are scarcely branched, they are nevertheless so entangled at the roots as not to be separable from each other. This mossy cushion is very soft and elastic, not growing hard by pressure. If it becomes too dry and compressed, its former elasticity is restored by a little moisture." —*Lachesis Lapponica*, vol. I. p. 171.

This principle of action is widely, perhaps universally, diffused among vegetables; and in some of the lower forms of this class, as Nostoch and the Lichens, it is the chief means of supplying the materials and mode of growth: as it is also in the various species of sponge.*

The Hydra (*H. viridis*), a species of Polyp, resembling the animal portion of some species of Coral, but destitute of a bony skeleton, possesses its natural faculties so equally diffused through the body, that if the cavity which has acted as its stomach be everted, and the creature be thus turned inside out, while the new external surface

---

* The animal body named acephalocyst is in reality the most simple separate existing creature in nature: if that can be called separate, that can only exist in another body. This therefore might have been taken as an example of primary animal life; but others have been preferred, though higher in the scale, and more organized, because they are better known to the public.

now loses its former digestive powers, the newly-formed cavity enters on the possession of all that the other has been deprived of.

The principle inherent in these tissues is widely extended among creatures even of high organization; though from their more complicated structure, and the preponderance of other tissues and organs, it occupies among them a less conspicuous place. Thus the common Snail (*Helix aspersa*), when the air is dry, will remain for a long time torpid; but when it becomes charged with moisture and warmth, the mucous surface of the animal immediately attracts and absorbs it; other sensibilities are quickened; and without any other stimulus, the torpid creature awakes to activity. The more highly-organized Frog and Toad, from the nature of their skin, are excited by similar influences; without the operation of which they might remain in a state of insensibility for an unlimited duration: a circumstance which will go far to explain the alleged fact of their existence for ages in cavities of trees and blocks of stone or coal, although not to account for the manner in which they have thus become enclosed. Several of the highest order of animals are known to be much affected in their sensations by similar causes; and hence the Cat washes its face, and the Hog carries straws in its mouth, prophetic of moist weather and of wind. The Leech in a glass, and even fish in the depth of the sea, are thus sensible to atmospheric changes: the latter, considering their immersion at so considerable a depth, remarkably so ; and even man himself, fenced about as he is by artificial protection, cannot boast of being exempt from similar influences. They have, indeed, an important bearing on his comforts, as well as on the pathology of his inward organs; and thus we are compelled to learn that an organization, which constitutes almost the whole existence of the lower forms of creation, is still important in the higher ; and if it be less taken notice of, it is only because it is mixed with other characters, to which it is subordinate, or by which it is concealed.

The next ascending step in the scale of existence is, when *organic* sensibility, or, as it may be more properly termed, irritability, is added to the former condition ; so that not only are there vessels and tissues adapted to receive and circulate fluids, or matters congenial to their nature ; but we perceive actions excited beyond the mere range of the immediate influence of these tissues ; and these again communicated, by sympathy of connection, to organs of another fabric, and tissues of another nature. They even expand or contract in such a manner as to convey to an observer the impression of suffering or enjoyment ; but as this sensation is clearly without consciousness, it would be an error to characterize it by a name that shall imply the presence of mental phenomena, or even animal feelings.

This irritability, therefore, is not something infused into the muscular structure, as capable of being distinguished from its living essence ; nor is sensibility, in a class of tissue of still higher

nature, to be regarded as something superadded
to a living nerve: "but in virtue of the power
which brought those forms into existence, these
forms have, with their existence, their properties
also. Every organ therefore bears within itself
the cause of its own phenomena. By means of
its own powers it is nourished, grows, performs
its office in the animal economy; and though its
connexion with the rest of the body, as part of
a whole, must be maintained as a condition of the
maintenance of its powers, yet this connexion is
but a condition, and not a cause of those powers."—
(*British and Foreign Medical Review*, No. IX. p. 79.)
The action, therefore, which flows from irritability
of fibre, does not stand in need of a nerve for
its development, as we see in many animals and
all vegetables, which are altogether destitute of
such structure; but the presence of a nerve conveys
a much higher faculty, and besides the bestowment
of its own powers, still more powerfully unites the
organs into one consentaneous whole. There is
reason to suppose that the existence of unconscious
irritability is not confined to the nerves of simple
sensation; but that some creatures which, in the
scale of natural progression, rise above the level of
the classes whose properties are comprised within
the limits of mere reactive sensitiveness, or irritability, are furnished with organs that, without
enabling them to discern visible objects, yet answer
peculiarly to the impressions of light. The ocel-
lated spots which are placed round the fringe of
the mantle in the Pectens, and some other shell-

fish, and at the extremities of the Starfishes (*Asteriadæ*), appear to possess this essential property of an eye, without conveying the conscious sight of any distinct object. It is not improbable also that the sensation of hearing may be possessed by some creatures without being endowed with a consciousness of the distinction of sounds.

This is not the place to enter on the anatomy of the nervous system; and of its physiology, it is unfortunate that little of a satisfactory nature has been discovered. It needs therefore to be only remarked, that it exists to two separate conditions, with a proportionate variation of function; and that one of these, termed the ganglionic system, (because where it exists alone, it is not accompanied by or united to any organ answering to a cerebrum or cerebellum; which are the centres of thought and voluntary action,) presides especially over the nutritive system, and the involuntary motions. The arrangement of this distribution is not symmetrical; or, in other words, the body is not divided into two corresponding halves, with nerves in each department answering to those of the other; and the creatures thus circumstanced may be said to live in a state of unconscious existence, with no movements beyond those of an automatic kind. By the influence of these the merely irritative functions are executed, but no instinctive feelings can be manifested; although it may happen that sympathetic and reflex motions may put on the appearance of something that resembles them.

This observation more especially applies to some genera of molluscs : in others of which a further advance is made, by a change in one of these ganglia, from its assuming a larger size ; and with this there is such an increase of function as may entitle it to the denomination of a Brain, though without a manifestation of approach to the higher functions of that organ. In this manner, in the molluscan Conchifera, there is a ganglionic distribution to the single organ termed the foot, by which voluntary motions are elicited ; and we are thus enabled to judge that this enlarged portion answers to at least a portion of cerebellum. And this is the earliest development of real brain to be met with in the ascending scale ; and the advancement undoubtedly does not consist in the mere increase of size, but in an acquirement of some additional organization. The common Mussel (*Mytilus edulis*) possesses this foot, and corresponding ganglion ; and therefore, though not capable of positive change of place, it is able to extend and direct the organ in such a manner as, with some approach to consciousness, to direct the application of its mooring threads or byssus, so as to secure stability of situation. The oyster, anomia, and kindred genera, which remain fixed by calcareous adhesion, are destitute of the foot and the ganglion, and are consequently among the lowest in the scale of nature of molluscan animals. But in the highest of these orders or families, the Gasteropods or Cuttlefishes, not only is this nervous system much more highly organized and developed, but the ganglia begin to assume the form of a real Brain, inclosed in a defensive case approaching to the nature of a cranium; and accordingly their faculties of intelligence and passion approach closely to those of fishes. They are capable of manifesting some degree of curiosity, as is seen in their moving up to a shining object to examine it; and in the presence of danger they become suddenly suffused with a decided blush of red, and then eject the contents of their inkbag, by which they become shrouded from observation, and baffle pursuit.

It has been affirmed, that it is possible for a process of nervous matter, not in the form of a ganglion, to possess the elementary functions of nerve and brain combined in one: but if this be true at all, it appears to be so only in the very lowest classes that are furnished with nerves; in some of which we do indeed discover a connexion of nervous threads, which possess no such ganglionic enlargement in any part. But the observation is not correct when applied to the optic, or, still more, to the olfactory nerve of the higher orders; though the latter more especially appears to combine in its structure the sensient and sensible faculties. This organ of sense is formed of an extension of the substance of the real brain, or cerebrum, rather than of the mere communicating nervous cord; and on this account only is it in possession of combined faculties; and if there be in any creature a nervous system which approaches to the nature of such an extension, without a primary nucleus or centre from which it springs, the question would resolve itself into one of form, and not of intrinsic nature.

A uniting commissure by means of nervous continuity between the larger or cerebellic ganglia constitutes a great advance in the subjects that possess it; which are such among the lowest classes as give the first indications of a true nervous system, as distinguished from its looser and less symmetrical arrangement in the inferior tribes. The class of Starfishes (*Asteriadæ*) shew the earliest manifestation of this: for though seemingly very inert, and destitute of intelligence, they display some sagacity in the discovery and choice of food, as well as in the manner of seeking it; and are liable to variations of habit in the different seasons of the year. The common Seahog or Seaegg (*Echinus sphæra*), though apparently destitute of every sense, or possibility of regarding external objects by sight or hearing, will travel up the rods of a crabpot, enter the opening, descend within, mount again to the situation of the bait, and select the particular one that pleases it best.

It is a remarkable circumstance, that, notwithstanding the employment of high magnifying powers, anatomy has failed to discover such a difference in the construction or organization of the different nerves, especially in their active fibrils, as can account for their diversity of function; widely different as some of them are in this respect. And this difference of function in different nerves is still greater in kind than in degree: so that the fabric which is sensitive to light cannot be made sensible to the impression of sound or feeling, nor can the organ of sound be in any manner rendered responsive to the influence of light. It is possible also, and there are circumstances which render it not improbable, that in some creatures there are nerves of sense which are capable of receiving impressions and conveying or exciting ideas of a wider range or different kind from any found in the human race, and consequently than man is able to form a comprehension of. Some actions of animals, and remarkably of insects, imply as much as this; and the corresponding influence on their instincts must be considerable. This would explain how it is that the cat washes its face when damp weather is approaching: a circumstance it seems reasonable to connect with the well-known disposition of that creature to the manifestation of electric phenomena. The Pig carries straws in its mouth, in anticipation of a high wind; and the actions of both these animals will occur many hours before the smallest indication of a change has become perceptible in instruments of man's invention. In such cases it may be judged that the creature itself is unconscious of the meaning or intent of its own motions, which are no more than a reaction of impulse: but in others we are compelled to conclude that it is connected with intelligence; since it leads to preparations for a change of place, which nothing short of under-standing could direct. We shall have occasion to bring forward some remarkable instances of the operation of this faculty in the course of this work.

Something very similar to the unconscious action here referred to, and illustrative of its nature, is seen in the human body, and especially in the ordinary process of swallowing. This becomes an involuntary action when a substance comes in contact with a certain part of the throat—the *Isthmus faucium*, close behind the tongue; and it is out of our power to imitate the action if nothing is placed in contact with that part. Our only choice consists in passing the received matter over the root of the tongue; at which instant the self-moving process immediately begins. It is probable that this compulsory state of the process of swallowing is the natural condition of the orifice of some animals; the approach of food to this aperture being the mere result of accident. In them also it may not be attended with consciousness: for, even in the human body, the muscular structure of the iris of the eye, moved as it is by the impression of light, performs its actions without our being at all sensible of them. The closing of its shell in the Oyster, on the contact of some objects, and its opening on the flow of the tide, are instances of this property; and regarded in this point of view, they display wonderful adaptation of structure to the wants and circumstances of the creature, itself unconscious of a want, or, if felt, how to supply it. But, recurring to the automatic action of swallowing which has been already mentioned, perhaps there is no one in which the dependence of each motion on its predecessor is so distinctly visible and inevitable as this — in which none can be exerted, except by beginning with the first link of the chain. A craving for agreeable food is the exciting cause of the motions of the mouth and jaws : but however agreeable to the palate, this food is not retained in the mouth to obtain the only enjoyment it is capable of affording; but being thrown over the hinder part of the tongue, it is conveyed into the stomach by the involuntary muscular contractions of successive portions of the œsophagus or gullet. And it is interesting to observe in some animals the interposition of certain actions which are not less necessary to the process; and which, though the effect of skilful arrangement, are yet so far automatic, or simply consecutive, that an interruption of their course would place the creature under much difficulty in resuming those which are necessary to the process. It is the habit of the Boa constrictor, a large serpent, to crush and break the bones of the animal it seizes to devour; and so necessary does this action appear, in order to enable it to swallow the prey whole, as it is obliged to do, that we are led to regard this creature as guided by a calculating intelligence of the best mode of conducting its proceedings. Yet this scarcely appears to be a right view of the matter. A friend who had carefully watched the actions of a snake of this species, of the length of about six feet, informed me, that being desirous of witnessing its manner of taking its prey, and not able to obtain a larger animal for the purpose, he supplied it with a pigeon, which the serpent immediately proceeded to devour. Having suffered a long fast, it seemed to experience much trouble in expanding its jaws, the joints of which had grown rigid from want of use. But when they had become flexible by repeated effort, it proceeded to draw in the bird by the slow but persevering action of its jaws and teeth ; and no difficulty appeared to hinder the easy accomplishment of the task. Suddenly however, and rapidly, the serpent threw the coils of its body, at a foot or two behind the head, about the object, (as would have been appropriate to a larger prey,) and compressing it tightly, the body and wings of the bird became pressed and lengthened; at which time, still holding firmly by the mouth, it drew the pigeon from the constriction of its coil, and swallowed it with ease. The interposed portion of this proceeding appeared to be entirely unnecessary, so far as concerned its capacity of swallowing this prey : but it seemed to be instinctively unavoidable ; and the age of the creature was decisive to shew that it could never have previously had an opportunity of practising it on any animal that by its bulk could have rendered so complex an operation necessary.

But in creatures such as these, a part of the process, at least, is voluntary. It is otherwise in the oyster and cockle ; which could not be tempted to expansion by an offer of the desirable object, if held at a small distance from them ; however they might be suffering from want of it. Actual contact is necessary to excite both the opening and the closing ; and in a higher order of animals this natural impulse is so strong, as to counteract or overpower the dictates of reason and influence of the will, in cases where refraining might be important to health and safety. And though it is sometimes brought into action in cases where it proves injurious even to man, the importance of this irritable function can scarcely be sufficiently valued ; for the promptness of its action in many instances of necessity is more than equivalent to a perhaps wiser direction of motion, when the latter must be the slow result of deliberation. Such is the case in the winking of our eyes, when hurtful objects are presented to them ; and of not a few beside of our unconscious actions, in cases of apprehension or sudden danger. Most of the merely animal functions in the higher orders of animals may be referred to this natural faculty ; and each internal one is so constituted as to be susceptible of its own proper stimulus, without which life could not be sustained : as the blood to the action of the heart, and air to that of the lungs. It is to the morbid or irregular influence of the same principle, that we must ascribe many of the diseases under which we suffer.

There are no living beings in which this faculty of irritability or excitability exists alone ; but there are families in which no other addition besides this is made to the principle that first came under our consideration. Creatures thus constituted possess the power of making selections of food, and of varying their functions according to extraneous circumstances, or internal changes ; but it is only among the highest of these natural classes that any one can be said to display a preference. And in some even of these it is still simply through the influence of a reaction, (such as by Dr. Marshall Hall has been termed a reflex action of the nerves,) that anything bearing resemblance to a bias of the will can be discerned.

It is proper in this place to remark, that, although it is an ascertained truth that there is a general tendency in the natural families of organized beings to rise above each other in complexity and perfection of organization and acquirements, we are not authorized to conclude that the nervous system and intelligence of every member of each class or family necessarily rises above the condition of those of the classes or families which, as a whole, are below it. We have a remarkable instance of the reverse of this in the lancelet (*Amphioxus lanceolatus*), a singular fish, first discovered in Cornwall, and which beyond question is a vertebrated creature; but of which the nervous system springs from a spinal cord, without a brain or cephalic ganglion, which otherwise is of great simplicity. Its powers of consciousness appear to be proportionately obscure; and in every respect it is far below those of the generality of insects, and perhaps also of some molluscs.

The next stage of our inquiry will bring us to a still higher class; where we shall find not only the existence of wants, but consciousness of such a deficiency as the idea of a want implies: from which we shall be able to discern a rising impulse prompting to the search for a supply, as well to satisfy the craving of desire, as to palliate the pain of deficiency, or defend against danger. It is in this condition that an approach is made to the border of that which is properly understood by the term Instinct; and here therefore we shall do well to pause, and consider the complication of circumstances included in that function or character.

CHAPTER II.

IT is necessary we should bear in mind that, though in the cursory view which has been taken of the essential circumstances involved in the existence of living beings, we have gradually advanced in our inquiry from one stage of capacity or function to another, yet that in so doing we have not left any of these organizations and their dependent faculties behind us; but that the most complicated and most highly endowed of creatures are only constituted such by the addition of new tissues, or the modifications of those already existing, with their attending properties, to those possessed by the lowest order in creation. Man himself—who is beyond doubt the highest creature in the visible world—a genus in himself, and rightly defined by Linnæus in the expressive signification of that high point of wisdom,—a capacity for self-knowledge,—is constituted by the plenitude of the natural properties which distinguish beings, whose whole existence is confined to the possession of a mere tissue; as well as of those in the ascending series, whose lives are comprised in the separate additions of sensibility and irritability.

It is also necessary to bear in mind, that in studying this transition from one being to another, it was for the sake of perspicuity that we have spoken of creatures as divided into classes, according to their natural functions : for in reality no well-drawn line of distinction in any of those respects can be said to exist in nature; since the visible creation constitutes an entire whole, without a gap or precise line of demarcation between the races.

Yet I would not be understood to advance the opinion, that there are no extended groups in nature to occupy a more important or *extended* sphere of affinities, than the collateral or connecting branches by which these groups are united. There are obviously well-known families of animals which stand prominently distinct from others : as the Mammalia—which cannot fail to be distinguished as a group from birds and fishes : as insects and plants may be from either of them; and though there are smaller groups which form so closely a connecting link from one of these to another, as to render it difficult of decision to fix the family to which they may be said to belong; yet this must not be regarded as leading to the confusion of races, but rather to their amalgamation.

This point of union is usually not so much constituted by a single animal or group, as by the separate portions or organs; which thus form the singular and influential character, that to an inattentive observer seems an exception to all the laws of Nature. Thus it is the feet of the Kangaroo that form its visible approach to the structure of

a bird; and yet there are some particulars in other
portions of its natural history, and especially in
the manner of evolution of its young, which shew
that the similarity is something more than a casual
or ideal agreement. The bill of a bird constitutes
the connecting link in another family of mammals;
of which the *Ornithorhynchus paradoxus* is an
equally remarkable instance; and from the same
principle the thighs and feet of the Ostrich bear
a closer resemblance to those of a quadruped than
to any of the feathered races. In the eighteenth
volume of the Linnæan Transactions, Professor Owen
has given an extended account of the *Lepido-
siren annectens*, which genus has been assigned
by different eminent naturalists to the classes of
reptiles and fishes; and after a minute examination
and a comparison of its characters with those of
both these families, the decision is made that it
ought to be arranged with the latter, because, while
the other portions of its structure are almost equally
balanced between them, the nostrils do not communicate with the trachea, but are simple, blind
sacs: that being the only well-established distinction
between them. But it is discovered to be the habit
of this creature, which is a native of African rivers,
to wrap itself into a ball of mud, and thus become
torpid, in the manner of a reptile; and therefore
we may venture to conclude, that it affords one of
many instances in Nature, in which there exists a
superior structural affinity with one class of animals,
combined with an assimilation to the manners of
another, thus establishing a bond of inosculation

through the whole. Among the sponges, able naturalists are not agreed whether some be animal or vegetable; and the only way of deciding the question seems
to be by a reference to the products of their chemical
decomposition, though this would be a fallacious test
in some other departments of Nature. And though the
distinction between the living and the dead may seem
in its own nature to be necessarily well defined, it requires close examination to be assured even of this:
for the chemical, electric, or galvanic powers give
proof that they are able to imitate in one, what as
instruments they are called upon to perform in the
other. Similar observations will apply to creatures
that are found on the borders—the aberrant groups
—of those tribes, in which the properties of irritability, or organic sensibility and instinct, reside.
They pass insensibly into each other; and the
distinctive characters of each conspicuous family is
formed, not simply by the possession, but by the
preponderancy, of these separate properties.

In this stage of our inquiry into animal propensities, it will be proper to offer some remarks
on two important subjects which have already
been mentioned incidentally, and which lie at the
foundation of our first principles. The first is life;
which, as Bichat expresses it, is to an animal body
what gravity is to dynamics:—a first principle, of
which the existence can be shewn, but not the
essence. The difference which its presence makes in
the tissues cannot be so easily seen in a membrane,
because the functions of that organization are chiefly
mechanical. It lines a cavity and contains fluids;

yet though acted on it scarcely acts on any thing.
But in a muscle, which is the moving power in all
cases, at least of voluntary motion, as well as some
others, it is the presence of life that makes the
fibre contractile : which it is in a degree exceeding
even its own actual strength of tenacity ; so that
it would become ruptured by a much less force
when dead than it is able to lift and move when
alive. But the most perceptible and decisive instance
of the influence of life is seen in a nerve, which in
itself is a mere feeble thread, unable to accomplish
anything, and easily broken. But when endued with
life it is rendered capable of conveying every variation
of the finest sensations: as those of light, of form, and
all the tints of colour, of heat, and musical tones or
feelings, with all the modulations of language, emphasis
and look ; or again, of returning volitions so exquisitely rapid and precise, that the most delicate and
intricate mechanism is ordered by its guidance ; and
nothing beside can be imagined in any degree equal
to it. Milton calls its actions instinctive ; by which
he seems also to mean intuitive :

> His volant touch
> Instinct through all proportions, low and high,
> Fled and pursued transverse the resonant fugue.

There is no part of an organized body, of
whose nature so little is known as that of the
nervous system : an arrangement that in its highest development includes the brain, (*cerebrum* and
cerebellum,) which is the organ of thought and of
the animal propensities : with the spinal cord, from

which most of the motive powers proceed. The manifestations of the powers of these organs are carried to the remoter parts by sensitive threads, the distribution of which is well known, but the intimate organization and connection of these origins of thought and feeling, sensation and action, is scarcely guessed; and whether the transmission of impressions is by the impulse of one particle on another, by polarity, or by the passage of a fluid from and to the centre. For our present purpose, however, it may be sufficient to remark, as a matter beyond doubt, that in any one Being the functions which different classes of nerves perform are exceedingly different: so that the ear cannot assume the office of sight, the eye of feeling, nor the tongue of hearing; and in like manner, though less perceptible to observation, that, in addition to the nature of the tissue which forms the chief portion of its bulk, and the arrangement of its blood-vessels, each class of organs derives much of its peculiar action, whether of secretion or nutrition, from the intimate and appropriate structure of the nerve distributed to it, which binds the function of the parts together as a uniform whole.

It is on this account that, when an organ is appointed to execute complicated functions, the branches of two distinct nerves are assigned to it: of which we find a familiar instance in the whiskers of the Cat, Rat, Hare, and Seal. To the root of each of these firm and elastic hairs proceeds a fibre, mostly from the infraorbitary branch, the duty of which is simply to convey the impression of contact or the sense of feeling; and, by acting on which, the whisker, after the manner of a lever, gives notice of any obstruction, as the creature moves about in the dark. The other fibre, which is derived from the facial nerve—a branch communicating with, and in part of its course forming a portion of the auditory or nerve of hearing—acted on in a similar manner by this lever, places the auditory apparatus more on the alert; and thus mere mechanical contact directs attention to the obscurest sounds. This last-named nerve is of large size in those fishes—as the Eel—that are known to be affected by noise; and therefore it may be said to be endowed in some degree with a portion of the faculties of the more immediate nerve of hearing, of which in its internal progress it forms a part.

And the principle here laid down, which appears to be of general application in the anatomy and physiology of animal bodies, must be extended in a far higher degree in the various natural families, if we would seek to comprehend their most intimate nature.

In the animal body, as we have already hinted, not only the different tissues, as the membranous, muscular and nervous, are subject to modifications that render them liable to a variation of functions, while they still possess the intrinsic nature common to each; but the arrangement and proportion also of each of these tissues differ in each organ : so that the complication of each result, which constitutes the entire animal, must be equally diverse.

In illustration of this, we observe, that though

the optic nerve, as it is expanded into a retina at the posterior part of the globe of the eye, may be of similar form in man and most other animals, yet that the most intimate and active structure of most of these sensitive organizations, whether in the receptive extremities—where only sensation can be said to exist—or the intermediate and conveying fibres, and their central perceptive terminations—is exceedingly different in the different families and species. And how wide an influence even a small difference in these respects may have may be judged by recollecting, that anatomists have not been able to appreciate any change of structure, when in the phenomena of diseased vision the human eye has become insensible to the impression of some colours, while it has retained a sensibility to others. It is not improbable that this variety of liability to impression, which in man amounts to disease, is in some animals natural and permanent; and thus we are able the more easily to explain how it happens that in the latter certain colours produce emotions of rage and terror. That the Bull, the Buffalo, and Turkey are excited to fury at the sight of a red garment, becomes thus as explicable, as that the melodious ear is tortured by discordant sounds, which to inferior organizations would be matters of indifference.

The conclusion, then, is this: that the essential difference by which one kind of animal is distinguished from another, and in which therefore its specific identity consists, is constituted by the peculiarity of tissue in its various organs, and the preponderance or complications of such tissue in its

whole structure : but more especially by the peculiarity of its nervous fabric, and the arrangement of
what is called its nervous system ; by which impressions are received, and through which they are
conveyed to the sensorium—according to the nature
of the objects impressing them; and still more
powerfully according to the nature of the organs
accepting and conveying, and of the nervous centre
by which they are finally perceived. By the same
influences also, acting in a reverse order, the
voluntary and organic actions are controlled to
uniformity of purpose, which, in its result, constitutes
one harmonious whole.

In illustration and support of this proposition, and
in extension of its truth to a higher series of intelligence, it is pleasing to me to quote an authority
to which little resort has hitherto been had—on
account, perhaps, of some frivolous or objectionable
sentiments to which men of the same order have
given utterance ; or, more probably, because it has
been wrapped up in a literature not generally
studied. Besides the acuteness generally displayed
in its mode of argumentation, it deserves closer
investigation from the fact, that, in addition to its
being the opinion of an eminent Jewish Rabbi, (a
class of persons who were much superior in learning
and common sense to those who are called School-
men,) it probably embodies the sense of the philosophy of the East ; which flourished at a remote
period in a favourable soil, but, for the most part,
has disappeared, leaving only its relics to be thus
preserved.

In that most ancient and glorious of poems, the Book of Job, which affords glimpses of deep philosophy in addition to its inspired character, the Great Supreme is found replying to the complaint of the sufferer by the question, (chap. xxxviii. 36.) " Who hath put wisdom in the inward parts? Or who hath given understanding to the heart?" on which Rabbi Joseph Albo comments: " The word *batuchoth*, ' wisdom,' has here the same meaning as in another place in Job, ' security' or ' assurance,' and is intended to express those *innate impressions* by means of which knowledge is secured to man. *Binah*, ' understanding,' denotes perception, and accordingly the whole verse reads thus : ' Who has secured to man those innate impressions from which alone wisdom arises? Or perception, in order to attain knowledge by means of comparison?' which faculty is in Hebrew called *binah*, ' understanding :' as our Rabbies say, *binah* is to comprehend one thing by means of another ; or to arrive at just conclusions from dissimilar premises. The divine reproof is consequently, ' Canst thou explain how thou hast obtained faculties which animate beings of another species have not ?' This is likewise the meaning of David, when he says, ' Thou desirest truth, *batuchoth*, ' in our innate impressions ;' and as these are from Thee, all knowledge is imparted by Thee.' In like manner Solomon saith, ' The Lord giveth wisdom : from his mouth is knowledge and understanding.' The meaning is, that all wisdom is from God, because *dangath*, ' knowledge,' the innate impressions, *uth-*

buna, 'and perception,' emanate from and are
implanted by him. Thence likewise the men of the
Great Assembly (Ezra and his companions) use the
following words in the authorized form of daily
prayer: ' Thou favourest the human being with
dangath, 'knowledge,' and teachest man *binah*,
' understanding.' The meaning of which is : Thou
hast deigned to bestow on the whole human race
innate impressions, by means of which thou teachest
man to perceive and compare. And the prayer
ends with thanks for the gift of *dangath*, or ' innate
impressions,' as they are the root of all human
knowledge. This also led our Rabbies of blessed
memory to say, that, if there is no *dangath*, there
is no *binah*, and *vice versâ :* meaning, that without
innate impressions there can be no *binah*, or ' perception ;' and that without the latter, the former
is vain."—*Book of Principles, in Hebrew Review*,
vol. i. p. 36.

The innate impressions here meant, is only another way of expressing the human comprehension
or intellectual consciousness in which wisdom is
implanted, and by the operation of which man is
distinguished from the brute ; as, by another kind
of comprehension or consciousness, one animal is
innately distinguished from another.

CHAPTER III.

In the course of this work it will be our business to trace the effects of the developments we have spoken of, as displayed in the familiar actions of animals;—and chiefly in those with which we are best acquainted, either from their inhabiting our own country, or from the narratives of naturalists who have studied the creatures of distant lands in their native haunts. For the sake of illustration, preference will generally be given to the animals of our own country, because of the superior interest we feel in the habits of creatures with whom we are most familiarly acquainted; and also because when, from the situations they inhabit and their secluded manners, they are less known, the beautiful figures and accurate descriptions to be found in the series of works on British Natural History, by Professor Bell, Mr. Yarrell, and Professor E. Forbes, will afford all the information regarding them that can be desired.

And our first instances will be of such actions as vary with the age of the individual, or with the season, before we proceed to those which are distinctive of the species: as by so doing we may obtain proof, that changes in the force or manifestation of instinct proceed from no other cause than fluctuations in the state of the animal body itself.

Whilst identity remains the same, the succession of changes in the constitutional balance of the organs is the cause of a display of properties exceedingly different from those which formerly characterised the creature : so that it is open to observation, how different is the aged individual of every kind when compared with those of early youth. The kitten is marked by playfulness, and, from restless activity in search of amusement, will for a long time run round and round after its tail; till at last, growing angry at its want of success in the pursuit, it attempts to avenge itself for the disappointment by a bite. Thus sportive, even to neglect of its food, it offers a strong contrast to the sedater animal, that sits motionless and silent in a retired corner for hours together, in patient expectation of the appearance of a mouse. And even the poor young Ass, destined to a life of slavery and hardship, enjoys the first weeks of its existence in gambols, with so much glee, that it is difficult to imagine it the same sedate creature which, when at liberty from toil, stands for hours in complacency so great, and so absorbed in its stillness, that not a muscle can be seen to move.

Instances in illustration of this fact cannot fail to come under our notice in all our paths; and in no creature is it more conspicuous than in man himself. Nor is this change in him, any more than in the inferior creatures, in the progress of infancy to age, the result of distaste, occupation, experience, or indeed any mental phenomenon whatever, though it may be modified by all of them; except in so far as the mental disposition is in subjection to these circumstances of the bodily frame. But it has one especial effect on the instincts in particular, whereby it comes to be observed in animals more distinctly than in man; and this is, that not only does the development of mutation vary in its force according to the difference of age, but the kind of manifestation shall also suffer the change; and that which predominated at one period to such an extent as to form the distinguishing character of the creature, will subsequently give place to another, while the former seems even to have become extinct: a circumstance which may be judged to arise, not only from a variation of balance in the tissue or organ, but also from the preponderancy of the stimulus which each may exert on the others.

In some cases also the active development of an instinct becomes periodic, from the cause last expressed, and revives again after a more or less definite period of suspension. This is remarkable in some well-known series of phenomena in the economy of birds, which have long excited admiration. One of these is the disposition to the formation of a nest, of which we shall have to speak hereafter. For the present, no reference is made to the skill employed in its structure, situation, or adaptation to use, but only to the formative impulse; which in some instances is so

c 3

strong, that, when the nest is formed, instead of waiting until the egg is ready to be deposited, the building bird proceeds in the construction of others, until, at last, the further duty of using it for its peculiar object puts an end to its labours. This practice is particularly observed in the common Wren (*Sylvia troglodytes*); and it has been supposed that the true reason why this diminutive architect builds more than one nest is, that .it has become dissatisfied with the former edifice, or with its situation. But this supposition is incorrect, since it is known that, in a more advanced period of the season, when this particular instinctive propensity is declining, the pair will return to the forsaken nest, and employ it as originally intended.

Another phenomenon, to which reference is now made, is the instinct of migration, which leads so many birds to seek a warmer climate at one season of the year, and a colder at another. And to remove the suspicion that the migratory races are led simply by habit, or the spirit of imitation, in passing from one region to another, we have the remarkable example of the Cuckoo; which is destitute of one propensity so universal in other birds as to be worthy of being characterised as an essential property of the feathered races,—that of forming a procreant cradle to receive their young. Those young ones therefore they have never seen, and consequently can never have taught the lesson, or guided in the voyage. They also depart long before them; and yet, so strong and unerring is the impulse, that this bird, in its infancy one of

the stupidest of winged creatures, is invariably found
to follow in the right direction.

It is obvious, then, that animals are endued
with a variety of instinctive properties, each of
which may operate singly, or many may combine
in a variety of proportions, with the occasional
suspension of some of their impulses. Many of
the Duck tribe are migratory, and it is this
additional propensity of which we have been speaking that causes them at all times to select the
neighbourhood of water, the preference for which
is not less powerful in the little creature just
escaping from the egg. It is possible that this
instinct might lie in an unconscious state of
development, if placed in the midst of an arid
desert; but even there it would be instantly manifested under favourable circumstances, uninfluenced
and undeterred even by warnings of maternal ten-
derness: as is often witnessed in the instructive
lesson of such a brood under the care of an agonized
hen, whose vociferations are a proof of her instinctive dread of that which is the delight of her
progeny.

The reverse of this is seen in the love of the
Ostrich for the waste wilderness; and, to come
within the range of a smaller circle, the different
species of a natural class,—as the Thrush (*Turdidæ*),
and Blackbird, with the Redwing, Misselthrush and
Fieldfare; of the Crow kind (*Corvidæ*), including
the Raven and Rook; and also the several kinds
of Larks—possess numerous properties and habits
in common, and yet every separate species will

display a variation so distinct, as to prevent their ever associating together.

An animal feels the want of food through an instinctive impression principally arising from the state of its stomach; and the complicated sensation thence arising, a mixture of the impression of pleasure and pain, impels it to exertion for obtaining a supply, of which the nature and taste are ascertained with little inquiry. But there are other sensations of the stomach, still more painful, and for which there is a relief in nature, but towards which there appears to be no propulsive tendency: so widely different is the instinct arising from a natural want and a morbid action. Nor is there any exception to this among wild animals, as has been supposed; where the feeling arises from a derangement of any organ besides the stomach. A sick animal will, it is true, find out a plant that is not its usual food, and devour it; but this occurs only when the disorder is confined to the stomach. There is no instinctive craving in derangements of other organs; and, in its nature, this of the organ of digestion can only be compared to that similar feeling in man, which leads him to drink freely in a fever, or to accommodate a weak or irregular stomach by fanciful craving for food.

But this state of hunger is only the instinct of a want; and the manner in which it is to be satisfied is that which particularly distinguishes the character of each species, and to which therefore a conventional use of the word has attached an emphatic meaning in the term Instinct, though it is an obvious error to confine this expression to the latter manifestation only.

The organs of taste and smell, from causes hitherto unknown, are gratified with different odours and impressions in different creatures; and therefore we need not feel surprised if, in beings so differently organized, the objects sought after to satisfy the craving of hunger should greatly differ. And as among men one individual prefers the salt and another the sour, so we may observe in one pasture the Sheep nibbling the short grass, the Cow preferring the long and coarse, the Horse searching out the fine and tender, and the Ass passing the whole of these by, to shew its preference for the sprouts of furze. It is from a similar variation of taste that the Tiger seeks for blood, and the Bear for roots and honey,—the Fox for birds, the Weasel for eggs; until at last we find that there is not a substance in the animal or vegetable world that is not the selected food of some creature,—a source of supply and happiness to some sentient being. And even the most filthy and loathsome things are a delectable treat to some of the creeping families, which, by devouring the putrid matter, play their part in purifying creation from what would annoy others, and perhaps generate disease and death.

When the organs in man are in healthy action, the perceptions of taste, smell, and sight are agreeable, and what are denominated natural. But without any real change in the nature of the object, if the

sensibility of these organs becomes deranged by what
must be considered a morbid action, the nature of
the perception is altered; and the impression of
what we must call the true taste, sight, or smell
is converted into another which is offensive and
unnatural.   The optic nerve, under deranged or
excessive excitement, sees every object in a changed
or aggravated condition*: the flame of a candle
is obscured, or is seen as a blaze; a sparkle appears
like a fire; and the painful sense of vision continues
even after the eyes are closed.

The senses of taste and smell are still more easily
and frequently deranged: a vitiation of the sense
of taste, or its suspension, is in some persons
permanent; and the former may be commonly
traced to a change in the nature of the secretion
of saliva: for this taste is often most perceptible
when nothing extraneous has been received into
the mouth.   At other times it is due to a false
perception in the nerve of that organ, when, even
if a naturally agreeable object be presented to it,
a disgusting sensation is experienced; which feeling
of disgust will be continued by sympathy of remem-
brance, long after the condition that produced it
has ceased: a circumstance that will account for

---

* That condition of visual perception, which is termed Daltonism,
is best explained on the principles here advanced: for as the only
natural stimulus to the optic nerve is light, it is easy to understand
how the fibres of the optic nerve may be in such a state, that a
peculiarly-coloured ray may produce no impression, or only an
imperfect one. The nerve may be incapable of receiving any other
than a morbid or modified impulse, and the sensation communicated
must be of a corresponding nature.

many of the antipathies to be found among mankind. On the other hand, it occasionally happens that a liking is felt for what to the natural taste is offensive or disgusting; and what thus in man is the result of diseased action—or, still more strangely, the liking of custom or fashion, when, having been weakened by excess, it can only be stimulated to sensation by powerful impressions—is in some animals the natural condition, which fits them to luxuriate in the delicacy of a putrid carcase, and the disgusting savours of a drain.

A modification of these appetites will explain the occurrence of longings for particular kinds of food in parturient women, and in persons beginning to feel a return of natural action of the digestive organs after severe diseases : in which cases, with a natural craving for nutriment is mixed a morbid choice of the particular quality that is felt to be the most agreeable. In severe diseases also the taste of medicine seems congenial to the circumstances ; but on returning to a more healthy condition it begins to be rejected, the sensation conveyed not being that properly inherent in the substance, but such as is received in the perceptive peculiarity of the nervous organization.

And such being the cause of the preferences shewn by animals for particular kinds of food, the manner in which the purposes of supply are carried into operation is not less characteristic. And while this is in part founded on the ascertained habits of the thing sought after, it is not less closely connected with other propensities of the species seeking it: by which is more distinctly shewn the aggregation of their organizations and properties, which become as much the cause as the instrument of their characteristic instincts.

Urged by a common impulse, the headlong Lion and the furious Tiger rush boldly on their prey, as if conscious of a degree of strength that renders unnecessary any precaution against danger: for the subtilty and concealment employed by them are for the most part only adopted to prevent their prey from becoming alarmed. In the former beast also it seems to be the consciousness of unrivalled strength that sets it above the fear of its being at all necessary to guard against fraud; and therefore gives it that unsuspicious openness, in so high a degree its prevailing character. But it belongs to the Tiger that, having been long impressed by the craving of hunger, it is urged by a feeling that no quantity of the prey can satisfy his appetite, and therefore the slaughter is much beyond what the stomach is able to receive. He also endeavours to strike the prey dead at once: for, besides the immense power of his muscles, he infuses into the blow a resolve that the creature which has so long by its vigilance disappointed his craving shall not again be in a capacity to escape. It is from a kindred feeling that a cat which has pounced on a rat will beat the prey with both its paws for some time after escape is hopeless. A polecat has been known to kill fifteen turkeys in one night, and to drag them beneath a stack of wood; as if deferring the immediate gratification of appetite, however keen, that it might satisfy a gluttony which existed more in the imagination than in the capacity of enjoyment.—(Loudon's Mag. of Nat. Hist. vol. vi. p. 207.)

The Fox goes warily to work; and having discovered from experience that he is in danger of a foe or a snare at every turn, he has recourse to that subtilty which a combination of fear, caution, and appetite, influencing a shrewd disposition, can bestow, and which have won for him a wide-spread renown. The obscurity of night suits him best, as it does most other wild animals that maintain their position in the midst of a populous nation. And this nocturnal disposition is not only caused by a greater feeling of security, and the absence of vigilance in the prey, but also by the organization of the eyes, which are best fitted to see in the absence of the glare of day: as is the sensation of moisture to its other sensations, and its quietness to love of secresy. Much noise is a source of terror to most animals: yet it is worthy of notice that a less noise is not always avoided; and a herd of deer in a park, not accustomed to be broke in upon, after a time perceiving themselves not to be the object of the clamour, have been noticed to approach the neighbourhood where a band has been playing, and listen to its sounds. The wild Deer of America, when no obvious pursuit and terrifying sight have been suffered to alarm it, has been attracted by the grunting sound uttered by the hunter; and the most certain method of getting within a convenient distance is, while removing alarm, to excite its attention. A singular object will also attract them, as it will also that most timid of all creatures the antelope. The Otter, in the silence of the night, will approach and examine a conspicuous object ; and its presence in a neighbourhood may be detected by the traces it leaves behind. The Seal (*Phoca vitulina*), with all its timidity, forgets to dive in listening to a strange sound ; and Scoresby reports that they may be attracted to the surface by music or by whistling. It is even said that the sound of a trumpet or a bell will cause Sturgeons to assemble in shoals, and thus aid the success of the fishery.

It is by an instinct common to all wild animals that the Hare and Rabbit, the Cat, Fox, Rat and Mole, endeavour to escape from their enemies ; but it is a modification of this action arising from the nature of the object which each of them dreads, and the powers which each of them is conscious of possessing, which makes the variation in the expression of that by which each gives prominency to what is distinctive of the race. The Rabbit runs to the hole from which it has not ventured far, conscious of its want of power for distant or continued flight ; whilst, trusting to superior fleetness, the Hare wanders to a greater distance, and seeks no safety but outrunning its pursuers. The Cat runs up a tree, not however by leaping, but by extending its claws and fixing them in its bark ; and there, as if aware that the enemy cannot follow, it remains under a slight shelter of concealment, at no great elevation above its foe. In a house, when desirous of escaping detection or injury, it does no more than creep into an unsuspected corner, and trust to obscurity and patience for the result. When roused, the extended claws display a consciousness of another resource, which none but creatures of the feline race are capable of exercising.

This consciousness in individuals of the powers by which their race is characterised is deeply stamped upon their actions, in a manner to modify the existence of the creature, so as often to bear exclusively the name of Instinct. It is even seen in cases where, from the influence of domestication, the instruments that rendered the manifestation formidable have disappeared. The absence of horns in the Cow does not prevent it thrusting at an adversary with its head.

The Cat kind, including the Lion and Tiger, endeavour to retain their prey by grasping with the claws, and not the toes; and these claws, when in a state of rest, by a skilful contrivance, are removed to the upper part of the toes, in the concealment of the fur. When wanted for use, by the effort of a moment, the middle bone of the toe, which trod on the ground, becomes raised; and this, by elevating the nearer extremity of the terminal bone, and so bringing down the further end, advances the claw into the extended position: so that its prey is held as by a fish-hook, and escape is impossible, unless the claw be torn through the substance —an operation which no creature, however terrified, possesses sufficient fortitude to inflict upon itself.

The Hawk tribe secure their prey in a somewhat

similar manner; and it is by the same means that
the Swift (*Cypselus apus*) fastens itself to a wall:
the whole length of the toes being straightened
by an action not practised by the generality of
Birds, so as to be opposed to each other in pairs;
while the claw is bent beneath, with the point
directed inward.

The teeth of animals are weapons of attack and
defence; but the manner of using them as such
varies greatly. In rodent creatures, as the Rat,
the Weasel, and Squirrel, this is done by a simple
but piercing incision: as is also the case with
the viper (*Pelius Berus*);—and the latter, conscious of the power of the poison which it knows
will follow its bite, remains quiet after the infliction, as if waiting for its expected influence. But
in addition to its bite, the dog shakes its head, by
way of worrying the enemy; and, different from
all, the Boar strikes a sidelong blow with its projecting tusk, and then rushes off in the midst of
the confusion it has created.

We have an example of another kind in the
Horse, which, conscious of the strength of its posterior muscles, defends itself by kicks that have
been known to subdue even the Tiger; but the
Ass, so nearly related to it in generic affinity, scarcely
employs these organs, from their comparative feeble-
ness. Its battling is mostly by biting, with which it
is able to inflict formidable injury; but its manner
of resisting an attack implies consciousness of the
part best able to sustain a blow: its hips are
first proffered; and the readiest way to move it

from the position which it obstinately assumes, is to urge it in the opposite direction to that which we wish it to take.

The horns of animals seem to be nearly alike destined for defence; and yet there are lesser differences in their structure and position, of which the possessors seem to be well aware. Thus the Bull, with its head lowered to the ground, offers its horns to receive an attack; but as they are too simple to repel the enemy long, a motion of the head is added at the moment of the onset, by which to toss the assailant over the shoulder. The better-armed Deer places its defence in such a manner towards the foe, that even the Panther has judged it prudent to desist; and a consciousness in the Sheep that its force is only in its forehead, excites the Ram to anticipate attack by rushing on the enemy, and the hardness of its front will secure a victory over a formidable opponent.

Mr. Waterton, in Loudon's Magazine of Natural History, (vol. vii. p. 1) well remarks, " that as every creature knows and observes a certain mode of attack, as that by which he can best employ his powers of annoyance and conquest, a knowledge of this will best enable man to resist such attack;" and he gives the following instances in illustration of the principle: "The dog and the lion are both most formidable foes to an unarmed man; and it is singular enough, that the very resistance which he would be forced to make in order to escape being worried by the former, would inevitably expose him to certain destruction from the claws and teeth of the latter."

All animals of the Dog tribe must be combated
with might and main, and with unceasing exertion,
in their attacks upon man: for, from the moment
they obtain the mastery, worry and tear their
victim as long as life remains in it. On the
contrary, animals of the cat tribe, having once
overcome their prey, cease for a certain time to
inflict further injury on it. Thus, during the
momentous interval from the stroke which has laid
a man beneath a Lion, to the time when the Lion
shall begin to devour him, the man may have it
in his power to rise again, either by his own
exertions, or by the fortuitous intervention of an
armed friend. But then, all depends upon quiet,
extreme quiet, on the part of the man, until he
plunges his dagger into the heart of the animal:
for, if he tries to resist, he is sure to feel the
force of his adversary's claws and teeth with re-
doubled vengeance.—" I will here mention a trivial
row I once had with two dogs. It will tend to
prove the advantage of standing up manfully, when
attacked by animals of the canine tribe; and I
will conclude with recounting an adventure with a
lion, perhaps unparalleled in the annals of hunting.—
In passing over a common I accidentally came upon
two dogs. One of them was a stout, ill-looking,
uncouth brute, apparently of that genealogy which
dog-fanciers term half bull and half terrier: the
other was an insignificant female cur. The dog
immediately bristled up; and I had just time to
take off my hat, and hold it shieldwise, in self-
defence, when he came on, and made directly at it.
I gave him a hearty kick under the breast, which

caused him to desist for a moment; but he stoutly renewed the attack, which was continued for above five minutes, he always flying at the hat, and I regularly repeating my kicks, sometimes slightly, sometimes heavily, according to our relative situations. In the meantime the female cur was assailing me from behind; and it was with difficulty that I succeeded in keeping her clear of me, by swinging my foot backwards at her. At last a lucky blow on her muzzle from the heel of my shoe caused her to run away howling, and the dog immediately followed her, just at the moment when two masons were coming up to assist me. Thus, by a resolute opposition, I escaped laceration. But this little affair is scarcely worth relating, except that it affords a proof of the advantage to be derived from resisting the attack of a dog to the utmost. But there are circumstances under which this mode of proceeding would be imprudent or impossible; and I have been furnished by a gentleman with the following observations, which point out another course, and which are not less illustrative of canine character. Homer informs us, Odyssey, B. 14, that the fury of a Dog in attacking an approaching stranger is appeased by the man's sitting down:

'Soon as Ulysses near the enclosure drew,
With open mouths the furious mastiffs flew:
Down sat the Sage, and cautious to withstand,
Let fall the offensive truncheon from his hand.'—POPE.

That this, even at the present day, is a well-understood mode of defence, appears from a paragraph in Mure's Journal of a Tour in Greece and the Ionian

Islands : ' At Argos, one evening, at the table of General Gordon, then commanding in chief in the Morea, the conversation happened to turn on the number and fierceness of the Greek Dogs ; when one of the company remarked, that he knew a very simple expedient for appeasing their fury. Happening, on a journey, to miss his road, and being overtaken by darkness, he sought refuge for the night at a. pastoral settlement by the wayside. As he approached, the dogs rushed out upon him ; and the consequence might have been serious, had he not been rescued by an old shepherd, the Eumæus of the fold, who sallied forth, and finding that the intruder was but a benighted traveller, after pelting off his assailants, gave him a hospitable reception in his hut. His guest made some remark on the watchfulness and zeal of his dogs, and on the danger to which he had been exposed in their attack. The old man replied that it was his own fault, for not taking the customary precaution in such an emergency : that he ought to have stopped, *and sat down*, until some person whom the animals knew, came to protect him. As this expedient was new to the traveller, he made some further inquiries ; and was assured, that if any person in such a predicament will simply seat himself on the ground, laying aside his weapons of defence, the dogs will also squat in a circle round him : that as long as he remains quiet, they will follow his example; but as soon as he rises and moves forward, they will renew the assault.' "

" And now for the Feline tribe. The story which I am about to recount will show that non-resist-

ance was the only plan to be pursued, when escape
from death seemed utterly hopeless. The principals
in this affair were a brave young British officer
and a full-grown lion of India. I was at Frankfort
on the Maine, and heard the account from the
officer's own mouth. I shall never forget the affable
and unassuming manner in which he related it to
me. I repeatedly urged him to allow me to put
it on record, and, at the same time, to make use
of his name ; but I plainly saw that his feelings
were against his complying with my request, and
I think I should not have succeeded, had I not
luckily brought to my assistance the plea of benefit
to natural history.

" Two fine lions made their appearance in a jungle,
some twenty miles distant from the cantonment of
Rajcote in the East Indies, where captain Woodhouse and his two friends, lieutenants De la Main
and Lang, were stationed. An elephant was dispatched to the place in the evening on which the
information arrived ; and on the morrow, at the
break of day, the three gentlemen set off on horseback, full of glee, and elated with the hope of a
speedy engagement. On arriving at the edge of
the jungle, people were ordered to ascend the
neighbouring trees, that they might be able to
trace the route of the lions, in case they left the
cover. After beating about in the jungle for some
time, the hunters started the two lordly strangers.
The officers fired immediately, and one of the
lions fell to rise no more. His companion broke
cover, and took off across the country. The

officers now pursued him on horseback, as fast as
the nature of the ground would allow, until they
learned from the men who were stationed in the
trees, that the lion had gone back into the thicket.
Upon this the three officers returned to the edge
of the jungle, and having dismounted from their
horses, they got upon the elephant, captain Woodhouse placing himself in the hindmost seat. They
now proceeded towards the heart of the jungle,
and found the beast standing under a large bush,
with his face directly towards them. The lion
allowed them to approach within range of his
spring, and then he made a sudden dart at the
elephant, clung on his trunk with a tremendous
roar, and wounded him just above the eye." After
this, the elephant could not be brought to face the
terrible enemy with confidence any more ; and the
officers sought him on foot. He was fired at by
one of them, " which irritated the mighty lord of
the woods, and he rushed towards him, breaking through the bushes in most magnificent style.
Captain Woodhouse now found himself placed in
an awkward situation. He was aware that, if he
retraced his steps, he would just get to the point
from which the lieutenant had fired, and to which
the Lion was making ; wherefore he instantly resolved to stand still, in the hopes that the Lion
would pass by without perceiving him. In this,
however, he was most unfortunately deceived: for
the enraged lion saw him in passing, and flew at
him, with a dreadful roar. In an instant, as
though it had been done by a stroke of lightning,

the rifle was broken and thrown out of the captain's hand, his left arm at the same moment being seized by the claws, and his right by the teeth, of his desperate antagonist. While these two brave and sturdy combatants were yet standing in mortal conflict, lieutenant De la Main ran up, and discharged his piece full at the Lion. This caused the Lion and the captain to come to the ground together, while lieutenant De la Main hastened out of the jungle to reload his gun. The Lion now began to craunch the captain's arm; but as the brave fellow, notwithstanding the pain which this horrid process caused, had the cool, determined resolution to lie still, the lordly savage let the arm drop out of his mouth, and quietly placed himself in a crouching position, with both his paws upon the thigh of his fallen foe. While things were in this untoward position, the captain unthinkingly raised his hand to support his head, which had got placed ill at ease in the fall. No sooner, however, had he moved it, than the Lion seized the lacerated arm a second time, craunched it as before, and fractured the bone still higher up. This additional *memento mori* from the Lion was not lost upon captain Woodhouse: it immediately put him in mind that he had committed an act of imprudence in stirring. The motionless state in which he persevered after this broad hint shewed that he had learned to profit by the painful lesson. He lay, bleeding and disabled, under the foot of a mighty and irritated enemy. The two lieutenants now hastened to his assistance; and a ball, coolly aimed by one of them, laid the animal dead by the side of his victim."

Other instances have been related, in which the Lion, after laying his victim prostrate, and incapable of motion, has reclined by his side for a time, and then walked quietly away. It is a remark of Pliny, that the passion of a lion may be known by the motions of his tail, as that of a horse by his ears.

A different mode of defence from either of the above must be adopted against such animals as the Rat and Weasel, which, when irritated, are exceedingly severe and pertinacious in their bite. But a very firm and tight grasp, compressing the chest or abdomen, will cause the creature immediately to let go its hold.

Against the Bull the most eligible method of escape appears to be, to offer it some object on which it may exert its fury, while the time thus engaged is made use of to effect a retreat. A hat or coat may well be so sacrificed; but care should be taken to cover your escape in a manner not to attract the notice of the animal. The effort will be most successful when the Bull is near his object; at which time he drops his head, and partially closes his eyes. A sudden turn to one side will then be successful.

The danger of interposing in the quarrels of contending beasts may be known from the following incident: for, remember that the poet says,

Those who in quarrels interpose,
Will often wipe a bloody nose.

A kindhearted gentleman, whose goodnature had often brought him into difficulties, was riding along the road, when he observed a couple of Rams engaged in battle, which each seemed to have determined should be the last his enemy should fight. They often retreated to obtain a better advantage in the onset; and butted each other with their heads, in a manner that none but the head of a sheep or a negro could sustain. After endeavouring in vain to separate the combatants while on horseback, he dismounted, and interposed between them; but in a moment, the fury they had been exerting on each other was directed to the intermeddling pacificator, who was soon laid prostrate in the dust; and, but for the providential interposition of a man who came that way, he might have paid with his life for his imprudence.

As further evidence of the consciousness which animals have of possessing peculiar powers of attack or defence, I may adduce the difference of manner in which different birds are seen to pursue even the same prey.

In a paper on the motion of birds, by Mr. Aldis, read at the meeting of the British Association for the Advancement of Science at York, in 1844, it is shewn, that the centre of gravity of their body is variously transferred, according to the object they have in view; but that it is necessary always to keep it precisely over or under the axis of motion; which in flying is immediately under the position of the wings, and in walking over the pivot of the legs. The legs assist in securing this object, by being gathered up or stretched out, according as they are long or short; and it is further secured by the co-operation of the curve or elongation of the neck, and the inflation of the body, from the air transmitted through the lungs to the bones and cellular membrane. The latter organization enables the larger birds to sail through the air with so little impulse from the wings, that it seems wonderful how their bulk is sustained aloft. In no way, perhaps, is this distinction of action better shewn than in the difference of manner in which birds take up food from the surface of the ocean. Thus the Gull, when on the wing, will only seek to take a floating object, and repeatedly flies round it, as if uncertain how to proceed; often dipping obliquely without success, and acting as if apprehensive of being jostled in the attempt.

The Gannet proceeds on a different principle; and as its humeral bones are of such a length that the elbow is situated at about the middle of the distance from the shoulder to the wrist, and the point of suspension is at that of gravity, a slight inclination forward causes it to fall headlong on its prey, and rarely without success. It is a stretch beyond simple Instinct that teaches this bird to obtain a higher elevation, when the fish it seeks is swimming deep beneath the surface.

To the same class must be referred the instinct noticed by Cicero and Pliny, whereby animals are led to defend the least guarded part of their body,

or that most susceptible of injury*. " Each kind
defends itself against violence and fear. The Bull
protects itself by its horns, the Boar by its tusks,
Lions by biting, others by flight, and some by concealment. The Cuttle defends itself by a discharge
of ink; the Torpedo by its powers of numbing. Some
repel by throwing out an intolerably offensive smell.
.... All animals are well instructed in this, and know
not only their own advantages, but also the weak
parts of their foes. They are acquainted with their
own weapons, and the opportunities for using them,
as well as the feeble parts of their enemies."

It is a beautiful provision of means to an end,
that the Hedgehog, which is not capable of distant
flight or ready concealment, is furnished with a
muscle of singular position and structure, that, by
encircling a large part of the body at a short depth
below the integument, enables it to assume the form
of a ball, with a formidable array of prickles pointed
in every direction; and in this attitude it is able to
remain long enough to wear out the patience of all
but human adversaries.

I once possessed a living specimen of this species,
which was so exceedingly timid, that I was never
able to see it in active condition, except by

---

* Contra metum et vim, suis se armis quæque defendit. Cornibus
tauri, apri dentibus, morsu leones, aliæ fuga se, aliæ occultatione
tutantur : atramenti effusione sepiæ. Torpore torpedines, multæ
etiam insectantes odoris intolerabii fœditate depellunt. — *Cicero de
Natura Deorum.*

Callent enim in hoc cuncta animalia, sciuntque non sua modo
commoda, verum et hostium adversa. Norunt sua tela, norunt
occasiones, partesque dissidentium imbelles.—*Pliny,* lib. viii. c. 25.

viewing it through a crevice. On the least sound, without seeking to run to shelter, it would roll itself up ; and so conscious was the creature of the security of its defensive armour, that it at last effected its deliverance from captivity by mounting a low wall, and throwing itself down to a considerable depth below. That depth happened to be the sea, but it swam in a right direction, and landed in safety.

An error in observation has been extensively circulated concerning the manner in which the Sharks take their prey. Their peculiar action in inflicting a bite is highly characteristic of the consciousness which these creatures possess of what their jaws are capable of effecting; but it would be difficult for them to bite through a large object by the simple clasping of the jaws, which, at the most, would then only pinch off a piece of their prey. The mouth therefore is brought round to some extent, in a direction opposite to that in which the necessary rotation is to be accomplished ; and with the advantage thus obtained, the sharp and serrated teeth are made to rotate in the manner of a circular saw, by which a substance of considerable thickness is speedily severed. When the Blue Shark has not succeeded in thus cutting away the line attached to the hook it has swallowed, it sometimes continues to revolve in this manner, until half the cord is twined round its body. The common opinion that Sharks are compelled to turn on their backs, in order to seize their prey, has arisen from a mistaken view of this action. But in reality the position is assumed with the intention of acquiring a greater advantage in the rotation which is necessary to sever the part on which they have fixed their bite. The mode by which the teeth are attached to the jaws, and the direction of their arrangement, admit only of this kind of action, in dealing with a prey of considerable bulk.

Superiorly armed as many animals appear to be for offence and defence in comparison with mankind, we can discover this to be more than counterbalanced by natural advantages on the side of man. If the deer and bull are furnished for all occasions by the kindness of Nature, the benefit is more than counterbalanced by their being compelled to carry their weapons with them wherever they go, and they cannot change them for any other which a different mode of attack might render necessary. The faculty of invention in man is calculated to meet a variety of emergencies, with the additional convenience of being able to lay his weapons aside when no longer needed. The same remark applies to the advantage of artificial over natural clothing.

CHAPTER IV.

An apprehension of danger, operating on great timidity, is the principal cause why some creatures are incapable of being rendered tame ; and this untamableness is produced by fear exciting such a degree of confusion in its perceptions, as hinders the creature from understanding the nature and intention of those kind actions which are shewn towards it, when an endeavour is made to conciliate its regard. When therefore we discover in an animal a natural inaptitude to receive such impressions of conciliation, it may be concluded that there is, in addition to an overwhelming fear, a deficiency in the capacity of the Understanding. For though the truth of the Brahmin's answer to Alexander the Great may be admitted, that the wisest creature is that which keeps at the greatest distance from man, yet when compelled to endure his presence, it is a higher degree of wisdom to accept his friendship than to provoke his enmity. A mixture of understanding, therefore, with timidity will lead to a perception and appreciation of the signs that are manifested in its favour ; and by compliance with them, enable it to secure the attachment of the object of its fears. And even where a state of liberty is maintained, a degree of understanding united with timidity leads to the existence of the valuable quality of cautiousness, which is the surest principle of safety; whereas the absence of the nobler qualification of intelligence produces such distraction, as will prevent a creature from using, even where life depends on it, the ordinary powers of which it is possessed. Habits illustrative of this have been observed in individuals of the common Hare. If, on being first roused, it rushes off with headlong haste, it will assuredly be taken by a dog; but if the creature be seen to stop, and erect its ears, as if listening to its pursuer, its escape may be regarded as exceedingly probable. The effect of terror on the same animal is witnessed when it is pursued by the cry of a company of weasels. Their speed is greatly inferior to that of the hare; but such is the influence of the terror infused into it by an instinctive consciousness of the insidious and cruel nature of the enemy, that these ravenous creatures rarely have the trouble of a long pursuit. Instances are common in which a Hare, after escaping to a considerable distance from the reach of its pursuer, has altered its course, and returned to the very seat of the peril; and if followed after with great clamour, with any very loud and unusual noise, it is sure to be thus overtaken.

A parent Weasel, with its young ones in training, has been seen in eager pursuit of a flying blackbird; and though a slight elevation in the direction of

flight would have carried the bird over a hedge
and out of the reach of danger, so great was its
terror, that it was unable to mount so high, and
consequently soon became their prey.

Openhearted understanding, added to ferocity, and
modifying its influence, constitutes the chief distinction of character between the Lion and the Tiger : for
the latter, being ever under the influence of fear as
well as of fury, cannot, like the former, be made
to contemplate a display of favour ; and the few
instances to the contrary of which there are accounts
in the history of this animal will tend to establish
rather than invalidate this remark. The attachment which the tiger has manifested in its adult
growth had received its foundation in early youth,
before its native fear or fury had been brought
into exercise : the animal had not forgotten the
object of its regard, though long removed from its
sight ; but it was not able to admit of any new
attachment.

It also weighs something in our estimate of
the influences which stand in the way of our
taming particular species, that some of them are
liable . to sudden starts of passion, which burst
the bonds of any restraint we have been able
to lay on it. There are even some insects which
have been rendered sensible of human attentions
and regard ; and the common honey-bee is known
to distinguish the presence of an accustomed friend
from that of a stranger : but the irritability to
which it is subject on any cross to its temper
renders it, according to its means, not a little

formidable when roused. The cat, however fond of its domestic friends, is prone, upon occasion, to strike a sudden blow with its expanded paws; and, if possessed of as much force as the lion, it would inflict as much injury.

It has happened occasionally that certain individuals of the most untamable races have partaken of this softening influence; so that the Hyæna has followed its master as a dog, and the Weasel has laid aside its shyness and fear. And it is no less worthy of notice, in our history of the variations of habit, that where portions of a race possess qualities which admit of being wrought upon, so that domestication becomes their second nature, yet that singular exceptions occur, wherein what we may denominate temper, or a wayward direction of the faculties, renders them incapable of a beneficial direction, or hinders them from being estimable companions. I have known a horse which no soothing was able to conciliate—no kind treatment render any other than what is denominated vicious, with the habit of doing everything but that which it was wanted to do. This spirit was at last subdued by fixing on its back a terrifying object, which its utmost efforts were not able to shake off: but when the conquest was accomplished, not a single worthy quality remained.

That, however, it may occasionally happen that a cross-tempered creature, and one not to be soothed by ordinary means, shall still be susceptible of the better emotions, the following anecdote of an ill-natured Gander will shew. It is taken from the public papers of April, 1845; and ought to redeem a despised race from a reproach which is at once the heaviest and most frequent to which even the human race is liable. "*A grateful Gander.*—An old bird, of surly habits, following and attacking every person that passed, in the neighbourhood of Clysthydon, in his wanderings chanced to get up a deep narrow drain, whence he was not able to get out again. A labourer, in passing, discovered the gander in this situation, and mercifully drew him out. Since this time, as if to evince his gratitude, the gander follows his deliverer about like a dog, and suffers himself to be handled in any way the man chooses. This special mark of gratitude is alone extended to his deliverer : to all else he is as spiteful as before."

That animals possess much individuality of character is well known, and it is amusingly illustrated in the history which the poet Cowper gives of his tame hares. I possess opportunities of frequently observing the conduct of a dog, who through life has displayed manifestations of a goodnature which distinguishes him from the generality of his canine brethren, and which, after subjecting him to much distress, has established him in a situation in which this amiable quality procures him proportionate esteem. He is of the Newfoundland race, and first saw the light in some part of North America. Being of robust stature, it was thought that he would be valuable on board ship, to which therefore he was consigned ; and he would have fulfilled the expectations of his owner, if he had been required to plunge into the ocean to save a man from drowning. But he could not be made to understand that man could be otherwise than honest, or an enemy to man ; and therefore, being judged too quiet for his situation, the poor dog was turned adrift in an English port, to obtain food and shelter wherever he could find it. His fine appearance and docility soon obtained him a master, but the same fault accompanied him ; and it could not be believed that he could be of any service, when he would not snarl at a stranger, or quarrel with a neighbour. Twice therefore was this poor dog turned out to seek his casual fortune ; and though a little food would suffice, and refuse fish as soon as any, poor Boatswain was in danger of being starved, when a little boy took compassion on his lank appearance and mild deportment, and by dint of entreaty obtained permission to assign him a resting-place ; with the condition that, to provide him food, he would, in case of necessity, share with him a portion of his own. By the superior authorities this was a reluctant permission ; but his affectionate behaviour soon succeeded in effecting a reconciliation. It is amusing to see how fondly this poor creature is attached to all the members of the protecting family. A slight notice is acknowledged rather by an inward than an outward rejoicing, and he will suffer without a murmur a rejection, and even expulsion from a favourite situation,—frequently even on the utterance of a simple command. But his most characteristic expression is when he manifests similar kindly feelings to his canine brethren, many of whom are too surly to accept them in the spirit in which they are offered ; and the appearance of mortified disappointment in his countenance, when his approaches to friendly intercourse are met by a growl, are exceedingly expressive. He appears pleased at the liberties taken with him by children ; and when these become an annoyance, the utmost amount of his displeasure is shewn by an unceremonious thrust that lays them prostrate. On one occasion, when a determination was manifested to ride on his back, after suffering it for awhile, he disposed of the inconvenience by dismounting the rider into the gutter. There is only one unamiable trait in his disposition, which is the pleasure he seems to take in annoying any stray ass he may chance to meet. His only spontaneous attacks are directed against that persecuted animal. A long walk is also to him an abomination ; and on one occasion, after accompanying a lady to the distance of half a mile from the beach to the next village, he returned to the seaside, sprung from the rock into the sea, and followed the boat that had brought him, in the confidence that he should not receive a rejection.

In some creatures we discover the ability to convert fear into caution ; or, rising above this, the caution itself amounts to a guard against what may appear as danger, before any actual signs of it have been discovered : of which examples may be found in many of the higher orders of animals.

The consideration, that excessive timidity is the chief obstacle to the taming of many creatures, enables us to discern the proper conduct to be pursued in seeking this desirable object. The process must be conducted by shewing the creature that its dread is groundless; that the supposed enemy may in truth be a friend; and while the outbreak of passion or fear is shewn to be useless, or is rendered harmless, the needless trepidation is soothed, and not irritated. Much coolness and patience are requisite for the performance of this task; and especially when the creature is subject to inequality of temper, or possesses great power to injure; but when accomplished in this manner, it is lasting.

There are many wild animals of which man knows nothing but their destructiveness, and from which he derives no benefit but such as accrues from their death; but from which, by judicious training, he might obtain valuable assistance in many of the conveniences of life. In a large part of Africa the Elephant is at this time hunted for no other purpose than the supply of ivory; whereas in former ages this noble creature was, in the same country, rendered docile and abundantly useful, as it is well known to be in other countries. The Dog is an abomination to Jews and Mahometans, who thus lose its valuable services. The Seal and Otter have been tamed, and taught to bring home fish for their master; and even a species of Cormorant was formerly employed in our own country for a similar purpose, as it still is, at this time, among the fishermen of China.

CHAPTER V.

RECURRING again to examples, so abundant in nature, of the variety of actions by which different races and species display their consciousness of the possession of organs and powers which enable them to escape, conceal, or defend themselves, I will mention those by which the two former are sought, by *running* in order to avoid observation, or by remaining *concealed*, without the manifestation of terror. And though by bringing forward these instances in this place, I am in some degree anticipating a subsequent part of my argument, on the whole they appear more appropriately in connection with the present division of the subject.

The Landrail (*Crex pratensis*), when alarmed, prefers trusting to the plainness of its colours and its tortuous course, rather than to its powers of flight; and is gone to an opposite part of the field, before an observer would suppose that it had discovered its foe. The Water-rail (*Rallus aquaticus*), Spotted rail (*Crex porzana*), and Moorhen (*Gallinula chloropus*), will creep off to some crevice or gutter, and there remain for hours after the patience of the pursuer is exhausted. I once kept in captivity a

Barbary partridge, and was surprised at the great strength it possessed in its legs, especially in leaping. This bird was fond of running; and, without the assistance of its wings, it was able to spring from the floor to the top of a table, without much seeming effort. But having taken it to a garden for exercise, the bird suddenly disappeared; and all the search that was made did not lead to a discovery of the place or manner of its escape. The only certainty was, that it could not have been effected by the use of its wings; and it was only on the following day that it became known that it had obtained the shelter of a narrow hole, in which it had remained so long consciously hidden from its pursuers. I have known the Wheatear (*Sylvia Œnanthe*) to seek to avoid my notice, by entering a shallow cavern beneath a large stone; and when about to come out, seeing me at the entrance, it retreated into a crooked passage, where it remained hidden so long as I remained in the neighbourhood. Most other birds would have fluttered out, on the first alarm, whatever the danger might have been, and in the present instance this was exceedingly small; but in the Wheatear secresy is preferred to seeking safety by flight.

Among the singular methods by which some of our native birds effect concealment, is that of immersing the whole body, and even the head, beneath the water, where they remain without motion, the bill only being kept protruded for the sake of breathing. The Water-rail and Dabchick (*Podiceps minor*) are possessed of a singular power of accomplishing this; but the manner in which it is effected is a matter of dispute. It has been contended that it can only be done by the creature's seizing hold, with its feet, of the herbage growing from the bottom : but the contrary of this is affirmed to have been witnessed ; and a probable supposition appears to be, that the most important agency in obtaining this effect is, the power of diminishing the specific gravity of their body, by expelling the air usually contained in the bones and cellular membrane lining the integument, with a portion of that which would otherwise have been retained in the cells of the lungs. The Swan performs a similar action when it sinks into the water, to enable its young ones to mount its back, that they may be conveyed through the more rapid currents in safety. It appears to be by a like power that the Whale (*Balæna mysticetus*) sometimes sinks from the surface, out of the sight and reach of enemies, when its situation prevents the possibility of its diving by the usual action of the fins and tail. This action in birds seems the reverse of that which prepares the body for flight : for in the latter case, the integuments being inflated through the inhalation of air from the lungs, and its subsequent diffusion over the body, a moderate effort is enough to launch it aloft; and some of the larger species are suspended in the higher regions, and move rapidly in a variety of directions, even in opposition to the wind, with no apparent action of the wings. But for the purpose of submersion in water or descent in air, compression of the body and absolute stillness may be sufficient to retain it; while in the former case a slight action of a small portion of the lungs is sufficient to continue the support of life.

There are species of fishes also that are in the habit of seeking the safety which arises from concealment; and that too, not only by frequenting places where the colour of the ground is most like that of their own bodies, but also by burrowing beneath the soil, or quitting the water altogether, and lying hid in secret crevices in the rocks.

In our own country, the kinds which most frequently resort to this are the Flat-fishes (*Pleuronectidæ*), as Turbot, Plaice, Flounder, and their congenerous species: the Conger and Eel (*Anguilla conger* and *acutirostris*, &c.), Launce (*Ammodytes*), Wiever (*Trachinus draco et vipera*), Lamprey (*Petromyzon branchialis*), and Lancelet (*Amphioxus lanceolatus*): an enumeration which comprises genera of very opposite kinds, but which possess in common a few characteristics which we may suppose to be connected with the habit in question.

It is easy for these Flat-fishes to obtain concealment beneath the sand—for a little is sufficient to cover them—and all that is required for the purpose is a tremulous motion of the fins bordering the body. The eyes, which, in comparison with other fishes', are unusually prominent, and the gaze of which is not at right angles with the body, are the only parts left exposed. It is perhaps to lift them instantly above the surface on the slightest appearance of danger that the dorsal fin is brought

so far over the head, and the ventrals made so
much more powerful than the pectorals. But the
other species of burrowing fishes completely hide
themselves from sight; and the facility with which
this action is accomplished in the Launces renders
it the most ready mode of escape when danger
presses. Both this fish and the Mud-lamprey are
able to move through a considerable depth of
their covering mud or sand with ease and quickness; and the slightest touch will cause them
to exert this power of motion. It is thus beneath the surface of even rough gravel that the
Launce sheds its spawn; and scattered as this
is, it remains safe from its numerous enemies.
The Conger accomplishes the task of inhuma-
tion with much labour, and therefore does not
attempt it where other modes of concealment can
be obtained; but in soft ground it begins the
operation by fixing first the point of its jaws, and
then, passing the body round as on a pivot,
it penetrates into a recess, on which the sand
is soon thrown in a manner which leaves little
mark of its presence below. I have some reason
to suppose that both the conger and eel deposit
their spawn in such situations : for multitudes of
the young of the latter have been seen to emerge
from an aperture in the bottom of a stream in
continued succession.

It is evident from this action of interment, and
still more in those of progression through the
ground and emergence, that these fishes possess
faculties of perception, of great accuracy and power,

especially fitted to these purposes. And though one seat of this is in the fins on the anterior part of the body, which are more sensitive than the fins of the species not possessed of such instincts, yet it resides still more remarkably in the tail, which is furnished with an organization that particularly ministers to the influence by which it is accomplished. This remarkable distribution of blood-vessels in the Eel was first pointed out by Dr. Marshal Hall, who has given a figure of it in his work on the Circulation of the Blood, Plate X; which is copied by Mr. Yarrell in his Natural History of the Eel (*British Fishes*, vol. ii.), though without notice of its probable nature and object. But though the minute arrangement may be different, something similar, or at least a remarkable enlargement of vessels, not included in the regular order of circulation of the blood, is seen in the Flat-fishes, Launces and Wiever; and if not yet discovered in the Lancelet, it may be accounted for in the transparent nature of all the vessels of this fish. I have noticed in the Lance that it is chiefly visible during life; that after death it disappears, and another set of circulating vessels is seen, which had carried on the usual supply of blood to the tail. Of this latter organ each ray is accompanied with a smaller vessel, which is most conspicuous at the edge of the caudal plate.

We may suppose this curious arrangement of blood-vessels to be more complicated in the eel and conger, because in those fishes the instrument, at the base of which it is placed, is endowed with higher powers of feeling, action, and especially of prehension. The conger is able to insinuate the point of its tail through a crevice, and so to dilate it as to obtain a passage for its body by a retrograde action ; or, if that cannot be accomplished, it will examine by its powers of sensation, draw itself along, and, using the tail as a fixed point, elevate its body as by a lever, and lift itself over an opposing obstacle of considerable height : so that neither the eel nor conger can be confined within a limited space, when their inclinations prompt them to wander from it.

There is scarcely a family in nature that might not supply us with some instructive instance of the influence of this principle ; but we will conclude with the mention of that which has excited the wonder of philosophers in all ages, and which has not lost its interest in our own day. That some creatures should be endued with an apparatus and natural powers, similar to those which constitute an electric battery, is indeed a subject that may well excite surprise, whether we regard the mode of its employment, or the use to which it is destined. But I will only regard it now as a means of defence ; and this it is proved to be, of an effectual kind, and of its force and direction the creature shews itself perfectly conscious. The Electric eel (*Gymnotus electricus*), the habits of which are particularly described in Travels to the Equinoctial Regions of America by Humboldt and Bonpland, vol. iv., buries itself in oozy ground at the bottom of rivers in Central America : on being disturbed it rises near the surface, and, laying itself side by side with the animal against which it is irritated, inflicts such chastisement as shall deter it from all intrusion for the future. The Torpedo (*T. nobiliana* and its congeners), conscious of being without the spines which constitute the means of defence of most of the natural family to which it belongs, when only just excluded from the egg, displays the will to exert the same power ; and none of the creatures furnished with it are known to resort to any other. It is a curious circumstance, that several species of fishes, which possess a formidable arrangement of spines, are yet furnished with them in such situations, and with the points so directed, as to appear the least likely to be effective against an adversary ; and yet, when brought into operation, some sudden motion shews how well acquainted they are with the uses of which they are susceptible. This is well exemplified in the spines, in many instances curiously incurvated or notched, of Sharks and Ray-fishes: in some of which these organs are so arranged, as if to render them incapable of inflicting an injury ; and yet, by some peculiarity of action, these fishes are formidable enemies to those who venture to attack them. Sticklebacks (*Gasterostei*) also, and probably the Scad (*Caranx trachurus*), employ their spines, and even their lateral plates, in lacerating such of the scaly tribes as seek to injure them.

To the observer of Nature it is a work of instruction and pleasure to discover the diversity and even opposition of contrivance, through the agency of which similar purposes are obtained. Thus, as we have remarked,

E

in many instances safety is secured by an effort of strength, and in others by rapidity of flight, or the timidity of concealment: whilst that which in man constitutes the most refined operation of science is the resort of a few; and there are some which trust their security to the nauseous influence which a disgusting discharge shall produce on the organs of smell. Another mode of safety exists in that which the generality of creatures is known to avoid,—the attention and gaze of the foe; and the means of escape are afforded by assuming such a terrific aspect as may confound the faculties of the pursuer, and strike him with an effectual though empty terror. The beauty of the peacock's plumage was a theme of admiration in the remotest times; and the bird was sought after as capable of adding splendour to the magnificence of Solomon. The chief display of this beauty arises from that arrangement of long and gorgeous feathers which spring from the space between the region behind the wings and the origin of the tail; but the use of this to the bird itself has been a subject of doubt. At first sight it seems to be no better than a luxuriance of nature, and an encumbrance, rather than a benefit. The action by which their splendour is outspread has also been deemed an absurd manifestation of pride.

But men are imperfect interpreters of the actions of animals; and a closer examination of the habits of this bird will afford a different explanation. The tail of the peacock is of a plain and humble description; and seems to be of no other use besides aiding in the erection of the long feathers of the loins ; while the latter are supplied at their insertion with an arrangement of voluntary muscles, which contribute to their elevation, and to the other motions of which they are capable. If surprised by a foe, the peacock presently erects its gorgeous feathers; and the enemy at once beholds starting up before him a creature which his terror cannot fail to magnify into the bulk implied by the circumference of a glittering circle of the most dazzling hues, his attention at the same time being distracted by a hundred glaring eyes meeting his gaze in every direction. A hiss from the head in the centre, which in shape and colours resembles that of a serpent, and a rustle from the trembling quills, are attended by an advance of the most conspicuous portion of this bulk; which is in itself an action of retreat, being caused by a receding motion of the body of the bird. That must be a bold animal which does not pause at the sight of such an object ; and a short interval is sufficient to ensure the safety of the bird : but if, after all, the enemy should be bold enough to risk an assault, it is most likely that its eagerness or rage would be spent on the glittering appendages, in which case the creature is divested only of that which a little time will again supply. A like explanation may be offered of the use of the long and curious appendages of the head and neck of various kinds of humming-birds, which, however feeble, are a pugnacious race.

Among the birds of our own country the Bittern (*Ardea stellaris*), the Pheasant and common Cock, are, in a less degree, examples of the same strategy in defence; and besides the terror they infuse, are instruments of protection, in offering an uncertain mark to a combatant.

Dr. Derham speaks of the hissing of the Wryneck (*Yunx Torquilla*) as sufficient to scare him from the examination of its nest; and a similar sound from the nest of a Titmouse (*Parus major*) is enough to frighten back the fingers of a bird-nesting boy.

CHAPTER VI.

AT an early stage of this investigation, reference was made to the poets and philosophers of a previous age, to shew the limited views which they possessed of the essence and extent of Instinct; and I had occasion more especially to remark that, by those who had attempted to consider it philosophically, the impression was conveyed that, in their apprehension, it was the motive power, or mind, of animals, as distinguished from that of the human race.

It has been one part of my object to shew that such an idea is too contracted in its nature, and has its foundation in error; but the mistake—*for which philosophers are chiefly indebted to the divines, whom in those days it would not have been safe to have contradicted*—consists in having treated it on what may be denominated metaphysical principles: according to which it was judged to arise from, and be constituted by, a simple and separate existence —a kind of soul—which formed the principle of the living nature of the beings actuated by it, in the same manner as the human soul was supposed to constitute the moving principle, the essence of the life as well as the intellect of the body it inhabited.

They proceeded from this to infer that it was not possible it should exert an influence on mankind, because they were not able to imagine the possible presence of two distinct ruling souls in a single being.

It is no part of our purpose to enter here on an inquiry into the nature of the human soul; but it is plain from what has been shewn, that Instinct, in its simple and unmixed manifestation, is no other than a vital property, which has its foundation in the living organization of a combination of tissues, of which that of the nerves, both in extent and function, is most predominant.

From this proposition it will follow, that as, in regard to his merely animal powers, man is furnished with similar organs, and is governed by laws parallel with those of the lower creatures, from which, so far as they extend, his manifestations do not differ more than do some of them from others, he must also be swayed by the influences of what must properly be pronounced Instinctive faculties.

And it is to be observed that even Cicero, who was willing enough to contend for the dignity of human nature, is an advocate for the general community of the instinctive nature of man and animals:*—"In the first place," he says, "it is a gift

* "Principio generi animalium omni est a natura tributum, ut se, vitam corpusque tueatur, declinetque ea quæ nocitura videantur; omnique, quæcunque ad vivendum sint necessaria anquirat, et paret, ut pastum, alit latibula, ut alia generis ejusdem. Commune autem animantium omnium est conjunctionis appetitus, procreanda causa, et curæ quædam eorum quæ procreata sunt." But his philosophy and

from nature to every kind of animal, that it should consult the preservation of itself, both in its life and limbs; and consequently that it should avoid everything which seems hurtful. And further, that it should obtain and prepare for food whatever is necessary to subsistence, as well for itself as its offspring. The desire of union for the sake of offspring, and the care of them when obtained, is felt by every kind of creature...... But there is this great difference between mankind and the beast: that the latter, as it is moved by the impression of sense, applies itself to present things, and little regards what is past or future. But man, who is possessed of reason, through which he discovers what is meet, perceives the causes, course, and remote connections of events, compares things that resemble each other, and brings together and connects the future with the present."

If this were the sole difference between man and the brute, it would at the best be only in degree, and not in kind. In proof of the law of human nature by which man is compelled to observe and obey instinctive impulses, it will not be necessary for us to enter upon a minute survey of the various circumstances of his

observation fail him when he adds: "sed inter hominem et belluam hoc maxime interest, quod hæc tantum, quantum sensu movetur, ad id solum quod adest, quodque præsens est se accommodat, paululum admodum sentiens præteritum et futurum. Homo autem, quod rationis est particeps, per quam consequentia cernit, causas rerum videt, earumque progressus, et quasi antecessionis non ignorat, similitudines comparet, et rebus præsentibus adjungit atque annectit futuras."—*De Officiis.*

existence, in his passage from youth to age: for, in attempting this, we should bring ourselves under the necessity of constantly endeavouring to separate and define the phenomena which have their source in one, from those which must be admitted to spring from another and higher origin.

In preference, then, I will select a period of his life when he has not acquired habits of any sort: when no instruction can have been received, when no opportunity has been offered of profiting by imitation—a principle so powerful in the education even of brutes — when, in fact, the only stimulus to which he has been subjected is that of the air, which has first excited the action of breathing, and has then entered the lungs to produce its specific effects on the blood. At this the earliest stage in the life of an infant, the sensation of hunger is the only want it has ever felt, or has been able to display. The manner in which this craving of nature is manifested is eminently characteristic of an instinctive faculty; and it is the more illustrative in this instance, since it is both appropriate to its present circumstances, and different from those which are equally appropriate to a more advanced stage of its life. No precept has instructed the little stranger that the mouth, rather than the eye or ear, is the entrance to that channel through which nourishment ought to be received; or that this food is furnished by an apparatus of one form rather than another; and yet, even if a finger be brought into contact with its cheek, the mouth is instantly directed to the object, and it pursues it in various directions, as the impression first made is removed to another spot. And when at last the lips are permitted to be closed on the supposed source of enjoyment, the action is not that of chewing—which is the instinctive propensity, under similar circumstances, of the being from whom the infant has derived its existence—but of sucking, which is the only one that for the present can be made available to the object in view.

We are drawn aside for a moment from the consideration of this fact to a reverent admiration of the goodness and wisdom of the Framer of our existence,—that thus, previous to a capacity for instruction, He formed our structure in such a connexion of cause, effect, and use, that human necessities are better supplied than if we had been thrown dependent on the latent capacity of reason ; and that, in the different races of animals, a corresponding variation is perceptible in the minuter parts of this proceeding, though all are directed to a common aim. The good feeling of Bewick induced him to place under one of his vignettes this question: " Who taught the lamb to suck its mother's paps ?" and he might have added, to strike the paps with blows of the head : a process which would be found not a little painful to other mothers, but which has the effect of causing the milk to flow more readily. By a similar instinct the nestling-bird, instead of closing its mouth, expands it to the utmost, to receive the food passed from the bill of the parent.

In this proceeding of a child, curious as is the

adaptation, the infant is at best only on a level
with the horse and cow; and in the last of these
animals a peculiarity of action is so decidedly
perceptible, that a calf would starve in the presence
of its appropriate food, if observation had not taught
the dairy-woman to convert her fingers into the
semblance of teats; and by holding them projecting
from a vessel, tutor it to suck up its first milk.

It is not a consciousness, though this might be
instinctive, of the difference between fluid and solid
nutriment, that leads to the practice of sucking, in
the early stage of existence, and of chewing in more
advanced growth: for in the animal tribes, as well
as in man, in subsequent life, it is by sipping or
lapping that fluids are absorbed. The lapping of
the dog bears little resemblance to its action when
young; and an infant will suck a solid substance,
though it yields no fluid, and is not able to grasp
it with its lips.

The propensity to playful gambolling is another of
these unconscious impulses, and is as much a
proceeding of instinct in the child as the kitten.
How earnestly it is followed, in either instance, is
an amusing portion of its nature; and few can have
failed to notice the eagerness with which the kitten will run round and round after its tail, and
snarl, and endeavour to bite it, when disappointed
in the attempt to secure it in its grasp. The
changes in disposition which are brought about by
the modification of organization through the progress of years are not less conspicuous in the
careful grimalkin that has laid aside her gambols,

and now directs her attention to the important
object of adding a captured mouse to her larder—
of feasting on a caged canary, or a coveted morsel
from the delicacies of the parlour; in the sober ass
luxuriating on a thistle, undisturbed by the intrusion of a tyrant master; than in the miser,
who has left the top and ball which amuse "children
of a larger growth," to dote upon his pelf; or
the sensualist, who has changed the sports of the
field and flood, for the idlest of amusements in a
crowded city. Many of even our most refined
gratifications have their foundation in this instinctive feeling; and while in their sanctity they
are recommended by reason, they are compelled to
find their permanent support in the humble but
energetic principle of Instinct.

It is interesting to examine in what manner
attempts have been made to account for this diversity of proceeding on the maxims of the received
philosophy: of which the most prevalent amongst
the Western sages, as we have seen, was the existence of a soul in brutes, which soul was supposed to be nothing less than the presence of the
Deity himself. The opinion of the Orientals was
of a different character; and it was probably from
this source that Hippocrates drew his idea of the
presence of three souls in humankind: the natural soul, or animation; the sensitive; and the
intellectual. It is according to the same principle
that the Jews call common life a soul; and the
opinion was widely spread among them that each
of the natural faculties had its origin in a separate

soul. The learned Jew, Maimonides, says, " But as each distinct species of animated beings has its own peculiar soul, the faculties of each species of soul must be peculiar to itself." And again: " We apply the word *soul* indiscriminately to the souls of men and those of all other animals, although each species has its own peculiar *soul*, the faculties of which must also be peculiar to itself." If we make this correction, that, in these opinions, the effect is mistaken for the cause, it will not be difficult to admit the truth of this opinion.

CHAPTER VII.

The portion of our subject to which we have last referred leads us on to new ground, and the investigation of another habit, which seems to lie on the boundary between what has preceded and that which is to follow: for in many of its properties it partakes of the nature of Instinct, while in others it claims a more lofty extraction.

It has been a favourite speculation of some writers—who have sought in the mere progressive laws according to which a supposed philosophical development is effected the whole cause and economy of creation, and who have professed to trace the manner in which this progression must necessarily have gone on from the early stage of misty and chaotic nebula, through the operations of gravity and attraction, in the lapse of unlimited ages, to their present state of completion—to suppose that when man first obtained consciousness of existence he was merely a savage, as ignorant of the amenities of life, as the natives of the wildest regions of the world at the present time * ;

* Vita fera similis, nullos agitata per usos:
　　Artis adhuc expers, et rude vulgus erant.
　Pro domibus frondes norant, pro frugibus herbas.
　Nectar erat palmis hausta duabus aqua.

Nullus

And wild in woods the noble savage ran.
The state of nature was the reign of God:—
Pride then was not, nor arts that pride to aid;
Man walk'd with beast, joint tenant of the shade;
The same his table, and the same his bed;—
In the same temple, the resounding wood,
All vocal beings hymn'd their equal God.—POPE.

It is true that even in this case God is represented as the *primum mobile:* so that the scheme is not one of mere atheism. But the following quotations shew that the representations of this secretly-working, philosophical Deity imply no more than a mere abstraction, destitute of personality—a simple fatality, with little of volition; and, in truth, nothing better than a diffusive æther or galvanic influence. " The philosophy of Pythagoras (which was full of superstition) did first plant a monstrous imagination, which afterwards was, by the school of Plato and others, watered and nourished. It was, that the world was *one*, entire, perfect, living creature : insomuch as Apollonius of Tyana, a Pythagorean prophet, affirmed that the ebbing and flowing of the sea was the respiration of the world, drawing in water as breath, and putting it forth again. They went on and inferred that, if the world were a living creature, it had a soul and spirit; which also they held, calling it *spiritus mundi*, the spirit or soul of the world. By which they did not intend God (for they did admit of a deity besides), but only

Nullus anhelabat sub adunco vomere taurus;
Nulla sub imperio terra colentis erat:—
Sub Jove durabant, et corpora nuda gerebant,
Docta graves imbres et tolerare notos.—OVID.

the soul or essential form of the universe. This foundation being laid, they might build upon it what they would : for in a living creature, though never so great (as for example in a great whale), the sense, and the affects of any one part of the body, instantly make a transcursion throughout the whole body. So that by this they did insinuate that no distance of place, nor want or indisposition of matter, could hinder magical operations : but that, for example, we mought here in Europe have sense and feeling of that which was done in China ; and likewise we mought work any effect without and against matter ; and this, not holden by the co-operation of angels or spirits, but only by the unity and harmony of nature."—(Lord Bacon's Natural History, 10th Century.)

In their ignorance of the nature and power of gravitation, it was a difficulty, in their system of philosophy, to imagine how the planets and the world we inhabit are kept in regular and consistent motion; and therefore, extending the principle of this spirit of the world, they supposed that the whole of them were animated or guided by separate intelligences : which Jewish sages believed to be created, but which the Gentiles held to be divine ; but the supposition of their mighty influence was in either case a necessary result. There can be little doubt that Pliny conveys the sentiments of the principal part of the philosophers of his day concerning the Deity that governs the world, in the commencement of the second book of his Natural History : " It is reasonable to believe," he says,

" that the world, and that which I will comprise
under the name of the sky, within the circumference
of which all things are enclosed, is a divine power ;
eternal, immense, neither created, nor ever to perish.
To explore its properties is neither the concern of
man, nor does it lie within the reach of human
conjecture. This Being is sacred, eternal, immense,
all in all, and he is truly every thing in its most
intimate portion ; finite resembling infinite, the established of all things, and resembling the least
established ; embracing within himself all things,
whether within or without : at the same time the
work of nature, and nature itself. It is madness
that some have disturbed their minds in attempting
to measure him, &c."*

How much more consistent with reason is the
representation afforded us in the only really ancient
history, in which the Deity is seen clearly distinguished from his works ; and man is described,
with all the attendant creatures, as springing into
existence from the actual creation of his Author,

* "Mundum, et hoc quod nomine alio cœlum appellare libuit,
cujus circumflexu teguntur cuncta, numen esse credi par est, æter-
num, immensum, neque genitum, neque interiturum unquam. Hujus
extera indagare, nec interest hominum, neque capit humanæ con-
jectura mentis. Sacer est, æternus, immensus, totus in toto, imo
vere ipse totum ; finitus et infinito similis, omnium rerum certus,
et similis incerto, extra, intra, cuncta complexus in se ; idemque
rerum naturæ opus, et rerum ipsa natura. Furor est, mensuram
ejus animo quosdam agitasse, atque prodere ausos : alios rursus
occasione hinc sumpta, aut his data, innumerabiles tradisse mundos,
ut totidem rerum naturas credi oportet, aut, si una omnes incubaret,
totidem tamen Soles totidemque Lunas, et cætera etiam in uno et
immensa et innumerabilia sydera, &c."

in the possession of all the acquirements that are necessary to the perfection of his being. It is true he had that to learn which only experience could bestow ; and such must be his state in every imaginable stage of his existence : but it is an injurious reflection on the excellency of his endowments to suppose that his earliest condition was not of a civilized nature. And such a state, as a principal qualification, implies the possession of conversible language, to no small extent and degree of refinement : as we are warranted to conclude, among other reasons, from the historical fact, that he was able to hold converse, not only with his own Kind, but with his Creator also, in such terms, and on such subjects, as that both should be gratified. It is consistent with this narrative to believe that animals also received their first powers of whatever language they are capable of at the same time, and from the same source ; and that each of this multitude of languages, the utterance of the matured sounds of each species, was well adapted to the expression of feelings and ideas appropriate to their several natures.

The song of birds has ever been a theme of poetic admiration, and a subject of interest to every lover of nature ; but the precise character of these sounds, with those of animals in general, and more especially the ideas which the creatures may be supposed to express in these modulations, have been little studied by naturalists.

It is obvious to a listener that, in the utterance of song, birds are intensely occupied by their feel-

ings ; and that they are listened to by others of
their race with an intelligence and earnestness
which prove that they possess an understanding of
the meaning of what is uttered. A thrush, blackbird,
or redbreast may be seen to stretch forward the
head, and direct the ear, to catch the notes which
come to it from some distant songster of its own
species ; nor will an effort be made to return a
sound, until the competitor is known to have
ended his lay. In such cases the contest is one
of rivalry, and not of imitation : for the series of
notes is in no case the same, nor is the beginning
or ending of each portion at all taken up from
one bird to another. And it is still more remarkable that the responses proceeding from those of
the same species are continued with distinctness,
and without distraction, their attention never being
diverted by the multiplicity of sounds that strike
the ear from birds of another species, which are
loudly singing close at hand. I have marked three
cocks, of superior size and majesty, engaged in answering each other from distant quarters in regular
succession ; but when at last a host of inferior
individuals were led to join their voices to the
chorus, the crowing ceased in those that begun it,
as if disdaining to mix their voices with the puny
efforts of the others.

The sympathetic feeling which is thus known to
exist between animals of the same species, and
the knowledge they display of the sounds of
kindred voices, to the general exclusion of others,
though more musical and obtrusive, besides the daily

experience we have of it in birds, is also witnessed in the uproar produced among dogs if one begins to bark in alarm. In the Jackal, so lively is this impression, and so powerful the impulse on all within hearing, that we are told when a multitude of them are abroad in pursuit of prey—where silence is requisite to escape danger and ensure success — if one of them utters the well-known note, even those whose safety is betrayed by its utterance are unable to resist the desire to unite their voices to the general cry.

As human language is the vocal expression of emotions and ideas of the mind, it is a natural conclusion that such also must be the nature of sounds in animals. But as the range of comprehension of the faculties of the latter is comprised within narrow limits, and, if compared with that of man, must resemble the imperfect colloquial powers we have in earliest infancy, when all expression is of necessity simply instinctive, we are compelled to conclude that the meaning conveyed is limited also, and rather indicative than conventional or conversational. And setting aside the aid which the understanding receives from the expression of the eye or countenance, there is reason to believe that many animals are sensitive to modulations of tone, of which the human race is unconscious. Our muscles are incapable of exceeding a very limited number of contractions in a given time; and thus our emotions are rendered proportionally slow. If called on to give more rapid utterance

to sounds, our tongues either refuse to execute
their office, or the distinction of words is lost in
confusion. Our sense of hearing is equally unable
to separate sounds which follow each other at a
very rapid rate : though, in fact, the sound made
by the string of a violin is as much formed of
separate pulsations, as that of the piano or harp ;
but are uttered so much more rapidly, that, from the
nature of our nerves of sensation, they are not to be
judged of separately. To the bee itself, its hum
probably is a succession of drummings. As there
are men able to discern, in this music, whether
the insect be angry or pleased, it is easy to
believe that there is much significant variety in
the modulation of what to us is unvarying and
senseless. There are many men who cannot be
taught to distinguish what by others is easily made
out ; and it is not libellous to extend this observation to the whole human race, as regards other
modulations, of which none of our ears can be
sensible : for it has been demonstrated that the
waves of air, by which vibrations are communicated, must assume a specific form, when about
to impress on the tympanum or drum each peculiarity of sensation ; and to some of these forms
neither the tympanum is perhaps able to re-
spond, nor the nerve to convey a corresponding
sensation. I have seen reasons to warrant the
belief that many fishes, which are supposed to be
condemned to the general silence of their race,
are not altogether destitute of the power of utter-

ance, by means of a vibration in front of the throat.

It may be concluded from observation, that, throughout the great classes of animated nature, there are certain sounds which, however diversified in other respects, are recognised by the whole of the families, and which seem to be of the nature of instinctive expressions of simple emotions : so that a scream of terror will scare away a variety of creatures within hearing, in the same manner as an outcry of alarm will be intelligible to men of many nations, though they may not understand a word of each other's language, and are consequently ignorant of the precise danger that is expressed. A groan is an indication of pain which will burst out spontaneously, though there be none to hear ; and a moan excites pity : while the sound of laughter is contagious, though no particular cause has been assigned : thus affording us a glimpse of the simplicity and force of all that can be termed language in some tribes of animals. It is this that forms the clamour of want in the young, so powerfully understood by the parents, and even by creatures of another genus ; and a reply from the parent is uttered on the same principle that a hush from a mother is expected to calm into silence the cry of an infant, which has not yet acquired a knowledge of the meaning of articulate sounds.

The congeniality of the senses to certain sounds is not less remarkable than the tone of the windpipe to their utterance ; and in both these respects there appears to be in most animals, and especially in birds, more sensibility, power, and accuracy than in man; and if it were not that, in some human individuals, remarkable instances had occurred of sympathy with peculiar modulations of sound, from which comparisons may be instituted, we should be altogether in the dark concerning them.

There is in souls a sympathy with sounds;

and some which are simply plaintive, without the utterance of a word, will melt to tears a susceptible hearer. An instance of this kind, which is one of the most common of the effects of music, will assist us to comprehend the real nature of the feelings conveyed in a variety of other cases: for if the persons thus impressed will endeavour to analyse the operation of their own minds, they will discover that the effect has been to recall some affecting thoughts or incidents of their lives, or in that of some who have been dear to them; and the sounds themselves were only remotely the cause of feeling, the self-application being the real source of the sympathy. The hired mourners of the East are only effective as they suggest ideas which the hearer adopts as his own; and to men in a different frame of mind they must appear only as a mockery.

The influence, however, is not always merely mental; or, at least, there are some organs which have been known to manifest a remarkable disposition to be operated on, independent of, or even contrary to, the impulses of the will. Dr. Derham observes, that not only could the famous Greek musician Timotheus excite and allay the furious passions of Alexander by the sounds of the lyre; and a king of Denmark be excited to fury, so as to kill some of his best and most trusty servants; but a knight of Gascony was compelled to the act of micturation by similar influences *; and Mr. Boyle reports the case of a friend, who was affected in the same manner, on hearing the noise of a running tap. And however rare such well-marked instances may be, those of a less degree are not uncommon; nor do they appear of difficult explanation, on the known principles of the vibration of tones, as they influence to sympathy the peculiarities of human sensations.

In this, however, as in so many other cases, what is only occasional or morbid in the human constitution is the permanent state of some of the lower creatures; and it is the key, more especially, to what is commonly understood by the term *charming*. The serpent and lizard tribes are not capable of uttering any sounds besides those of a disagreeable hiss: but their hearing is for the most part acute; and some species appear to lose all self-command when brought under the influence of instruments and tones with which the nervous sympathy has special connexion. It is less seen in the species of our own country, perhaps for other reasons besides susceptibility; but it has been noticed in the green lizard of the south of Europe, which may be lured from its

* Cui phormingis sono audito vesica statim ad urinam reddendam vellicabatur.—(*Derham, Nat. Theol.* p. 134.)

hiding-place at the sound of a flageolet. The story of the East Indian serpent-charmers is known to all, and confirmed by those who have visited the East. It is the more remarkable, as the influence is exerted on one of the most dreaded and dangerous of the serpent race, the hooded serpent, or *Copra da capella*. Attempts have been made to explain this fact in a variety of ways, especially on the supposition that the poison-fangs have been extracted, before the charmers ventured to take such liberties with these serpents; but, on the evidence of those who have witnessed the occurrence, such interpretations appear to be without foundation. We shall have occasion to mention that some species of fishes are liable to similar influences.

The tone or quality of a note is decided by the number, as its intensity is by the strength, of the vibrations elicited in a cord or tube in a given instant of time: to which must be added, as an important element, the form which the waves of air thus set in motion are made to assume by the impulse received: of which there are some curious illustrations in Mrs. Somerville's Connexion of the Physical Sciences, p. 165, and in the figures.

It is also known, that when sounds or notes are thus elicited, whatever substance, as a string or vessel capable of being thus thrown into vibration and in unison with them, shall be in the way, it will be so affected as to be similarly sonorous; while others, by construction or situation not in a right key, will remain uninfluenced. It is not the force of the sound, considered as a gust of wind, nor a merely tremulous motion produced by the instrument, to which this effect is to be ascribed; but the more obscure unison of vibration, of which the most intelligible idea is to be found in the waves above referred to: yet the effect is so powerful, that, on the sounding of the bass notes of a good organ, the whole structure of a large church will be found sensibly to tremble. Derham quotes the case of a Dutchman, who was able, by the force of his voice, to fracture rummer glasses. In this case the coherence of the particles of the glass was not sufficiently firm to withstand the tremor into which the strength of his tones was able to throw it; and we may easily imagine the possibility of the demolition of a building through similar means.

This exertion of the power of sound may strike us more forcibly in its effects; but it is not more remarkable in its nature than other influences, which owe their peculiarity to *kind*, and the natures on which they operate, rather than to degree; and which therefore pass unperceived, except where the physiological condition of the nerves is peculiarly constituted to receive them. It is in this point of view that Pliny's observation is correct: " In man the voice is an important part of the countenance * :" for even the tone of expression conveys a meaning, which it is not in the power of a multitude of words

* Vox in homine magnam vultus habet partem.—Lib. x. c. 15.

F

otherwise to express. The varying of an accent in some languages, and in English particularly, greatly modifies the meaning ; and a slender tone of utterance will mar the noblest passage of oratory.

I have already endeavoured to shew that the difference in capacity of the senses, in man and a variety of animals, is owing to a difference in the constitutionally organized life of the nerves, on and through which the impressions are conveyed to the brain ; together with a peculiarity of organization or development of the brain itself. It is from this cause that the optic nerve cannot discern anything besides light : that the ear cannot taste, nor the fingers hear ; but a more minute and precise inquiry into these functions tends to show, that even in these organs, as well as the more ordinary nervous system of particular individuals, there exists a great variety of function and acquirement : so that not only shall one person see, hear, or feel better than another, but also there shall be a variation in the nature of the perceptions conveyed to the brain, by each or all of the senses, although the object viewed be identically the same. It is thus that some eyes can only be made to discern certain colours, or peculiarities of tint ; while others are exquisitely alive to every variety, and *feel* their beauty rather than *judge* of them. Mr. Boyle (on Colours, Works, vol. ii. p. 10) gives the case of a man who at certain times could distinguish colours by the touch of his fingers. This was John Vermaasen, at that time about thirty-three years of age, who, when he was two years old, had the small-pox, which rendered him absolutely blind; and he is at present an organist in a public choir. The Doctor discoursing with him overnight, this man affirmed that he could distinguish colours by feeling, but not unless he were temperate at the time; for any quantity of drink deprived him of that exquisite touch which is required for so nice a sensation. Upon this the doctor provided against the next morning seven pieces of ribbon of these seven colours, black, white, red, blue, green, yellow and grey; but as for mixed-coloured, this Vermaasen could not undertake to discern them: though, if offered, he could tell that they were mixed. To discern the colour of the ribbon, he places it betwixt his thumb and his forefinger, but his most exquisite perception is in his thumb, and much better in the right than in the left. After the man had four or five times told the doctor the several colours, whilst a napkin was tied over his eyes, the doctor observed he twice mistook, for he called the white black, and the red blue; but still, before his error, he would lay them by in pairs, saying, that though he could easily distinguish them from all others, yet these two pair were not easily distinguishable from one another. Then the doctor desired to know what kind of difference he found in colours by his touch. To which the blind man replied, that all the difference he observed, was a greater or less degree of asperity : " For," he says, " black feels like the points of needles, or some harsh sand, whilst red feels very smooth. Black and white are the most rough and unequal of all colours, and so like, that

it is very hard to distinguish them; but black the
roughest of the two. Green is next in asperity;
grey next to green; yellow the fifth in degree of
asperity; red and blue so alike, that it is as hard
to distinguish between them as between black and
white, though red be somewhat more rough than
blue: so that red has the sixth place and blue the
seventh in asperity." The same author (vol. i. p. 94)
gives several remarkable instances of peculiarity in
human constitution, illustrative of the proposition,
that from bodily, and so far probably from nervous,
susceptibility men may be variously affected by
different sympathies and antipathies: from which
we are authorized to conclude, that much of the
difference of character and propensities which is
discerned in men, and still more decidedly in the
various races of animals, derives its origin from the
variations of this physiological structure and action.
It is not the man of a delicate sense of hearing
that is most alive to the beauty of sounds: for a
fine musician has sometimes to complain of an inability to distinguish the notes which when heard
excite him to rapture; and it has been already
remarked that some creatures, of the lizard and
serpent tribes, are sensitive to the sounds of a flute,
though they are incapable of harmonious sound. The
effect of sounds, in exciting disagreeable sensations,
exclusive of any sympathy with the understanding,
or mental feeling, is familiarly known in the teeth
being set on edge by the harsh notes elicited in the
process of sharpening a saw; and I remember that,
several dogs being kept in the court of a gentleman's

mansion, the ringing of the evening bell has, in only
two of them, failed to excite a loud and painful
howling, which does not cease so long as the
ringing continues, and is invariably renewed on
the same occasion.

It can only be ascribed to a similar peculiarity
of nervous temperament, that certain musical instruments, without reference to measure or tune, are
capable of influencing individuals in a manner to
which others are insensible; and thus the trumpet
will stir up that ardour which other instruments cannot excite, and which its own sounds are not able
to allay. In the well-known instance of the relief
afforded to the melancholy depression of spirits
in Saul by the musical skill of David, it is
not improbable that what was accomplished with
the harp would have failed with any other instrument. Something also must be ascribed to the
power, possessed by appropriate perception or intelligence, of distinguishing and separating the
expression of rapid or peculiar modulations; so
that every touch will excite and receive its own
sympathy; and how ready animals are in compre-
hending this may be seen in the first expression
of utterance of their youthful existence. On the
day of its birth the cry of the babe excites a feeling
in the heart of her who has only now begun to be
a mother, and has many times heard the like
sound with little emotion. The new-born lamb not
only awakes a like feeling in the heart of its dam,
but soon learns to distinguish the tones of its

parent amidst the variety of bleating on every side,
when an observer is unable to separate one from
another. It is surprising how speedily this distinguishing knowledge is acquired; and it can only
be explained by the fact, that all the instinctive
acquirements of animals are manifested with corresponding celerity: in this respect far exceeding
man, who is compelled to be dependent on maternal
care for a much longer season than any other
creature in existence.

The following instance of the communication of
ideas between the parent and its young, is not
only a proof of ability in the dam to accommodate its proceedings to new circumstances, and
to communicate them in a way calculated to
secure willing obedience, but it also shews the
early age at which intelligence is possessed by
the cubs: "An Otter produced a pair of young
ones in the Zoological Gardens in London; and
on the twenty-second of December these young
ones got into the pond when but half-filled with
water, and were unable to climb up its perpen-
dicular sides. When they had remained in the
water some minutes, the mother appeared anxious
to get them out; and made several vain attempts
to reach them from the side of the pond. She
then plunged into the water; and after playing
with one of them for a short time, she put her
head close to its ear, as if to make it understand her intention, and then sprung out of the
pond, while the young one clung tightly by its

teeth to the fur at the root of her tail. Having landed it, she rescued the other in the same manner."—(*Athenæum.*)

If we take a solitary walk in a neighbourhood where there are many nests of the Chough (*Corvus monedula*), a clamour may be heard from the brood, which the parents are at no pains to silence; but on discovering the intruding stranger, a deep and expressive note is uttered by the old birds, and in an instant the noise is hushed. A corresponding warning from the parents of a nest of Gulls will send the young ones off to the shelter of some close crevice in the rock: but another note from the parents in either case proclaims that all is safe; and the Gull returns to its seat, and the Chough to the exercise of his vociferation.

A person accustomed to the walk may pass among the haunts of the most timid birds without occupying much of their attention; but a stranger is immediately noticed, and a chirp of inquiry is passed from one of the concealed songsters to another, as if to set them on their guard. If he enters a room occupied by a family where birds in a cage are hung, the same note is elicited; and if we approach a company of Linnets, who are amusing themselves without seeming to be conscious of what is passing around, a twitter is first heard from one or other observer of the flock, and, on the slightest further advance, all within hearing become so much alarmed as to fly off to a quieter station. When the Blackbird flies off to a closer cover, it communicates the alarm to all its race; and from frequent repetition this sound becomes a signal of caution, which the young cannot fail to associate with the idea of danger, even when no object of terror is seen. My attention was once attracted to the rapidly-repeated utterance of the scream of a blackbird, and the twittering of many other individuals of the same species, which were directing their eyes towards a circumscribed spot in a thick bush; and on approaching to examine what could be the cause of so much clamour, the presence of a cat was discovered. The sly creature had evidently been endeavouring to escape observation, and was therefore not a little annoyed at being thus made " the observed of all observers." But the birds were determined that the whole neighbourhood should know of the presence of the intruder : instead of flying off, they continued their vociferation; and peace was not restored until puss had been compelled to retreat.

It is from frequent exercise that the corresponding organs of perception and intelligence become considerably developed; and in the lower orders of animals more than in man, it is among the established relations of nature, that the great development of organization thus produced becomes permanently propagated in the race. The long absence of a cause of alarm among wild animals is observed to produce an inaptitude for the understanding and expression of the sign: the instinct of vigilance in consequence is suffered to pass into a state of rest; which will explain how it is that in newly-

discovered lands wild animals, and birds more especially, have manifested such unconsciousness of
danger as to excite the surprise of their destroyer.
A gentleman informed me that, when the Island of
Ascension began to be frequented by ships, as his
vessel approached her anchorage the yards and
bowsprit were abundantly covered with birds, attracted in a great degree by curiosity, and unscared
by the active operations of the sailors; and a similar
circumstance, in a still more remarkable degree, has
been narrated by other sailors. One species of bird
has acquired the appropriate appellation of Noddy,
and another that of Booby, from their inaptitude
to acquire habits of suspicion, and their apparent
stupidity. In well-sheltered parks and preserves
the hare, pheasant, and partridge, from conscious
security, become indifferent to the presence of
man. It is from the same cause that creatures
who have escaped from captivity so commonly
fall a prey to enemies which experience has not
taught them to suspect.

It is from experience also, though of an opposite
kind, that the most timid and cautious birds, when
living in the midst of alarms, are in the habit of
distinguishing enemies from those, however formidable in appearance, that have done them no
harm; and hence we see the observant magpie, the crow, rook, wagtail, and lark mingling
with sheep and oxen, and even alighting on their
backs, who at the sight of man will immediately fly
away.

It may be from an association of our ideas of
F 3

the song of birds with the beauty of spring and
glory of summer, that the former has been supposed
to constitute in a particular manner an expression
of amorous feeling, or an exuberance of joy; and
the supposition has derived some countenance from
the fact, that the utterance of their liveliest expression is reserved for the season when all nature is
beginning to exult in the renewal of the spring.
But, analogous as this is to similar principles in the
human race, (by consulting the emotions or impressions of which we are sometimes best enabled
to interpret our observations on the native actions
of the lower animals, but by which we are also liable
to form a wrong judgment,) the conclusion from
other particulars tends to the idea, that, in most
cases, it is neither love nor joy that swells the note.
In autumn, when many of the smaller birds are
engaged in shifting their residence, a little party
may be seen flitting along, without any intention of
resting on their way; but the call of a bird
placed for that purpose in a cage will arrest
their progress, and if left to themselves a contest
is the result. In these cases it is scarcely possible
to imagine a previously existing cause of antipathy; and therefore we must suppose that a
challenge was intended and accepted: excited by
such a feeling of alienation or insult as there is
proof of having often arisen between birds in
captivity and those who are in the enjoyment
of freedom. In a wild condition, birds of the
same species will not sing near each other; and
if the approach be too close, and the courage

equal, a battle follows. Redbreasts offer a frequent example of this; and if an intruder ventures on the accustomed domain, the song may be low and warbling, or apparently reserved or suppressed; and neither of them will appear to condescend to notice the efforts of its competitor. But this restraint cannot endure long: the music becomes more developed: it rises higher: the attack is sudden, and the fight so violent, that they fall to the ground together; and one is killed, or both may be taken with the hand. Two birds, even if bred in captivity, will not sing in the same cage; and when two cages are hung near each other, in order to secure a song, it is necessary to place a screen between them, and hide them from each other: for, without this, the bird who is conscious of inferior powers either of song or prowess will not venture to excite the anger of its opponent by an effort of music. For a similar reason the confidence of superior powers elicits a louder and more frequent strain from the sole songster, which it is not difficult to interpret as the exultation of triumph and insult.

"A friend of mine," says Mr. Bold, in the Zoologist, vol. ii., "informs me that by placing a mirror before an old male mule in his possession, he could at any time be induced to sing, beginning with a gentle cadence, and gradually rising as he became excited: at length he poured forth his notes with rapidity and vehemence, and if not prevented by a timely removal of the mirror, dashed madly forward to the attack of his imaginary rival. That his song was not one of love was proved by introducing a bird of the opposite sex into the cage: for, after singing his usual song, he attacked it with fury, and would soon have destroyed it, had it not been removed. The same party kept a Redbreast in confinement for nine months. On placing a mirror near its cage, it immediately expressed the recognition of its fellow by a particular low and sweet note, and would give vent to its satisfaction in a loud song. In fine weather this bird was generally placed outside, and daily carolled his gay notes to his own image reflected from the window."

How large a share of the spirit of contention for supremacy in musical strength and duration is engaged in such competitions, will appear from the methods employed to urge a pair of Canaries to vie with each other. The scraping of a pan, or the noise of a crying child, excites them to exertion, or revives it when it begins to droop; and how much passion is contained in these modulations may be learned from the tale of the Nightingale who entered into competition with the instrument of the musician, and fell exhausted at the foot of the player. A friend informs me: " I remember an eccentric barber living at the corner of the gateway of the Whitehorse Cellar, Fetter-lane, who was very successful in breeding and rearing Nightingales, hung up all round his shop in cages. He could set them singing at any time, late or early, by simply turning the cock of the cistern in the corner of the shop, and letting the water fall into a pewter basin."

The disposition to rivalry in song, arising from conscious powers, was noticed by Pliny *, who has written of this bird with an evident study of the subject : " They contend among themselves, and evidently with much passion. The conquered yields the victory only with life ; the strength failing sooner than the song."

There is reason to believe that when a Thrush is pouring forth from some elevated branch his luxuriant harmony, to solace his mate in her nest, besides the assurance he conveys that no insidious enemy is near, there is also an exultation of defiance to his hearers, and an announcement that he is prepared to defend the prerogative which the affection of his mate has confided to him.

The alteration which for the most part takes place in the song, when the young are excluded will admit of a similar explanation, the modification being in conformity with the altered circumstances. In some, and especially those which are not furnished with what can be termed a song, as the Partridge, the note conveys the anxiety of caution, on the first sound of which the young move off to the nearest shelter, and lie as if insensible, until a cluck from the parent assures them of safety. The Misselthrush, Fieldfare and Redwing, on the

* Certant inter se palamque animosa contentio est. Victa morte finit sæpe vitam, spiritu prius deficiente, quam cantu.

contrary, will assail an intruder with repeated threat-
enings, which are uttered with such angry vociferation as is well adapted to scare away any of the
smaller animals: in all which, however, there is no
more evidence of individual meaning than in the
hissing of a spiteful Cat, or of the Wryneck in
its hole.

But though, from numerous instances, I conclude
that the simple sounds of animals possess no further
meaning than the expression of a feeling, and from
this I judge of the general nature of their language,
yet there can be no difficulty in proceeding a step
beyond this, and conceding, that the superior sensibility they exhibit to minute impressions may give
effect to variety in the utterance, which our duller
aptitude may prevent us from feeling or com-
prehending. And so far as this it may be granted
that a specific meaning is expressed in the modulations of the utterance. How well such meaning
is understood appears from the proceedings of
the Otter just now mentioned, and also of a pair
of Swallows, who were observed on the wing engaged in a chattering contest close to an opening
which led into a solitary barn. It was the evident
intention of one of them to obtain an entrance;
and equally the determination of the other that
no admission should be permitted. They flew in
various directions about the only aperture, with
incessant and angry chattering; but the bird which
appeared to be the rightful occupier always maintained his advantage in keeping nearest the opening.
When at last nothing that he was able to do or

utter seemed capable of repelling the pertinacious
intruder, another bird suddenly darted out through
the opening, with a double portion of indignation
marked in her motions; and, without uttering
a sound, joined her mate in repelling the foe:
after which she again returned to her solitary station within the building. The rapidity of the
action seemed to say, that, though in the dark,
still she had been listening to the contention, until
her patience had become exhausted; and knowing
that further threatening must be useless, she was
resolved to suffer such insolence no longer. It will
assist in explaining this incident, the similarity of
which has been observed in other instances, that
so powerful is local attraction in the breast of the
swallow tribe, that the young commonly return to
the nest where they were bred, on the first season
after migration; and it is only when repelled that
they consent to seek another situation.

There are many instances to shew that song has
been employed to attract the attention of a human
enemy; and that the station of the songster has
been changed, or the voice reduced into a kind
of ventriloquism, for the purpose of withdrawing
him from the place of the nest. A bird in captivity has been known to sing more and louder
than usual, until it fell dead at the bottom of
the cage, to solicit attention to its deficiency of
food, from the want of which it at last perished;
and another instance is related where the little
creature sung earnestly when surrounded by the
flames of a burning house.

Under such circumstances we may be allowed to suppose, that an attentive ear might have detected a variation in the notes from the usual song; for under much less exciting circumstances a change is known to occur in the modulation. Some also are in the habit of imitating the song of other kinds: in learning which it has been remarked by Lord Bacon —as a proof that mind is principally engaged in the effort—that the acquisition is obtained by listening with the ear, and not by watching the expression of the mouth and throat.

The application of my remarks on the aptitude of certain organizations of the nervous fabric to the reception and propagation of some kinds of modulations in preference to others, is displayed in the development of the power of imitation; to the obtaining of which some persons, from motives of profit, have directed much attention: for a bird that sings a tune not natural to its race, and especially if the song be such as is arranged in the form of human harmony, has been known to fetch a high price.

The aptitude of creatures in a state of nature to receive congenial instruction is so great, that the acquisition has much the appearance of being the result of intuition. A Thrush in a cage, who can have had few, distant, and cursory opportunities of listening to the song of its species, if at all, will be able to sing at the age of four or five months. But we shall the less wonder at this precocious maturity, when we recollect that the same bird will have acquired all the intelligence of its kind, and will build itself a nest, at the end of a year. I have known a Goldfinch, taken from its nest at the age of a fortnight, in the month of May, who never could have heard anything of a sound from its kind, beyond the twitter that announced the presence of its food ; and yet by the end of July it had begun to utter low but imperfect notes. In the first week in August the tone was louder, and with evident modulations ; but displaying the nature of the sounds, by its manner of singing—not to communicate with any other, which it could not have imagined to exist in the world, but by singing to solace itself, and shewing itself best pleased when perfectly alone and uninterrupted. Thus a short infancy in most of the animal races will teach accurately all the lessons they have to learn, where the subject is limited and superficial ; but where the subjects are multiplied, or of deeper consideration, a longer state of pupilage is necessary. Even in man precocious powers are no certain proof of future excellency ; and a certain firmness of the structure of the brain, as well as of activity of function, is required to produce the higher efforts of thought. There are those who cannot attempt abstruse reasoning without suffering the penalty of headache, and confusion of sight ; nor enter upon a multiplicity of subjects without dimness and distraction : which are signs that the organ of thought is not in a condition for the exercise. The faculty of intellect will therefore require a long infancy of preparation ; but those which are derived from imitation are the first to be acquired, and are the most easily retained.

Considered as the expression of a feeling, there is just as much in the song of a bird as there is in the humming of a tune by man, which, without the expression of a word, would indicate by its measure the lively or the gloomy feeling which occupies the heart of the musician. And in this point of view, both in man and bird, there is no difficulty in supposing that the utterance may be properly termed innate. And in a higher degree, in both instances, the case is not much altered when study and instruction are employed: for it is still tune, rather than language, that is improved. It is thus that Pliny says of the Nightingale, "The younger birds study the older, and catch and imitate the song. The scholar listens with the utmost earnestness, and replies to it at intervals. He comprehends the correction of error, and every little slip in the lesson *."

But while thus a native and congenial note of spontaneous origin is readily received and tenaciously retained, that which is only the result of imitation and opportunity is acquired with difficulty, and is liable to be soon forgotten. Mr. Yarrell reports that a Hawfinch (*Fringilla coccothraustes*) was found to have learned the song of the Blackbird, but after-

---

* Meditantur aliæ juniores, versusque quos imitentur accipiunt. Audit discipula intentione magna et reddit, vicibusque recidit.— Intelligitur emendatæ correctio, et in docente quædam reprehensio. (Lib. 10. c. 29.)

wards entirely forgot it (British Birds, vol. i. p. 486); and Bechstein says of the Bulfinch (*Pyrrhula vulgaris*), one of the few birds who can be induced to learn a tune which may be reduced to the form of musical notation, that, with regular and continued instruction, it will take nine months to become firm in its lesson; and that in many instances the task learned is again forgot during the season of moulting. It is with them, as with the human race: those which are quick in attaining are also rapid in losing their acquirements; while those which are slow to learn, are equally slow to forget.

A similar difference of propensity, analogous to what is often found in the human race, shews us why it is that some species of birds are distinguished by the character of marking and imitating the strains of others; and that individuals belonging to a race not generally characterized by this faculty will imitate the vocal sounds of a variety of animals, but will still prefer some to others. The Mocking-bird (*Turdus polyglottus*), an American species of thrush, is sufficiently distinguished by it to have thence derived its name; and instances are recorded where the Blackbird has not only imitated the crow, but, as if to shew that the particular imitation was directed by a natural congeniality, it has practised other familiar actions, of the dunghill Cock. In Loudon's Magazine (Nat. Hist. vol. iv. p. 433) is an account of a blackbird who imitated so correctly the crowing of a cock, that more than one of these heroes of dunghills in the distance

were led to answer it. It occasionally indulged
in its usual song for a second or two, and then
resumed the imitative sound; while at other times
it commenced with crowing, and broke off in
the middle into its own native whistle. In an
instance of the like habit recorded in the ninth
volume of the same work (p. 572), the bird carried the trick of imitation further, by flapping
his wings when he crowed: "He crows three or
four times, and then sings like a blackbird; and
then crows again. The crowing resembles that of
a Bantam cock, and is full as loud." Mr. Yarrell
(British Birds, vol. i. p. 204) speaks of its imitating the cackle of a hen; and, from several
instances that have fallen under my own observation, I have no hesitation in concluding that
there is in the nature of this bird an aptitude
to imitate most of the habits of the cock and hen.
A Blackbird which was kept tame in a house,
without being confined to a cage, when irritated
would peck the hand held out to it, and rise to
strike with its claws after the manner of a cock.
When in past years I have been engaged in taking
birds with a hook and line, I have observed that
the Thrush and Redwing would endeavour to dis-
engage the bait by running to the end of the cord,
and there pulling at it with all their might; but
that the Blackbird would rub the bait on the
ground with its feet as the hen digs for food.
The ground-scraping Thrush (*Turdus strepitans*), a
native of south Africa, obtains its food by scratching the earth in a similar manner. An instance

of the Blackbird's imitation of the song of a Nightingale is recorded in Loudon's Magazine, (vol. ix. p. 378.)

It was first remarked by Pliny, and since by Dr. Prichard (Natural History of Man), "that the use of conventional speech has been regarded as one of the most remarkable characteristics of humanity : its universal existence among men is not less remarkable than its total absence among the inferior tribes." And it is with a consciousness of this, as implying a difference in intellect and sympathy of feeling, that man does not seek to converse with the ape or lion as he would with a stranger to his own nation, though he knows that the latter must be ignorant of his individual language. And in regard to those creatures which approach him most closely in their form, and in some of their habits, this difference in the mode of communication and sympathy is the more striking, because we are less prepared to expect its entire absence,—from an opinion extensively spread, that, in the descent from the superior to the lower races, the decrease of intellect and expression should keep pace with the gradation of structure. "The organized world," says Dr. Prichard, "possesses no greater contrasts and resemblances than those which we discover in comparing mankind with the inferior tribes. That creatures should exist so nearly approaching to each other in all the particulars of their physical structure, and yet differing so immeasurably in their endowments and capabilities, would be a fact hard to believe if it were not manifest to our observation. The differences are everywhere striking: the resemblances are less obvious in the fulness of their extent; and they are never contemplated without wonder by those who, in the study of anatomy and physiology, are first made aware how near is man in his physical constitution to the brutes. In all the principles of his internal structure, in the composition and function of his parts, man is but an animal. The Lord of the earth, who contemplates the eternal order of the universe, and aspires to communion with his invisible Maker, is a being composed of the same materials and framed on the same principles as the creatures which he has tamed to be the servile instruments of his will, or slays for his daily food." But although there is much general resemblance in form, internal and external, between man and the higher Simiæ*, it refers to the merely animal functions only. Their nervous system, and especially the brain, differ as greatly from those of man as those of other animals—as much as brains and nerves can do in the *vertebrata*, and remain *vertebrata*: as may be seen in that author's plates of skulls, at page 111. And the fact that it is so, and that the difference exists as much in the qualification of speech as in every other particular, should be taken as one of those providential and wise arrangements which eternal foresight has devised to prevent the confusion which might have crept in and degraded the lord of the creation, without benefitting the condition of any creature be-

* Simia quam similis, turpissima bestia, nobis !—*Ennius.*

low him. After an invited inquiry, by the command of his Maker, man at his first creation was wise enough to discover that among mere animals there was no helpmate suited to him. Our researches confirm the same opinion; and especially that it is not the oran outang or the monkey that is formed for human friendship, and to share in our interests or amusements. The dog, elephant, and horse are better capable of appreciating man's intentions, of aiding his efforts, and sharing in his confidence, than those creatures which approach so much nearer to him in form. But when we inquire after a creature capable of imitating human language, we find it only where our theoretical impressions would still less dispose us to seek it—among the feathered race. It might be agreeable to us, and in some respects useful, if the dog were able to utter, as well as understand, our language; but if the articulation exercised by the parrot, and understanding united to affection in the dog, were exercised by the oran outang— though it might better accord with our notions of graduated subordination in the succession of groups—it might lead to danger, in associating too closely what it seems the intention of the Creator to keep widely distinct.

It would be a matter of interest to know what kind or extent of ideas the parrot, magpie, and raven attach to the words they utter, more especially as stories have been told which support the opinion that they are not ignorant of meaning in what they utter. It should be remembered, that even in these cases they would have uttered no more than the dog gives proof of understanding : but in them the corresponding comprehension seems not to be sufficiently attested to warrant our belief ; and the multitude of examples to the contrary render it little doubtful that the human voice it imitates is merely regarded as equivalent to their own simple vociferations.

Among the remarkable, because unusual, instances of imitation of the human voice, that of the Canary deserves mention, as recorded by Mr. Charlesworth : (Mag. Nat. Hist. N. S. vol. i. p. 548.) " A curious fact came under our observation a short time since, in connexion with the power which some species of the feathered tribe have of imitating the articulation of the human voice. A lady, residing at the West end of the metropolis, wrote to Mr. Yarrell, saying, that she had a talking canary, and requested him to visit it, that he might be convinced of the fact. Having received an invitation to accompany Mr. Yarrell, we called on the lady, and had an opportunity of witnessing a performance which greatly surprised us. The canary repeated words and whole sentences, certainly as distinctly as any parrot we everheard, and that as often and as naturally as its own song. The lady stated that she had reared the canary, which was a male bird, from the nest ; and on one occasion, whilst addressing to it some endearing expressions, to her surprise it repeated the words after her, and has been in the daily habit of talking ever since, a period of about six months."

If similar attention were paid to this and other species, in teaching them human sounds, as is practised in the instruction of the bulfinch and redstart, with special reference to and preference of those accents which are best adapted to their utterance, there is little reason to doubt of its success : for there are few persons who have attended to the rearing of the smaller birds from the nest who have not observed their attempts to modulate certain sounds of kindness addressed to them at the time when they are fed or cleaned. The quality of the tone is of much importance, as encouraging to imitation ; and as there are sounds which a parrot will not attempt to follow, because its organs are not able to utter them, so what could be readily caught by one species, will be passed over as impossible or uninteresting by others. Ancient writers record instances in which different kinds of birds have been heard to utter words of human language : in which, besides the universal linguist, the parrot, we find the thrush, starling, nightingale, and even the partridge ; but when a hen uttered distinct words (Pliny, lib. x. c. 21,) it might well have been regarded as an omen or prodigy worthy the attention of the Augurs.

There is no question, then, that sounds uttered by animals are expressive of meaning ; and that it is by variety of modulation that expression is made of a difference of feeling or intention : for it is easy to see that they possess a power of communicating to others very minute particulars of the impressions which actuate themselves. In the

G

more simple cases it is proved that the sounds
are comprehended by more than one race; but
in instances involving a more elaborate song, the
sympathy is only excited in individuals of the
same species. In such cases they appear to possess more of the force of language, though without
the enunciation of anything that can claim the
nature of a word or grammatical sentence; and
hence, when a couple of cats have drawn the
attention of their feline neighbours to their dispute, until one of the opposite sex interposes her
authority, still the sounds are only such as convey
the impression of deep indignation, modulated by
its varying ebullitions, but significant only as angry
sounds.

That in animal nature it is possible for modulated sounds, not having the qualities of human
speech, to produce impressions which assimilate
it to conventional conversation, solely by sympathetic and instinctive influence, will not seem
strange, if it be considered that the same has
occurred in man, when the sounds themselves were
of merely artificial and even mechanical contrivance; and their influence was solely brought
about by an obvious association of ideas. It was
from this groundwork that the ancient practice
sprung of employing, what appears to us an
unnatural practice, hired professional mourners
at funerals, who by a doleful melody invited
and incited the outward expression of the feeling
which laboured for utterance in the hearts of
sorrowing friends, and which perhaps finds the

readiest entrance into the dullest of sensitive intelligences.

It is by association of ideas with sounds, not otherwise significant, that we see many actions performed among the lowest of intelligent existences.   Mr. Ellis, in his Polynesian Researches, speaks of a native chief of the island of Hawaii, who, having brought Eels to a degree of tameness, could call them from their retreat with the shrill sound of a whistle. Carew, the historian of Cornwall, was in the habit of calling together his Mullets to their food by the sound of chopping with a cleaver. A farmer's servant will assemble her company of pigs, and set them scampering with more than their wonted speed, at the rattle of a bucket and the accompaniment of a peculiar cry, which conveys no sound to which in a state of nature they could have been accustomed.   And in the west of England, where oxen are universally employed in labour, a particular sound is employed to encourage them, which some boys are far better able to exert than others, and thus become more successful drivers; and of the variation of this, as it is drawled out, the cattle shew themselves duly aware, turning to the right or left, and proceeding more or less slowly, or stopping altogether, at the expression of tones altogether destitute of individual meaning.

CHAPTER VIII.

The habit of some creatures, which leads them to change their station with the revolution of the seasons, is so remarkable, and, while stimulated in its exertion by an active instinctive impulse, is so clearly guided by calculating intelligence, that it could not fail to attract attention in the earliest ages, when the worshippers of God believed themselves best exercising their rational powers in closely studying his works. Accordingly we find it referred to in the sacred Scriptures as an instance of wise foresight, finely contrasted with the besotted inattention of man to his spiritual interests: " The stork in the heaven knoweth her appointed times ; and the turtle and the crane and the swallow observe the time of their coming: but my people know not the judgment of the Lord," says Jeremiah (viii. 7.)

But the observations thus made chiefly referred to the creative Wisdom, which implanted such a useful propensity in his creatures ; and the physiological causes which direct it in its individual application,

as well as the mode in which it varies in the
different regions of the globe, have been left, for
the most part, unobserved and unexplained to the
present day. With these deficiencies, a general
history of this interesting portion of natural science
cannot yet be written; but enough may be remarked, as coming within our local observation,
or conveyed to us on the authority of travellers,
to shew its bearing on our argument. It is
already known to influence in some degree a
portion of almost every race or family in nature,
though with much diversity of time and circumstance; and from these particulars we may judge
that the predisposition, as well as the exciting
causes, are various. But until more extended and
minute observations are collected, our attention
must be confined to the facts derived from the
study of the creatures of our own country, or the
immediately neighbouring nations; with such illustrations only, from more remote regions, as appear
to be well established.

And of these, Birds will afford us the most
instructive examples.

It is true that in some parts of the earth
mammiferous animals regularly migrate; but this,
as commonly observed, is influenced by the obvious causes of scarcity or abundance of food—
or, as was remarked by Bruce in Abyssinia, to
escape some natural inconvenience; and the An-
telopes and Deer of southern Africa, which furnish to the Bushmen a periodical harvest, cause

the Lion and Leopard to become the scourges, in succession, of particular districts. The really wild Horse, in the steppes of Asia, is also migratory, in a more decided manner than the same animal returned to freedom from domestication. In another part of this work will be noticed a more obscure and limited migration of the smaller animals; of which some instances occur at uncertain periods in our own country, but the causes of which are little understood.

But our principal object is to elucidate, so far as the present state of our knowledge of comparative physiology will enable us, the chief causes of the phenomena of migration in that class of animated beings among whom it most extensively operates, and which are best able to obey its impulse. And this we will seek to accomplish on general principles, rather than attempt to penetrate into the variety in which it may shew itself, from modifying influences in the separate classes.

The principal flights of British migratory birds are those which come to this country in the spring, and leave it again in autumn. Soon after their arrival they enter upon the great natural duty of continuing their race; and in a short time after the young are capable of flight—and in one remarkable instance, even before such is the case—they depart to some other regions of the globe, commonly at a considerable distance from their summer haunts. The Swallow tribe affords a well-marked example of this habit; and to the ascertained circumstances regarding them our attention shall be first addressed.

It is believed that all the species comprised in the Linnean genus Hirundo, scattered as they are in almost every corner of the earth, are impressed with a migratory character, and that their nests are generally formed in some country remote from and possessing a cooler temperature than that which receives them at the opposite season of the year. And though it is known that in the island of Madeira, of Ceylon, in Surinam, Egypt, and probably in some other parts of Africa, swallows are found throughout the year, yet it seems that in all these the numbers vary with the season, which implies a migration of part of them; and it does not appear that any of those which remain produce a brood.

It is understood also that, as in most other of our summer immigrants, the *line* of their flight from one station to another is in a direction approaching to a right angle with the equinoctial line; and, for the most part, they pass with little delay from their winter to their summer station. As the time when the formation of a nest may be entered upon is more or less early according to the climate—and to which perhaps they are as much guided by local attachment as by congeniality of constitution—it follows that the time of their arrival is different, in the proportion as their vernal constitutional influence is more easily established.

The poet Ovid, who seems to have been a good

observer of nature, places the earliest appearance of
the swallow at Rome in the last week of February*:
in Sardinia it is noted on the last day of the same
month (Trans. of the Royal Academy of Brussels):
Mr. Davis says that at Pekin, in China, in lat. 40°,
they return in March; and the Prince of Musignano
saw them at sea, within 200 miles of Madeira, in the
middle of that month (Trans. Linnean Soc. vol. xvi.
p. 754): but from the beginning to the middle of
April may be regarded as the regular season of
their appearing through the greater portion of
Europe. There is, however, in most published ca-
lendars of natural history, a source of error in
recording the arrivals of migratory birds which
ought to be borne in mind; because it tends to
vitiate our conclusions, when the subject is brought
to bear on the character of the season at which
they arrive, or at which they depart. The mistake has its origin in the custom of confining the
record to the arrival of the first two or three birds
of a species: after which their increase is no further noted, although the great multitude may not
come for a month afterward, and they have been
known to be still crossing the Channel until the
middle of May. So long a time as three weeks
has been known to pass between the discovery of
two or three swallows in the first fine days of
April, and the arrival of the next party: so that
the season of migration, with the economy of the
spring, more especially as it refers to vegetation,

* Fallimur? an veris prænuntia venit hirundo?
  Et metuit neque versa recurrat hyems?

has been very late, when a calendar which noted only the earliest specimen seen would have represented it as unusually early.

A want of accuracy concerning the time of departure is of the opposite kind: so that it is only the last seen that is entered on the record; although the impulse to migration must have exerted itself powerfully long before, and perhaps first on those individual birds which were the first to visit us. It is uncertain whether young birds in general go off sooner or later than their parents, although the opinion of naturalists generally inclines to the latter supposition; but it is probable that in their wanderings they do not long keep together. On the 25th of August, 1845, a late season for vegetation and periodical actions of most natural kinds, a young Shrike (*Lanius collurio*) was brought to me that had flown on board a fishing-boat in the preceding night, at the distance of four or five miles from land, while apparently in the act of migration, though its age from the nest was so little that it could scarcely be supposed likely to have crossed the Channel in safety.

The time of arrival of the swallow, martin, and barkmartin (*Hirundo rustica, urbica,* and *riparia*), swift (*Cypselus apus*), and goatsucker (*Caprimulgus Europæus*), is in the order in which their names are placed; and the swift is seen in Sardinia in the middle of April, but with us not until the first few days of May. The goatsucker is perhaps the last of our migratory birds, and does not usually come until towards the end of May.

G 3

The time of the withdrawal of these birds is more irregular than that of their coming ; and begins with the swift, which usually takes its flight in the first or second week of August—the whole colony commonly disappearing at once—the actual departure being preceded, for a few days, by exercises in flying, which seem to be practising in sport what they soon expect seriously to be obliged to execute. They may be witnessed ascending in a spiral manner, and in very close phalanx, with even more than their usual rapidity, to a very great height ; and having two or three times executed this movement, they suddenly sink down to their nests : after which, until the next day, they are no more seen.

A remark often made appears to be correct—that the swallow tribe go away earliest in the warmest seasons ; but whether there be any physiological reason for this is a matter of doubt. The principal cause of their early readiness for migration seems to be, that less interruption has been thrown in the way of the formation of the nest, and there has been a greater abundance of insect food for the support of the young, which has accelerated their growth. In an unfavourable season in these respects, or when other causes have occurred to retard the maturity of the brood, the birds have not only been kept later, but in many instances the migratory instinct has grown sufficiently strong to overcome the force of parental affection, and the brood has been left to perish in the nest. To attend on a helpless young one, a single swift has been known to remain for a fortnight after the departure of its race ; and it is a frequent occurrence for the swallow to leave its late brood to perish in the nest.

The older individuals of the swallow tribe that come to us have usually paired before their arrival, and none of them pass the season in Europe without attempting to rear a brood. The swift confines itself to one laying, which comprises a single pair of eggs; and the young acquire their well-known power of flight in a very short space of time: so that very soon after quitting the nest they are prepared to accompany their parents in their migration; and so constantly do these birds depart immediately after bringing out their young, that no doubt can be entertained of the nature of the motive which led them hither. If we sometimes discern in other members of this family (*Hirundinæ*) a greater delay in entering upon this great duty of nature, it is not difficult to trace it to the destruction which the nests have sustained from the insecurity of their situation or materials—to the meddling interference of birdnesting boys—and, more frequently, to the thoughtless or wicked destruction of one of the parents by children of adult growth, to shew their mischievous skill in gunnery. The perseverance displayed in spite of these obstacles is a lively proof of the force of the instinctive feeling which during the summer forms the pleasure and business of these happy creatures, and sometimes enables them to bring forward three broods in safety.

As autumn approaches they return to their nests only for the sake of sleep, or as a convenient resting-

place ; and about the middle of September, after
having shewn their social disposition by assembling
in companies, the earliest of them enter upon their
autumnal migration, for which the proper season is the month of October. The flight to their
winter's destination is less direct than their coming ;
so that it is not uncommon for small parties to appear again, long after they have seemed to have left
us. Such is frequently the case in November. In
the year 1845 we have an account that a small
party of martins were seen at Penzance on the 14th
of December; and some swallows were observed there
a few days after that date. Mr. Peach communicated to the Royal Institution of Cornwall that
three swallows were seen at Mevagissy, in that
county, on the 25th of December, 1843; and they
extended their stay to the third day of January
following. These birds may in some instances be
such as are passing from more northern stations,
and have been delayed on the route; but the recognition they bestow on old nests and resting-
places leaves no doubt of their being the rightful
proprietors.

It is somewhat remarkable that, with such un-
doubted courage, and strong powers of flight, the
swallow seems to feel a degree of hesitation in
venturing on the passage of the Channel, and will
keep along the coast, for a considerable distance,
before it will adventure over the expanse. And this
is the more surprising, since we know that the
wheatear (*Sylvia Œnanthe*), various species of willow
wren, and even the little goldcrest (*Sylvia regulus*), are

able to cross in safety. But the greater distance of the autumnal flight of the swallow, and the habits of flight of these families, may afford an explanation of the singularity.

The shorter-winged birds are seen to hurry along from one margin of the sea to the other, with no more effort than is absolutely required to enable them to cross in safety. But the mode of flight of the swallow tribe is in circles; and they seem less careful in arranging the time, manner, and distance of departure : so that the journey becomes extended much beyond its natural limits. I have seen a troop of martins, which may have been baffled by contrary winds, approach the shore from the sea, late in autumn, in such an exhausted condition, that they were compelled to alight on the sills of windows, where it would have been easy to have taken them with the hand.

It is known to naturalists, that the physiological change which birds, and perhaps most wild animals, exhibit at certain seasons of the year, in a periodical development of energetic action, and which in many of them is accompanied with such changes in the strength and arrangement of their colours as for a long time to have led to errors in the identification of the species, is necessary to the desire and power of providing for the continuance of the race ; and that in numerous instances in each species, (though more in some than in others,) there are individuals which, in the midst of similar external circumstances, display

no signs of sensibility to the impression. Influenced
by this new development of organs and energy,
their very nature seems altered ; and while the
climate they formerly delighted in has thus grown
irksome, they feel a craving for one in which
the procreative impulse may best be carried into
effect. A peculiar temperature is felt to be necessary for this, as well for the sake of the parent
as of the egg ; and as, to provide for the latter,
a bird will confine itself for a long time to
the nest, in order to maintain a due degree of
warmth, and will leave it for a longer or shorter
time as its sensations decide to be necessary,
so, in the former case, that temperature or
moisture of the air which would be agreeable in
its ordinary condition, becomes irksome and unnatural. Instinctive feeling then decides that a
change is necessary, to obtain such a combination
of circumstances as is congenial to the newly-
developed vital actions ; and while such individuals
as are uninfluenced remain behind, those whose
faculties are thus urged into action wing their
way to a cooler sky, to which they are guided by
sensations which lead them along a line that
varies little from a meridional direction.

It is no adequate objection to the sufficiency
of this explanation of the vernal migration to
urge that many birds prefer to remain and raise
a brood in the warmest climates ; since the necessity of a change in some species, and the absence
of it in others, must depend on the natural influences which in either case are requisite to the

successful performance of the function. We may even admit that in different individuals of the same species the constitutional aptitude may demand a variation in this particular; and this appears the more probable, when we notice that many swallows prefer to bring out their young in the warm climates of Palestine, Greece, and Naples; while others will not be satisfied with anything short of a laborious journey to Zetland or Lapland.

We learn from Mr. Kitto (Pictorial Palestine), that the cuckoo is found in Palestine in winter; and its note has been heard in that country in April—a probable reason for believing that it also breeds there: for in England, though it may have arrived in March, it is commonly silent until some time in April, when near the time of depositing the egg. There is reason to suppose, however, that in no instance will any of the swallow tribe which visit Britain produce a brood in the country of its winter residence. They were noticed by Adanson in the interior of Africa, at about eighty or ninety miles from the coast, during the summer; but it could not be ascertained that they there brought out a brood.

But, besides the influence that may impel to the selection of a colder or warmer situation, the exact choice of habitation is further determined by other causes which have hitherto eluded observation. Thus the Nightingale is not found in Cornwall, nor in a large part of Devon, though the temperature, shelter, and food of those counties

might be supposed well fitted to its habits. With
some degree of affinity to this indisposition in
certain creatures to attach themselves to particular places, Pliny remarks the absence of the
Dormouse in a certain wood (lib. viii. cap. 58);
and it is a common observation, that some birds
are exceedingly fastidious in the choice of situation : so that they will take a distant flight to
obtain that which a little change of accommodation
would have furnished them with at home. The
Woodcock has begun to frequent situations, and
form a nest, where formerly it was only a winter
visitant ; and where the grey Wagtail (*Motacilla
boarula*) regularly visited the south of Cornwall in
winter only, a single pair, which successfully built
a nest, have left a colony of residents, who neither depart in summer, nor perceptibly increase in
winter.

It is here also that we can perceive a new
principle of action coming into play, by which
a bird is led to select one residence, whether
it be a country, district, or a much more limited
station, rather than others which might appear
equally eligible. This is the principle of local
attachment ; which is strong also in Quadrupeds,
and is even perceptible in some of the inhabitants of the ocean. Immediately on their arrival, the swallow, martin, and swift are seen
to approach the old-frequented nest ; and this,
in many instances, where it is situated in places
of a singular character, and which would not have
been recognised by those who were ignorant of

the spot.   Mr. Blythe records an instance where a Redstart was known to have revisited the same garden for sixteen seasons in succession, which may be said to include the whole of its life. The bird was sufficiently distinguished by being lame.   (Loudon's Mag. Nat. Hist., N. S., vol. i. p. 133.)

We can easily suppose that where the conditions of the air, which render any situation—as the top of a Mountain or the expanse of a Plain—congenial to the feelings, were extended to a much wider district, that then the animals which before had confined their range within narrow limits would be induced to wander through a greater extent of country.   It is not, therefore, that they are driven from their haunts, but they are invited to extend their rambles, by finding equal comforts over a larger space of ground.   It may be from a similar cause that so many of the summer migrants are found in regions far to the north, when the principal motive for emigration might have been as well answered by a much shorter flight.   The swallow and cuckoo are found in summer as far north as Lapland ; and Captain Parry discovered the bankmartin at Melville Island in the month of June.

The further impulse, by which the vernal immigrants are impelled to undertake an autumnal journey, and which does not consist in a mere subsidence of the constitutional affection that led them hither, is a new and active bias towards mutation, which, in spite of powerful counteracting influences, they are unable to resist; and which, even in birds long subject to the unnatural restraint of the cage, still excites them to display urgent signs of restlessness for the space of two or three weeks at the accustomed time for departure.

The exciting cause of this regular autumnal departure is more doubtful, and perhaps more diversified, than that of their coming. It cannot be from deficiency of food: for, at the time when the swift and cuckoo leave us, Nature is in her richest abundance. The temperature has not decreased; and when some individuals of a migrant race remain through the winter, it is not easy to imagine why the chief part might not also find subsistence, and defy the climate. But whilst it may be allowed that more than one powerful cause is in operation, there is reason to believe that the most prevalent and decisive influence exists in the predisposition to the physiological function already mentioned, and from which none are exempt, though there are collateral circumstances which vary its operation, and render it more or less intense.

Such birds as continue in this country through the year are found to require a more than usually stimulating food, which they obtain in the abundance of insects then prevalent, whose vital juices for the most part possess peculiar chemical qualities; and also in aromatic seeds, which become ripe at this appropriate season. The warm and genial temperature of Autumn is also of importance, to enable them to force forward the renewal of their plumage. Excited action is requisite to this process; and by increasing it artificially and prematurely bird-catchers are able to obtain call-birds, which by vigour and activity attract the wild ones who are passing along in that more limited migration, which amounts only to a change of quarters, who are thus brought within reach of the fowler. This feverish condition, as in a similar influence on the human body, is accompanied with a higher degree of sensibility, which renders irksome those impressions of the air which before were pleasing. An appetite for new kinds of food may be a natural accompaniment of this state of the body, as it is under corresponding circumstances of a morbid or altered condition in the human system; and thus is formed another inducement to change of place, though this latter can have no share in the impulse that orders the direction. The influence of these combined causes is at least rendered probable by the fact, that none of the autumnal migrants pass through the condition of moulting their feathers before they leave us, though in many cases they continue in this country after the time when the greater part of our constant residents have accomplished that change. It is some explanation of the very late detention of the swallow and martin, already given in connexion with this account of the exciting cause of departure, that in instances recorded by Bewick and others, where swallows were preserved in cages through the winter, they did not undergo the process of moulting until the month of January.

But while a persuasion may be felt that this

peculiar influence is most powerful in the most migratory races, it can scarcely be deemed a satisfactory explanation of some of the less regular variations noticed by observers. Linnæus remarked that female chaffinches (*Fringilla cœlebs*) commonly migrate from Sweden in winter, while the males remain behind. Some races, at uncertain intervals, and without apparent cause, assume, as if by mutual agreement, a spirit of emigration; and though usually living solitary or scattered, as by a general summons, they assemble in a body, and proceed to some distant region, leaving the district they have long inhabited altogether destitute of the race. The same rage for travelling has fallen on a single individual, or a portion of a tribe ; and species, of which it is not common to find more than two or three in a large extent of country, occasionally assemble in numbers, and boldly venture on a flight which their former habits would have led us to suppose impracticable. The goldcrest (*Sylvia regulus*), which is a continued resident in some countries—where, even in severe cold, it is always able to support itself in good condition—and a solitary migrant in others, in Scotland, and the north of England and of Europe, performs this movement in combination with considerable numbers; and seeking close to the shore the most convenient station for departure, they hurry across the sea with the utmost expedition. Spern Head, in Yorkshire, is said to be a favourite place for such assemblages and flights. For a week or more in the month of October, they come thither in a succession of small parties; and when they have formed into flocks of a few thousands, they all at once disappear. (Zoologist, vol. iii. p. 281.) The same habit is more rarely seen in the western part of the kingdom; and in the month of November 1844, a flock, some hundreds in number, was driven from the sea, perhaps by baffling winds, to the east coast of Cornwall, where they found a resting-place on Looe Island, from which again in a few days they took flight, though the few native birds of the neighbourhood were satisfied to remain.

With a disposition akin to this, an assemblage of thousands of Thrushes (*Turdus musicus*), who can only have congregated from an extensive tract of land which their emigration must have exhausted, is not unfrequently seen flying westward in a continued stream, as if journeying to escape from the clouds of snow which press closely behind them. They alight in some favourable situation for the night, and perhaps remain through the following day; but before another morning they are gone, and none of the species remain, except the scattered individuals of the neighbourhood : not one of whom, though exposed to the same cold and lack of food, has been induced to accompany them in their flight.

Another noticeable circumstance is, that in some countries certain species are permanent residents; while in others, which do not appear to differ from the former in any remarkable circumstance, they are uniformly migrant. The common Thrush, as well as the Fieldfare and Redwing, forsake colder Norway in winter, and help to increase the multitudes we see in our hedges in the cold season. But what seems exceedingly strange is, that over most part of the Continent of Europe, including Belgium and some districts of France, the Thrush is also a regular migrant, though with us it scarcely passes from one parish to another.

It is easily understood why the Starling (*Sturnus vulgaris*) spreads itself over the county of Cornwall in the winter; but when the spring returns, the immense flocks which have there obtained food and shelter again quit the country, though only to proceed to the distance of a few miles, for the sake of a place in which to hide their nests, which it is difficult to suppose could not have been as well secured in the place of their winter's residence.

It may be classed among the irregular migrations which have no ascertained cause, that some species are observed to quit a country in one season, for the apparent purpose of avoiding cold: but in another season they will encounter it, in even a higher degree, with impunity; while others will expire under its influence, without having recourse to so obvious an expedient as removal. Such is the case with some of our smaller birds; and the Redwing (*Turdus iliacus*), after accomplishing a flight from the extreme north of Europe to the west of England, is not unfrequently disabled by cold in the course of the winter, when further removal for a few leagues would have secured its safety. The only explanation I am able to imagine of the circumstance of their not

undertaking a second migration, even to the south
of Italy, whither so many of the species had
preceded them, in continuance of the first impulses, and for the same object, may perhaps be
the fact, that the constitutional action, which led
to the original change of quarters, has come to
an end, and that indisposition to more distant
flight has taken its place. There is no British bird
continuing with us through the winter which is so soon
subdued by cold as the Redwing.

It has only lately been known that the Goldfinch
performs a regular migration in the west of England; from which it departs, in companies of from
twenty to fifty, at the middle of October, and
returns about the middle of March. It is remarkable that the Blackstart (*Phœnicura tithys*) is seen
in Cornwall only in winter; and since attention
has been directed to it, that rare bird, the Firecrest
(*Regulus ignicapillus*), has been found to visit the
same county at the same season.

It may be added, that some single birds will
take what might be imagined a perilous journey
across a wide expanse of ocean, with no apparent
inducement beyond the desire of change ; and these
aimless strangers are commonly young birds of the
first year.

The invariable direction in which migration is
prosecuted is not the least interesting portion of
the proceeding: for though it is known to us
that southern climates possess the warmest temperature, and the most nutritious and stimulating food, at the time when the summer haunts

of migrants are becoming deficient in these particulars, still it cannot be supposed that a bird is in possession of this speculative knowledge; or, possessing it, that, without compass or guide, it should unerringly pursue the route that leads to it. Yet they rarely deviate to any great extent in the journey, uninfluenced by mountains or oceans that intervene; and even the young cuckoo, new from the nest of a foster-parent who is itself indisposed to the effort, and destitute of any guiding influence besides its own instinctive feeling, quits the land of its birth, and fails not to reach the country of its search.

Inscrutable as this directing skill appears to our duller perceptions, it is not only constant in its manifestation among our little summer insect-hunters, but it is also possessed by birds whose opportunities of using it are only occasional. Domestic pigeons have been taken to remote distances from their home, and that too by a mode of conveyance which must effectually shut out all possibility of recognition of the local bearings of the direction, and yet they have returned thither with a rapidity of flight which marked a conscious security of finding it. I have known some of the most timid and secluded of our birds, as the Wheatear and Dipper, to be taken from their nests, and conveyed to a distance, under circumstances which must have impressed them with feelings of terror, and in which all traces of the direction must have been lost; and yet, on being set free, they were soon at the nook from which they had been taken. Even the common Hen, which has been carried in a covered basket through a district intersected by a confusion of hills and valleys, in a few hours was seen again scraping for grain on her old dunghill.

The only explanation, in these cases, must be sought in the existence of perceptions to which the human race is a stranger; their possession of which is proved by the exquisite and ready susceptibility of most animals to changes of weather, long before the occurrence of anything which our observation can appreciate, or which can be indicated by instruments. While the atmosphere seems to promise a continuance of fair and calm weather, and the wind maintains the same direction, the Hog may be seen conveying in its mouth a wisp of straw; and in a few hours a violent wind fulfils the omen. The Cat washes, and some wild animals shift their quarters, in compliance with similar indications; and even Fish, at considerable depths in the sea, display, in their motions and appetite, sensibility to the coming change. The latter circumstance especially, which is well known to fishermen, is a proof that mere change of temperature, or moisture, is not sufficient to explain the phenomenon.

· I will notice, in conclusion, some migrations in a class of animals, in which the modes of proceeding, and the motives which lead to them, are so obscure as to preclude any attempt at explanation.

" On the 8th or 10th of the month of June,

Madame de Meuron Wolff, and all her family, established during the summer in the district of Grandson, Canton de Vaud, perceived with surprise an immense flight of butterflies traversing the garden with great rapidity. All these butterflies were of the species called the Painted lady, the Belle dame of the French, the Papilio cardui of Linnæus, and Vanessa cardui of the modern system. They were all flying closely together, in the same direction, from south to north, and were so little afraid when any one approached, that they turned not to the right or left. The flight continued for two hours without interruption, and the column was about ten or fifteen feet broad. They did not stop to alight on flowers; but flew onward, low and equally. This fact is exceedingly singular, when it is considered that the caterpillars of the *Vanessa cardui* are not gregarious, but are solitary from the moment they are hatched. Professor Bonelli of Turin, however, observed a similar flight of the same species of butterflies in the end of the March preceding their appearance at Grandson. Their flight was also directed from south to north, and their numbers were immense. At night the flowers were literally covered with them. Towards the 29th of March their numbers diminished, but even in June a few still continued. They have been traced from Coni, Racconi, Suse, &c. A similar flight of butterflies is recorded, at the end of the last century, by M. Loche, in the Memoirs of the Academy of Turin. During the whole season those butterflies, as well as their larvæ, were very abundant, and more beautiful than usual." (Mem. de la Société de Phys. et d'Hist. Nat. de Genève, quoted in Loudon's Mag. Nat. Hist. vol. i. p. 387.)

" On the 30th and 31st of last May (1839) immense cloud-like swarms of Dragonflies passed in rapid succession over the town of Weimar and its neighbourhood. The general direction of the migration was from south by west to north by east. The migration had been likewise observed in all the villages situated a few miles to the east or west. The insects arrived in a vigorous state, some of the flocks flying as high as 150 feet above the level of the river Ilm, and striking against the windows of a house situated on an eminence ; others passing through the streets. The specimens caught there were those of *Libellula depressa*, at least all those I have seen were of that species.

" Being anxious to ascertain the range of this migration, I tried to collect every possible information from various papers ; but all I could learn from that source was, that cloud-like swarms of Dragonflies had been seen at Gottingen on the first of June : at Eisenach on the 30th and 31st of May (flying from east to west) ; and at Calais on the 14th of June, on their way towards the Netherlands. Those seen at Eisenach were likewise *Libellula depressa* : those observed at Calais appeared to belong to a different species, as they were described as being thick, and about three inches long. Being rather disappointed in my expectation of finding news from many quarters respecting the same

phenomenon, I endeavoured to procure more information by means of a public advertisement;
whereby I learned that the swarms of dragonflies
had been seen, about the same time as they were
here, in the neighbourhoods of Leipzig, Alsleben,
Ascherleben, and Halle. The information which
Dr. Buhle, the inspector of the Zoological Museum
of Halle, had the kindness to impart was particularly valuable. The specimens caught at that place
belong to *Libellula quadrimaculata*. The first swarms
arrived there in the afternoon of the 30th of May,
a short time before a thunderstorm; and I see from
my meteorological journal, that we had a thunderstorm here both on the 30th and the 31st of May,
and two on the first of June. They flew very rapidly
from south to north. On the 31st of May similar
flocks followed their predecessors in the same direction : most of them passed at the height of seven
or eight feet, catching insects as they flew on. On
June the first and second, straggling parties of five
or six were observed, always keeping the same
direction. Within a league to the east of Halle
these swarms were everywhere observed. To the
west the whole valley was inundated by the river
Saale. *Libellula quadrimaculata* is rather scarce at
other times about Halle, as *Libellula depressa* is about
Weimar. As far as the information which I have
been able to collect goes, this migration has extended
from the 51st to the 52nd degree of latitude, and
has been observed within 27° 40′ and 30° east of
Ferro. But the instance of Calais renders it probable that it has extended over a great part of

Europe, wherever the same meteorological circumstances have prevailed.

" Several of the larger species of *Libellula* do occasionally migrate, but the phenomenon is of rare occurrence ; and the circumstances which bring about such an uncommonly numerous development of the perfect insect must be very peculiar. The last migration of dragonflies (before that commemorated in this article), which was observed at Weimar, took place on the 28th of June, 1816. The insects in that instance also belonged to the same species—*Libellula depressa.* They were then, as recently, taken for Locusts by the common people ; and the superstitious saw in them the harbingers of famine and war. The year 1816 was extremely wet, and 1817 equally so ; but it appears that the dragonflies did not migrate that year. Though such migrations must be very destructive to the species, yet this cannot be the reason why the phenomenon was not observed in 1817, as the *Libellulæ* require more than one year to become perfect insects. The difference of the dates of the 30th and 31st of May, 1839, and the 28th of June, 1816, is also remarkable ; but I cannot account for it.

" As to the great multiplication of these insects about the end of May in the present year, it is by no means mysterious. From the beginning of that month to the 21st the weather had been exceedingly rainy ; rivers and lakes overflowed, and spread their inundation over immense areas of low grounds, whereby myriads of the *pupæ* of the

Libellulæ, which, under other circumstances, would have remained in deep water and become the prey of their many enemies, were brought into shallow water; and the hot weather from May 21st to May 29th converted those shallows into true hot-beds. Numerous thunderstorms (at Weimar there were four) during that week must have greatly encouraged their rapid development into perfect insects; and so those clouds of winged insects rose almost at once from the temporary swamps, and were immediately obliged to migrate in order to satisfy their appetite, as these species are very voracious.

" In these migrations they follow the direction of the rivers, and they appear always to fly with the current, to whatever quarter the river may flow, near which they happen to be, although they do not keep close by it, as they must spread over wide districts in order to subsist. If, with the directions above-mentioned, we compare the following statements, I think my opinion will be found sufficiently established. Near Weimar the river Ilm begins to flow from south-west to north-east, after having flowed from the north: near Halle the Saale flows due northwards: near Eisenach the Nesse follows a westerly direction towards the Werra." (W. Weissenborne, Weimar; Loudon's Mag. Nat. Hist., N. S. vol. iii. p. 516.)

But, however rare the event, it is certainly true that the common or devastating Locust (*Gryllus migratorius*) has been known to visit the British islands; and the circumstance is more deserving of notice, since its re-occurrence may enable us to form some opinion of the particular influences which brought them hither. Ruysch (Theatrum Animalium, vol. ii.) says that, in the year 874, after devastating France, they attempted to cross the British Channel; and such multitudes were drowned and thrown on shore, that their putrefaction was said to have caused a pestilence, which soon after followed. But the Channel has not always proved an impassable barrier: for it is recorded that, in the year 1593, clouds of Locusts were seen in Wales; and in the 8th volume of the Philosophical Transactions is an account of another visit to this country, in the year 1748.

It was probably for want of observers that the notices we have of these visitations are limited to parts of Britain excluding the north and west: it is therefore a matter of interest to know that in the visitation of these creatures, in the autumn of the year 1846, though the numbers were diffusely scattered, so as but in few instances to bear the denomination of flocks, yet they were actively alive in Scotland, and to the extremity of the Land's-end in Cornwall.

In an earlier part of the same summer, vast clouds of a species of Butterfly were seen to cross the Channel from France; and these concurrent circumstances lead to the inquiry, What can have been the cause, through the influence of which, at considerable intervals of time, these creatures—and especially the former—can have been impelled

from a distant and warmer climate, to visit the
extremities of the British islands?

It is obvious that these visits are not to be
ascribed to boisterous winds, which may have irre-
sistibly driven them from their native haunts. This
summer was, for the most part, calm; and for two
or three months previous to their visit, remarkably
so. But with this general tendency to calm, there
was also a condition of temperature and climate
which was not, indeed, exceedingly warm, but which
conveyed an impression or feeling of congenial
warmth and comfort, much resembling what is
described as usual at corresponding periods in
more southern regions; and which therefore may
be supposed the most agreeable to the habits of
these creatures.

It seems to be an instinctive repugnancy to certain conditions of the atmosphere—among which
perhaps a chilly humidity has the greatest influence—that proves a more effectual hinderance
to the disposition of wandering in a variety of
animals, than the mere geographical limits of
mountain or ocean. And when, for a time, as
during the summer of 1846, the atmospheric condition of a region has undergone a great change,
it ought not to be thought surprising that creatures which have hitherto been repelled, should
extend the range of their motions to such a
district.

An associated migration of caterpillars has also
been described, both in Europe and Australia; of

which latter the account given by Mr. Davis, in the same Magazine, is an instance : "On the third of May, I saw a procession of caterpillars. They were evidently Bombyces, and in form somewhat resembling *Arctia caia,* very hairy, but the hairs white ; the body dark brown, but marked with paler lines. These caterpillars were crossing the road in single file, each so close to its predecessor as to convey the idea that they were united together, moving like a living cord in a continuous living line. At about fifty from the end of the line, I ejected one from his station : the caterpillar immediately before him suddenly stood still, then the next, and then the next, and so on to the leader. The same result took place at the other extremity. After a pause of a few moments, the first after the break in the line attempted to recover the communication : this was a work of time and difficulty, but the moment it was accomplished by his touching the one before him, this one communicated the fact to the next in advance, and so on till the information reached the leader, when the whole line was again put in motion. On counting the number of caterpillars I found them to be 154, and the length of the line 27 feet. I next took the one which I had abstracted from the line, and which remained coiled up, across the line : he immediately unrolled himself, and made every attempt to get admitted into the procession : after many endeavours he succeeded, and crawled in, the one below falling into the rear of the interloper. I subsequently took out two caterpillars, about fifty from the head of the procession : by my watch, I found the intelligence was conveyed to the leader in thirty seconds, each caterpillar stopping at the signal of the one in his rear. The same effect was observable behind the break, each stopping at a signal from the one in advance : the leader of the second division then attempted to recover the lost connection. That they are unprovided with the senses of sight and smell appeared evident, since the leader turned right and left, and often in a wrong direction, when within half-an-inch of the one immediately before him : when he at last touched the object of his search, the fact was communicated again by signal ; and in thirty seconds the whole line was in rapid march, leaving the two unfortunates behind, who remained perfectly quiet, without making any attempt to unroll themselves.

"I learn from a medical gentleman here that these caterpillars feed on the Eucalyptus ; and that, when they have completely stripped a tree of its leaves, they congregate on the trunk, and proceed in the order here described to another tree. The caterpillars I saw must be nearly full-grown, measuring about two inches and a quarter each in length."

CHAPTER IX.

In the course of our inquiry it has been seen
that the manifestations of development of the different stages of advancement in natural beings
is shewn in the addition of tissues and organs,
with their corresponding faculties; and that the
principle understood by the term Instinct is one
of the conditions, a step in this progress from the
state of unintelligent existence to that of the
highest intellectual power. It has been shewn,
also, that man is in possession of this faculty of
Instinct, in common with the inferior creatures;
and from this proposition we shall rise to the
observation—as a fact too plain to stand in need
of lengthened proof—that he is also endowed with
powers of a higher nature, which are included
in the term Reason: from which point our inquiry
will proceed to shew whether, and in what degree,
these inferior creatures are partakers of the same
lofty qualification.

But it may be necessary to make the introductory remark, that it is not intended to include
in this research any disquisition on the nature

and faculties of the human soul, the spiritual seat and spring of man's nobler nature. The existence within him of such an essence is here assumed as a truth; and I do this so much the more readily as it is not essential to the argument, and because our reasoning will rather be built on the phenomena manifested, than on the nature of the original source from whence they may be derived.

Of all natural arguments for the existence of an essence in man separate from the material organization of his frame—though there are others of no small force—I regard the faculty of initiative volition as the most obvious and unanswerable; and whilst I am ready to admit that some of the arguments advanced in favour of this proposition—as well, indeed, as most that are against it—derive their force rather from our ignorance than our knowledge, yet it must be contended for, as of no small weight, that the acknowledgment of the existence of this essence affords a simple and consistent explanation of many phenomena, which without it lie in impenetrable obscurity. I consider it also my duty to add, that the conviction of its being a doctrine of Revelation would with me be decisive, even if the objections which have been advanced against it were more numerous and formidable than I believe them to be.

In thus advancing my own convictions on this important subject—which has rarely been discussed in a philosophical spirit, but usually, whether in affirming or denying its truth, with a leaning to the right or the left of the question, from its supposed bearing on religious faith, and the ulterior consequences of the chain of reasoning— I feel great pleasure in being able to support my views with the authority of Dr. Prichard, from whose Natural History of Man I have already made a quotation expressive of the near organic relationship of some brutes to man :— " If it be inquired, in what the still more remarkable difference consists, it is by no means easy to reply. By some it will be said, that man, while similar, in the organization of his body, to the lower tribes, is distinguished from them by the possession of an immaterial soul—a principle capable of conscious feeling, of intellect and thought. To many persons it will appear paradoxical to ascribe the endowment of a soul to the inferior tribes in the creation : yet it is difficult to discover a valid argument that limits the possession of an immaterial principle to man. The phenomena of feeling, of desire and aversion, of love and hatred, of fear and revenge, and the perception of external relations manifested in the life of brutes, imply, not only through the analogy which they display to the human faculties, but likewise from all that we can learn or conjecture of their particular nature, the superadded principle, distinct from the mere mechanism of material bodies. That such a principle must exist in all beings capable of sensation, or of anything analogous to human passions and feelings, will hardly be denied by those who perceive the force of arguments which metaphysically demonstrate the immaterial nature of the mind. There may be no rational grounds for the ancient dogma, that the souls of the lower animals are imperishable, like the soul of man ;—and we may venture to conjecture that there may be immaterial essences of divers kinds, endowed with various attributes and capabilities : but the real nature of these unseen principles eludes our research ; they are only known to us by their external manifestations."

But the inquiry into the essence of which this existence consists seems to be of so difficult a nature, that what is usually the first crude conception of a reply is founded in error.

In the minds of those who have sought to frame in the intellect an idea of the nature of Spirit, an obscure conception of materiality has always found a place. There has always been an opinion or impression of some substratum, in which the spiritual faculties are fixed, or by which they are exercised : which is about as near the truth as if, with some writers, we were to endeavour to form an idea of simple matter, in which length, breadth, thickness, and gravity should be no more than accidents, and not essential properties. For, in the same manner as these properties enter into the composition of a substance, so the action of thought and consciousness demonstrates the presence of spirit, its capacity for which forms in fact its essence.

Considering Spirit as an existence, of which

Thought is as much an essential property as Gravity is of Matter, the *necessary* immortality of all such existence is rather taken for granted than proved; and the abstract demonstration of this immortality is far from being made out by the arguments *à priori* which have been advanced to establish it. A much stronger argument in its favour may be derived from what may be denominated the Instinctive aspiration, which is manifested in certain conditions of the mind: for obtaining and enjoying which felicitous existence, Immortality is indispensable.

The simple love of life is possessed in common by man and the brute; and in the latter it is often manifested in powerful attempts to escape from danger, under circumstances of such bodily injury as must render the continuance of such existence nothing short of continued suffering. But a close inquiry into human feelings and conduct renders it evident, that in man there is a principle of still more extensive and powerful operation: that in him the love of life yields to a desire after immortality, which is in the nature of an instinct, separate even from its moral consequences: so that even though his conscious condition, in regard of good or evil, be such as to render the prospect awful, he would tremble still more at utter annihilation. To the question,

—— Why shrinks the soul
Back on herself, and startles at destruction?

the proper answer is,

'Tis *this* divinity that stirs within us.

It is asking no more from the acknowledgment of all men than it is supposed the confession of all who have studied the works of nature will readily grant, that they will admit the truth of the proposition : That in framing the constitution of universal nature, the eternal Author formed his work on the contemplation of all the properties and capacities which he intended it to possess : so that wherever there is an internal organ, a function necessary to the creature is supposed and supplied ; and if an outward organization, whether of attack, defence, or of simple utility towards the means of life, there will certainly be found enemies to be repulsed or overcome, victims to be subdued, or advantages to be secured. The mental properties of a Being are the complicated result of many combinations ; but wherever there is found, common to the whole of a race, an aspiration after a special object, it would suppose an infraction of the laws of Nature to believe that there nowhere existed the object by which this aspiration is to be gratified.

It is possible that the possessor of such an instinct may be far removed from the presence of the object towards which it is directed, and he may have no definite idea of the thing desired. In confirmation of this supposition, we have adduced the case of a duck, which might have been hatched in the deserts of Africa ; where it could have had no opportunity of acquiring an idea of the nature of water, of the want of which it is sensible, and into which, as to its congenial element, it would instantly plunge, when presented to its view. The houseless dogs of Asiatic cities, who know nothing of man but as a stranger or enemy, are degraded to the condition of scavengers; and yet they possess a capacity for being the friends and protectors of the human race which would be sought in vain in many of their kindred tribes: let man but proffer to them a friendship congenial to their affections, and it is soon seen that this instinct does not exist in vain. The aspiration of the poet Burns is in this point of view as just as it is poetical:

> —— And if there is no other scene of being,
> Where my insatiate wish may have its fill,
> This something at my heart that heaves for room,
> My best, my dearest part, was made in vain.

In this, then, consists the universal, decisive, and permanent difference between the spiritual nature of man and animals; and its fruit is necessarily seen in his faith in God. And, singularly reserved as the Book of God is in its references to so curious and interesting a subject as the nature and prospects of the lower animals, there is no more, I believe, than a single text which comes so close to it as to touch on the subject of the superior aspiration of Man. By the wisest of mankind, who had the advantage of divine teaching to aid him in his studies especially directed to the nature of animals, the essential difference in the human and the bestial instinct is pronounced to be,

that the propensity of the former is to objects
of a nobler nature, and to a progressive rise in
intellect and purity; whereas the bias of the
mere animal is to descend, and be satisfied with
what is here below. (Eccles. iii. 21.) The nature of
religion therefore is, to furnish motives, assistance,
and guidance to reach this perfection of human
existence; and in the midst of so much ignorance
of its real nature, so innate and universal is
this instinctive craving for the higher good—
immortal existence—that, Cicero remarks, no nation, however savage, has ever been known, in
which some religious consciousness has not found
a place, even where every other mental endowment has failed. And whenever the idea of a
God, a future state, and invisible things, has
been presented to the mind of the savage man,
it has been received as congenial to his apprehension, although the sectarian doctrines which
have accompanied it have been rejected. The
universality of such an impression among all who
bear the name of humanity, is strongly contrasted
with the universal destitution of it in all animals,
who have lived among us, and have been within
reach of the means of acquiring such knowledge, if
the capacity for its application had existed.

It would be an error to confound this instinctive
aspiration after something of a higher kind than
earth and our present nature affords, with the
motions and dictates of another principle of our
nature—the influence of Reason; because the latter

assumes the task to support, explain, and exalt it. It does the same for other of our instincts, from which its difference admits of no dispute.

A further well-marked distinction between the human and animal spirit is seen in the use to which their share of this nobler attribute—reason— is appropriated; and which might even be supposed to designate a difference in the nature of that principle itself, were there not examples to shew a capacity in man to degrade his reason to the level of that of the brute. My proofs of the existence in animals of a reasoning faculty are yet to come; but in the proportion in which it exists I shall have to shew, that its sole appropriation is as the servant of Instinct, to guide the latter in its development; and the result is, that the possessors of it are rendered more completely the creatures of appetite and earth. In direct opposition to this, the instincts of man are only designed to be the servants, not the masters of his reason, to whose perfection they contribute; and while the one rises in the scale of created things, and is, in his highest excellence, but " a little lower than the angels," the other is either stationary, or, degenerating, retrogrades. That this, in either case, is the proper relationship, is evident from the common feeling of mankind at large, who admire the stratagems of an animal which employs consummate skill in defence against an enemy, or to secure its prey, and satisfy its appetites, but despise the man whose aims and desires are on a level with the brute; and having no higher object than that which dignifies them, he incurs their contempt.

Of the higher demonstrations of intellect, the capacity of reasoning is one of the most prominent; and it is defined by Dr. Johnson as " the power by which man deduces one proposition from another, and proceeds from premises to consequences." What has been regarded as a still higher faculty—that property of the intellect termed Intuition—appears to differ from reasoning in nothing but celerity and certainty of action ; which arise from the unclouded view which clear intelligence is able to take of every possible circumstance and contingency involved in any case.

A predominant error in the minds of those who deny to the inferior animals the capacity of reasoning, is the omitting to take into account a possibility of the existence of instinct in connexion with it ; or that it may lie at the foundation of that building, of which the rational faculty is the consummation.

In proof of the operation of instinct in human beings, reference has already been made to its early display in the first stage of our existence, when reason as a guide could have no foundation or means of action. But, to demonstrate its presence at a more advanced stage of life, it is only necessary to analyse the ordinary combinations of human proceedings, to shew that it is the basis on which even reason itself, with its attendant affections and imaginations, erects its loftiest excellency. The highest of these affections is the passion of love—an emotion which assimilates man the most closely to the highest spiritual existences; which is the most pure, refined, and excellent of human feelings; but which, even in its highest exaltation, is rarely found separate from a mixture of instinct.

Those forms of love which take the condition of parental, fraternal, or sexual affection may assuredly be said to elevate, and not degrade the feeling of attachment, even in minds of the highest order. That the lower animals are capable of a similar mingling of refined feeling with instinctive passion, there are numerous instances to prove. Referring to the habits of the Mandarine duck (a Chinese species), Mr. Bennet says, " Mr. Beale's aviary afforded a singular corroboration of the fidelity of the birds in question. Of a pair in that gentleman's possession, the drake being one night purloined by some thieves, the unfortunate duck displayed the strongest marks of despair at her bereavement, retiring into a corner, and altogether neglecting food and drink, as well as the care of her person. In this condition she was courted by a drake who had lost his mate, but who met with no encouragement from the widow. On the stolen drake being subsequently recovered and restored to the aviary, the most extravagant demonstrations of joy were displayed by the fond couple. But this was not all: for, as if informed by his spouse of the gallant proposals made to her shortly before his arrival, the drake attacked the luckless bird who would have supplanted him, beat out his eyes, and inflicted so many injuries as to cause his death."

The Journal of a Naturalist relates the following

instance of affectionate attention in the Thrush.
" We observed this summer two common thrushes
frequenting the shrubs on the green in our garden.
From the slenderness of their forms and the freshness of their plumage, we pronounced them to be
birds of the preceding summer. There was an
association and friendship between them that called
our attention to their actions. One of them seemed
ailing or feeble from some bodily accident ; for
though it hopped about, yet it appeared unable to
obtain sufficiency of food. Its companion, an active,
sprightly bird, would frequently bring it worms or
bruised snails, when they mutually partook of the
banquet ; and the ailing bird would wait patiently,
understand the actions, expect the assistance of the
other, and advance from his asylum upon its approach.
This procedure was continued for some days ; but
after a time we missed the fostered bird, which probably died, or by reason of its weakness met with
some fatal accident."

Pliny relates a somewhat similar instance of affectionate care of the aged in the Rat ; and it is so ordinary a portion of the character of the Stork, as to
have given origin to its name. This feeling sometimes
characterizes a race. Thus, though living usually
apart, Jackdaws are fond of associating with Rooks,
and sometimes venture to place their nests in the
rookery, although the latter bird appears to tolerate,
rather than encourage the intimacy. Starlings also,
when assembled in flocks in the winter, will often
court the friendship of Rooks ; and on this account
permit the neighbourhood of men, whom otherwise they

would have carefully avoided. This habit of affectionate association is the more remarkable, as contrasted with the antipathy which some creatures manifest to each other. The Crow is always ready to buffet the Buzzard and Kestrel; and the annoyance inflicted by the smaller birds on the Owl, and sometimes on the Cuckoo, has often been described. It cannot be for food that the Sword-fish (*Xiphias gladius*) attacks the Whale; and yet its approach towards any of the tribes of the latter creature causes them to fly with terror. The love of the human race so powerfully shewn by the Dog is the more surprising, as man is the only creature in whose favour it is displayed: for to individuals of its own kind its savage propensities are never wholly extinguished.

In animals, as in the human race, this affection is also sometimes attended with the feeling of jealousy: " A wood-dealer residing near Quai St. Michel, Paris, had a fine English bulldog, which was a great favourite of his wife, who used to caress the animal. On the 10th of August last she was sitting not far from the kennel caressing her child which was five years old; the dog became jealous of it, and at last so furious that he burst his chain, rushed at the child, worried it, and did not quit his hold until he was killed with a knife. The child was so severely hurt, that its life was despaired of." (Loudon's Mag. Nat. Hist., N. S. vol. ii. p. 568.)

A proper idea of beauty is, that it is the foundation of this emotion in the mind; and this impression

obtains a place in every being, in proportion as
it possesses intellect and predisposition : but the
particular modification through which it may be displayed is rightly termed a sentiment; by which is
especially meant the abstract feeling of excellency, as
applied, not to the gratifying of a want, but to such a
mental emotion as is accompanied with respect for
the object, and an earnest desire to conciliate its
regard. That simple beauty either of form or colour
is not the thing of which possession is coveted
by intellectual affection, appears from the fact that
it is not in our power to feel such love for a
statue or painting, however exquisite the workman-
ship or grace. As far as probability is concerned, the
story of Pygmalion is felt by every one to be unnatural; and the slightest analysis of our sensations
is sufficient to shew that the influence of beauty
is solely owing to the principles of physiognomy
implanted within us. We, however unconsciously,
regard the outward expression of countenance, form,
or action, as expressive of qualities of the mind
corresponding with an ideal image in the intellect ; and the possession of which in the object
constitutes its value in the feelings of the observer.
This explains the sudden attachments we see formed
between persons hitherto strangers to each other ;
and which consist in the filling up of a void that
has long been suffered, but to supply which a proper
object has not before offered itself. In others the most
earnest endeavour has laboured in vain to acquire it,
the very endeavour having lead to its own disappoint-

ment, by bringing into action some defect, or placing
the individual under circumstances of unnatural effort
and constraint.

As man is pre-eminently a social creature,
every human being is influenced by a wish to
win regard and respect from some one, and,
however otherwise blest with the gifts of fortune and talent, cannot be satisfied without it.
It is an instinct; and, in proceeding to fulfil its
craving, the preference for a particular individual
is founded on the impression, first, of likeness
to himself in feelings, tastes, and opinions; and,
secondly, on the admiration of some quality in
which he is consciously deficient, but of the value
of which he is abundantly sensible.   It is what
the scriptural history of man's creation aptly terms
a help *against* himself; and the lover who founds his
regard on external appearances may be said to trust
his happiness to the amount of his skill in the science
of physiognomy.   Beauty then, in its proper character, is to be regarded as an index, by which
we learn that the mind, of which it ought to
convey the lively expression, is of the required
order and degree; and hence the beauty, however
exquisite, which does not succeed in raising such
an impression must necessarily fail in securing
the admiration of attachment.   The sign may
prove fallacious, by exciting expectations which
experience does not fulfil; but it is more frequent
for the excellency to exist without an expression
of it in form or countenance.   The principle,
however, is not the less of universal application

I

in the feelings of every intelligent creature. Animals of the same species form attachments of affection from labouring together, though one of them may be unlike the general type of the species. A bird in one stage of plumage has been known to pair with another apparently so dissimilar, that naturalists, unacquainted with the fact that birds which are liable to much variation of plumage at different stages of growth are capable of continuing their race before they have attained the adult condition, have been inclined to judge them of different species. A brown field-mouse has been found occupying the same nest with an albino, their conscious mental communication disregarding the apparent dissimilarity of nature.

In connexion with this, we may instance the passion for personal adornment that pervades human nature in the most savage as well as in the most refined condition. The naked man, who knows little of the comforts of life, even as measured by his own ideas of conveniency, is found to paint his skin with a fanciful arrangement of colours ; and he even renders them indelible with long labour and the infliction of much pain. The miserable natives of the neighbourhood of Cape Horn, exposed to the wet and cold of their inhospitable climate, gave the preference to a strip of red serge, to be worn as an ornament round the head, to a whole piece for clothing to the body. The mode may differ, but the feeling is the same, whether it ornaments a monarch's crown with gold and diamonds, or emblazons with feathers the head of an Indian ;

whether it works into fashion the expensive pro-
ductions of the loom, or lays on the sable countenance the conspicuous lines of white or yellow
clay. The hand of Nature has lavished ornament
on the wing of a bird, and the shard of a beetle ;
and though excess or bad taste in the human
race have rendered this instinct ridiculous or con-
temptible, it may be questioned whether, if we
had been admitted to a sight of the youthful Eve
in her garden of innocence, we should not have
discovered the rose and the lily entwined among her
tresses—her only drapery.

A disposition to receive and bestow protection
constitutes another instinctive feeling, of which a
consciousness exists in the opposite sexes, and
deeply influences their actions. In woman there
is the impression that this is due to her from
man ; and hence the expression of her weakness
and timidity, so far from being a reproach, is
felt to be graceful and becoming, and amounts
to a tacit invitation to him to protect her. She
shrinks from danger, and is not ashamed of her
weakness ; but she would despise the man who was
as weak as herself. In him, on the other hand, there
is a feeling that protection of the weaker sex becomes
him, and that it is his place to offer it. And in
this lies the foundation of the attachments and
alliances which constitute the chief blessing of
life ; but which, though approved by reason, and
even by a much higher principle, are shared by
the bird and the beast. Birds preen themselves,

and shew consciousness of natural elegancy of form and colour; and the fur of animals is smoothed and cleaned, and every matter which would soil it is carefully avoided. They are also prompt to shew that they are able to protect, where protection is needed.

CHAPTER X.

AMONG the lowest, in point of excellency, of the emanations of Instinct, is the sensation of hunger, and the craving for food—an impulse common to all sensitive creatures, whereby they are instigated to the exertion of a variety of faculties, which partake alike of the nature of instinct and reflection.

And the mode of securing this object is in each race and species skilfully varied to suit the necessity of their case. If the proceeding be less elaborate in the more limited intellect, it is not the less appropriate to the nature of the creature to be supplied. It is no small effort of skill in the farmer to fit the cultivation of his crop to the course of the seasons and the nature of the soil. He employs instruments of complex structure in the preparation of the ground ; and supplies it with manures compounded and varied with chemical skill. His method of proceeding is changed, according as it is a rainy or a dry season ; and finally, if he employs his knowledge of mechanism in reducing his corn to food, we refer the whole proceeding to the exercise of reason : he has acted from a comparison of a variety of known causes with their anticipated consequences.

But although they do not possess, as they do not need, a mill to grind, or an oven to bake their food, we know that a storehouse is constructed by the rat, mouse, squirrel, polecat, and, among foreign animals, the hamster ; and bushels of corn, potatoes, apples, and nuts have been stored carefully away, as if in the persuasion that, however plentiful the present supply might be, it was wise not to trust to the continuance of such abundance, but to provide for all future contingencies. The conveyance of a large quantity of corn must be the work of time, with the combination of many individuals ; and there are not a few instances narrated, in which the work done must have been as well devised as the associated perseverance of man in executing any important and difficult enterprise. The appetite also must have been suspended, with no small degree of self-denial, during the progress of the undertaking.

The Rev. Mr. Bury (Zoologist, vol. ii. p. 787) says, " When I was in Hertfordshire, a few years back, I had, on one occasion, laid in our winter stock of walnuts : on the second evening it was discovered by the rats, and though I did suspect that mischief was going on, from certain noises that issued from behind the wainscotting, I had not surmised the extent of the mischief likely to be committed : for on the following morning, to my chagrin, the whole stock, amounting to two bushels, had disappeared, excepting only three or four that were bad."

The motive must have been the same in the mind of the Polecat described and figured by Bewick : for if the mere satisfying of immediate appetite had been the object, enough fish had been captured for its present wants ; but this did not satisfy it, and therefore it made eleven excursions to the rivulet, and laid up a treasure for the future.

The caution and skill of the Fox in securing its safety, while in search of prey to satisfy its hunger, are proofs of a capacity for reasoning by induction, to the full as decided as the elaborate preparations of man for the like purpose ; and it has been observed, " Whenever a Cat is tempted by the bait, and caught in a fox-trap, Reynard is at hand to devour the bait and the Cat too, and fearlessly approaches an instrument which the Fox must know cannot *then* do it any harm. Let us compare with this boldness the incredible caution with which the animal proceeds when tempted by the bait in a *set* trap. Dietrich aus dem Winkell had once the good fortune of observing, on a winter evening, a Fox, which for many preceding days had been allured with loose baits ; and, as often as it ate one, it sat comfortably down, wagging its brush. The nearer it approached the trap, the longer did it hesitate to take the baits, the oftener did it make the tour round the catching-place. When arrived near the trap, it squatted down, and eyed the

bait for ten minutes at least : whereupon it ran
three or four times round the trap : then it
stretched out one of its forepaws after the bait,
but did not touch it : again a pause, during
which the Fox stared immovably at the bait.
At last, as if in despair, the animal made a rush,
and was caught by the neck." (Mag. Nat. Hist.,
N. S. vol. i. p. 512.)

The cunning of the Fox has indeed been ever proverbial ; and, even so long since as the days of Æsop,
he figures as chief personifier of that quality. But, in
many of the instances which have been related, we
cannot refuse it the higher appellation of wisdom,
as possessing the excellency implied in the definition
of its being " the means best adapted to the ends
most conducive to its own well-being." The following instance is illustrative of the remark of
Pliny, that no degree of taming will entirely divest
this animal of the habits of its ancestry. A
Fox had been partially tamed, and was kept fastened by a chain to a post in a court-yard, where
he was chiefly fed with boiled potatoes. But the
animal seems to have thought that a desirable
addition might be made to his fare from the
numerous fowls that strutted round him, but whose
caution kept them beyond the reach of so formidable an enemy. His measures were soon taken ;
and having bruised and scattered the boiled potatoes which he had received for his dinner at the
extremity of the space that the length of his
chain enabled him to command, he retired, in an
opposite direction, to the full extent of his chain,

and assumed the appearance of utter regardlessness of all that was passing around him. The stratagem succeeded; and when some of the fowls had been thrown so much off their guard as to intrude within the circle of danger, the Fox sprung from his lurking-place, and seized his prey.

The habits of cautiousness displayed by this animal are also significant of conclusions drawn by observation from experience. For, when followed by dogs, it will not run through a gate—though this is obviously the most ready passage; nor in crossing a hedge will it prefer a smooth and even part—but the roughest, where thorns and briars abound; and when it mounts an eminence, it proceeds obliquely, and not straightforward. And whether we suppose these actions to proceed from a desire to avoid those places where traps may probably have been laid, or from knowing that his pursuers will exactly follow his footsteps, and he has resolved to lead them through as many obstacles as possible, in either case an estimation of causes and consequences is to be discerned.

We quote the following anecdote from the Zoologist, vol. ii. p. 790:—" While an old man was wandering by the side of one of the largest tributaries of the Almand, he observed a Badger moving leisurely along the ledge of a rock on the opposite bank. In a little time a Fox came up, and after walking for some distance close in the rear of the poor Badger, he leaped into the water. Immediately afterwards came a pack of hounds, at full speed, in pursuit of the Fox, who by this time was far enough off, floating down the stream; but the luckless Badger was instantly torn to pieces by the dogs. An instance of still greater sagacity in the Fox occurred a few years ago, also in this neighbourhood. As a farm-servant was preparing a small piece of land for the reception of wheat, near to Pumpherston Mains, he was not a little surprised on seeing a Fox slowly running in the furrow immediately before the plough. While wondering why the sly creature was so confident, he heard behind him the cry of the dogs; and turning round, he saw the whole pack at a dead stand near the other end of the field, at the very spot where Reynard had entered the newly-enclosed trench. The idea struck him that the Fox had taken this ingenious way of eluding pursuit; and through deference to the sagacity of the animal, he allowed it to escape." Derham quotes Olaus, in his account of Norway, as having himself witnessed the fact of a Fox dropping the end of its tail among the rocks on the seashore, to catch the Crabs below, and hauling up and devouring such as laid hold of it. On our own seacoast Rats also have been known to add a new dish to their dietary by taking Crabs, though it is not easy to imagine how the capture is effected; and certainly it is not by angling with the same pensile organ. On the credit of several persons, however, it is known that Rats have skilfully employed their tails in drawing oil through the narrow neck of a jar, when unable to reach it in any other manner. Mr. Murray observed a Dormouse to dip its tail into a dish of milk, and then carry it, smeared with the fluid, to its mouth; and similar ingenuity has been witnessed in its conveyance of water, when the little creature could not otherwise obtain a supply.

The modes employed by dogs of different races in capturing and devouring the Crab, and especially that pugnacious species the Velvet Crab (*Portunus puber*), well illustrate the experience which has become propagated in the breed, over the ignorance of the un-initiated. On the first discovery of the prey, a Terrier runs in to seize it, and is immediately and severely bit-ten in the nose. But a sedate Newfoundland Dog of my acquaintance proceeds more soberly in his work. He lays his paw on it, to arrest it in its escape : then tumbling it over, he bares his teeth, and, seizing it with the mouth, throws the Crab aloft : it falls upon the stones : the shell is cracked beyond redemption; and then the dainty dish is devoured at his leisure.

As the Hare is more timid, so it is less fertile in resources than the Fox ; but books that treat of hunting give examples of the exercise of much subtlety on its part also, when its object is to escape from pursuit. It is especially conscious of the scent left by its feet, and of the danger which threatens it, in consequence : a reflection which implies as much knowledge of the habits of its enemies as of its own. When about to enter its seat for the purpose of rest, it leaps in various directions, and crosses and recrosses its path with repeated springs ; and at last, by a leap of greater energy than it has yet used, it effects a lodgment in the selected spot, which is chosen rather to disarm suspicion than to protect it from injury. In the Manuel du Chasseur some instances are quoted from an ancient volume on hunting by Jaques du Fouilloux. A Hare, intending to mislead its pursuers, has been seen spontaneously to quit its seat, and proceed to a pond at the distance of nearly a mile; and, having washed itself, push off again through a quantity of rushes. It has too been known, when pursued to fatigue by dogs, to thrust another Hare from its seat, and squat itself down in its place. This author has seen Hares swim successively through two or three ponds, of which the smallest was eighty paces round. He has known it, after a long chase, to creep under the door of a sheep-house, and rest among the cattle; and when the hounds were in pursuit, it would get into the middle of a flock of sheep, and accompany them in all their motions round the field, refusing by any means to quit the shelter they afforded. The stratagem of its passing forward on one side of a hedge and returning by the other, with only the breadth of the hedge between itself and its enemies, is of frequent occurrence; and it has even been known to select its seat close to the walls of a dog-kennel. This latter circumstance, however, is illustrative of the principles of reflection and reasoning: for the Fox, Weasel, and Polecat are to the Hare more dangerous enemies than the Hound; and the situation chosen was such as these ferocious creatures were not likely to approach.

A gentleman was engaged in the amusement of coursing, when a Hare, closely pressed, passed under a gate, while the dogs followed by leaping over it. The delay caused to her pursuers by this manœuvre seems to have taught a sudden and useful lesson to the persecuted creature : for, as soon as the dogs had cleared the gate and overtaken her, she doubled and returned under the gate as before, the dogs again following and passing over it. And this flirtation continued backwards and forwards until the dogs were fairly tired of the amusement : when the Hare, taking advantage of their fatigue, quietly stole away. (Loudon's Mag. Nat. Hist. vol. iv. p. 143.)

In many instances the escape of the Hare from her pursuers has been so sudden and unaccountable, as not only to baffle the expectations of the hunter, but to confound his inquiries into the means. In such cases superstition has been called in to account for what was found so much to mar the pleasure of the chase; and accordingly it became the received opinion that nothing but witchcraft could account for it ; and, in fact, that the Hare itself was a witch in disguise. The terror of the poor old woman selected by popular prejudice for the imputation, at the sight of her enraged accusers, was taken to be a sufficient corroboration of the charge. The frequent escape of the Hare from the shot of the unskilful sportsman led also to the belief that the metamorphosed animal could only be killed with a gun charged with a crooked sixpence,

and fired by a first-born son. The evasions of the
Hare are, indeed, almost as numerous and as well
contrived as those of the Fox; but, unfortunately,
the great terror to which it is liable on hearing
of loud and unusual noises prevents the poor creature from experiencing all the benefits of its stratagems. The sudden sound of a horn, or a shout will
cause it to run into the very face of danger, and
make it die with fear. A gentleman met a Hare
in a road inclosed on both sides by the ordinary
hedges of Cornwall; and he succeeded in driving it
before him for a quarter of a mile, until it was compelled to take shelter in a pound, where he caught
it. This singular exploit was performed by following the Hare at a smart gallop, and when it shewed
a wish to attempt the hedge, or pass through a
gate that sometimes offered itself, a smart crack
with the whip so alarmed the animal as to deter
it from taking the leap that would have ensured its
safety.

But the Hare resorts to concealment, rather
than to swiftness, to escape her enemies; and
this she seeks from consciousness of the likeness
of her colour to the herbage or soil on which she
is seated. The better also to elude suspicion, her
form is selected where a single clump of fern or
tuft of grass may remove the supposition that any
creature could there lie hid. The following is a
minute description of such an attempt at secresy;
and that it is generally successful may be believed
from the fact that, even when pointed out, none but a

practised eye is able to detect its presence. "As we wound our way up a steep field, I was within a little of stepping on the back of a Hare. She had scratched out just enough of the sandy soil to bring her back level with the surface: one forefoot was stuck straight out before her, and on this rested her head: her ears fell on her neck on each side, and touched the ground: her eyes, large, bright, and black, were fixed intently on me; and the instant that my own eyes caught hers, I saw a slight movement. The nose had slid off her foot to the ground, and the other foot had been stretched out: this movement had lowered her head, which was now but a fraction above the level of the hill side; and so exactly was she the colour of the surrounding soil, that, but for the lustrous eye, I could not have persuaded myself that there was a living creature there. I pointed her out to my friend, who in his eagerness had as nearly stepped on her as I had. There we stood about two yards apart, and Puss motionless as a stone between us." (Loudon's Mag. Nat. Hist., vol. vi. p. 194.) In such a situation, if its hope of successful concealment be encouraged by the indirect approach of the observer, and especially if he walk circularly round it, with his eyes fixed on those of the Hare, he may come so near to it as to take it with his hand; but if the eye be taken off from it for a moment, the opportunity is seized to dart away and escape.

The following note, by Mr. Yarrell, is significant

of a process of reasoning derived from observation of the course of Nature, such as would do no discredit to a higher race of creatures :—" A harbour of great extent on our southern coast has an island near the middle of considerable size, the nearest point of which is a mile distant from the mainland at high water, and with which point there is frequent communication by a ferry. Early one morning in spring two Hares were observed to come down from the hills of the mainland towards the seaside ; one of which, from time to time, left its companion, and proceeding to the very edge of the water, stopped there a minute or two, and then returned to its mate. The tide was rising, and, after waiting some time, one of them, exactly at high water, took to the sea, and swam rapidly over, in a straight line, to the opposite projecting point of land. The observer, on this occasion, who was near the spot, but remained unperceived by the Hares, had no doubt that they were of different sexes, and that it was the male (like another Leander) which swam across the water, as he had probably done many times before. It was remarkable that the Hares had remained on the shore nearly half an hour ; one of them occasionally examining, as it would seem, the state of the current, and ultimately taking to the sea at that precise period of the tide called slackwater, when the passage across could be effected without being carried by the force of the stream either above or below the desired

point of landing. The other Hare then cantered
back to the hills." (Loudon's Mag. Nat. Hist.,
vol. v. p. 99.)

The following narrative, from Mr. Lander's Travels in the North of Europe, is also illustrative of
this capacity in animals for observing phenomena,
and by inductive reasoning employing their observations to their own purposes.—" A man set off
one morning (in Sweden) to shoot the Tjader or
Tjor (Cock of the Woods), which is effected in
this wise:—the bird is so extremely shy, that he
may rarely be met with, except in the pairing
season, when every morning he renews his song.
He usually commences just before sunrise, beginning in a loud strain, which gradually sinks into
a low key, until he is quite intranced with his
own melody: he then droops his wings to the
earth, and runs to the distance of several feet,
calling 'Cluck! Cluck! Cluck!' during which time
he is said to be incapable of seeing (so wrapt up
is he in his own contemplations), and may be
caught even with the hand by those who are near
enough. As the fit lasts only a few moments,
the sportsman must, if unready, wait for the next
occasion: for, should he advance a step, except
when the bird is thus insensible, he will certainly
be overheard, and the victim escape. The man
I began to speak of being, early one morning, in
pursuit of this bird, heard his song at a short
distance ; and, as soon as the clucking commenced,
of course advanced as rapidly as he could, and
then remained motionless till those particular notes

again sounded. It was quite dusk, the sun not having yet risen; but the song seemed to come from the centre of an open space in the forest from which the sportsman was just emerging. He could not see many yards before him, and only followed the direction of the sound. It so happened that, from another point, but at no great distance, a Bear was advancing on the Tjader, just in the manner of, and with the same steps, as the man. The hunter, while standing motionless, thought he perceived a dark object on one side of him, but it did not much engage his attention; and at the usual note he moved on towards the game, but was surprised to see that the black object had also advanced in an equal degree, and now stood in a line with him. Still he was so eager after the bird, that he could think of nothing else, and approached close to his prey before he perceived that a large Bear stood within a few feet of him; and, in fact, just as they were both about to spring on the bird, they caught sight of each other, and each thought proper to slink back. After having retreated a short distance, the man began to think it would be rather inglorious to yield the prize without a struggle; and there being now a good deal more light, he returned to the spot, when it appeared that the Bear had also taken the same resolution, and was actually advancing over the open space I have mentioned, growling and tearing up the moss with her feet. Though the man had only small shot in his gun, he fired without hesitation, and immediately took to his heels and fled, conceiving the Bear to be close in his rear." The animal was afterwards found to be killed.

To what extent necessity is the mother of invention is seen in the following anecdote of the Roebuck. " Some few years ago one of these animals, after being hunted out of Scotland, at last took refuge in the woody recesses bordering upon the banks of the Tyne, between Prudhoe Castle and Wylam. It was repeatedly seen and hunted, but no dogs were equal to its speed: it frequently crossed the river, and, either by swiftness or artifice, eluded all its pursuers. It happened, during the rigour of a severe winter, that, being pursued, it crossed the river upon the ice with some difficulty; and, being much strained by its violent exertions, was taken alive. It was kept for some weeks in the house, and was then again turned out; but all its cunning and activity were gone: it seemed to have forgotten the places of its former retreat; and, after running some time, it lay down in the midst of a brook, where it was killed by the dogs." (Bewick's Quadrupeds.)

I have purposely avoided drawing any illustrations of intellect from the history of the Dog; because, however sagacious many of its actions are, an objection might be raised, that its proceedings are influenced by the long-continued habit of receiving instruction from man. This animal also has been the subject of separate volumes of anecdotes, to which it is here sufficient to make a general reference; and I will therefore content

myself with the following traits of character,—
in the first of which the Dog shews itself a
nobler creature than the Man. " The hero of the
story figures in Captain Southey's History (of the
West Indies) with great propriety among the con-
querors of Puerto Rico : for, though only a Dog,
the full pay of a crossbowman and half as much
more was received by his owner for his services ;
and he was thought to have done as much toward
what is called the pacification of that island as a
third of all the Spaniards who were employed in
it. Bezerillo was his name :—of a reddish colour,
with a black face, not large of his kind, nor finely
made, but of great understanding and courage ;
and, indeed, what he did was such that, *sans*
doubt, the Christians believed God had sent him
for their succour. He would select among two
hundred Indians one who had escaped from the
Christians, or who should have been pointed out
to him, and would seize him by the arm, and
make him come back with him to the camp, or
wherever the Christians might be ; and if he attempted to resist, or would not come, he tore him
to pieces, and did other things which were very
remarkable, and worthy of admiration. At midnight, if a prisoner got loose, and were a league
distant, it was but to say ' The Indian is gone !'
or ' Fetch him !' and away Bezerillo went upon the
scent, and brought him back. The tame Indians
he knew as well as a man could know them, and
never did them hurt ; and among many tame
ones, he could distinguish one wild one. It seemed

as if he had the judgment and intelligence of a man, and that not of a foolish one. Salazar had one day taken an old Indian woman, among other prisoners, after a defeat of the natives, and for no assigned or assignable reason, but in mere wantonness of cruelty, he determined to set this dog upon the poor wretch. But it was to be made a sport of, a spectacle for the Spaniards, or the Christians, as their contemporary historian and fellow-Christian calls them, even while he is relating this story. Salazar gave the woman an old letter, and told her to go with it to the Governor at Aymaco. The poor creature went her way joyfully, expecting to be set at liberty when she had performed her errand. The intent was merely to get her away from the rest, that the dog might have a fair field, and the beholders a full sight. Accordingly, when she had proceeded little farther than a stone's throw, Bezerillo was set at her. Hearing him come, the woman threw herself on the ground; and her simple faith in Salazar's intention, and in the animal's sagacity saved her: for she held out the letter to the dog, and said, ' O, sir dog, sir dog! I am carrying a letter to the Lord Governor: don't hurt me, sir dog!' The dog seemed to understand her; and did understand her, in fact, sufficiently to know that she did not look upon herself as a condemned person, and that she implored his mercy; and he came up to her gently, and did her no harm."

The sagacity of this animal, as shewn in the following incident, will be better understood if we consider, that it is probable this dog had never before seen an instance of similar danger from fire, and had never before contemplated fire in any other form than as a useful contrivance for his own and his master's comfort. In the spring of the year 1845 a mastiff-dog in Cornwall, having discovered that the roof of his master's house was in flames, ran indoors, howling dismally, and, pulling at the garments of the inmates, urged their retreat from the building; and, hurrying out of the house, howled again, and directed their attention by his looks to the flaming roof.

Dr. Caius, in his tract De Canibus Britannicis, says of the sagacity of the English Bloodhound, that in the darkest night it would follow the track of a robber, however cautiously concealed, through a long distance, and single out his footmarks in a multitude of other traces: that it would search through the most secret and difficult places, and even cross rivers: where, when it had reached the farther bank, if the scent were not readily regained, it would take a circuit, in order to intersect the path he must have followed. In the pursuit it was seen to manifest reflection, reasoning, and a decision of choice; but the author justly remarks, that however surprisingly accurate in his proceedings, the sagacity of a dog is confined within narrow limits: so that none of the race can be put upon a multiplicity of pursuits; nor even made to hunt various kinds of animals with the same degree of intelligence:—a re-mark which is as applicable to men as to the canine races—

" One business only will one genius fit,"

the only difference being the extent of the limitation.

The following instance of a conclusion drawn from observation, which by practice has acquired the nature of an hereditary instinct, is witnessed in the Dogs inhabiting the borders of the river Madeleina, in central America, and resembles the trait already told of the manner in which a Newfoundland Dog disposed of that awkward thing to handle—a crab. When hunting the Peccari, the address of these dogs consists in so moderating their eagerness in pursuit, as not to attack an individual of the flock, but to keep the whole in check; and young dogs of the race employ this skill without any particular instruction, whereas strange dogs are found to run in furiously on the flock, to their own destruction. (Prichard, Nat. Hist. of Man, p. 35.)

The Badger is the most formidable of British animals; and though usually of secluded habits, and eager to escape when assailed, there are instances of its voluntarily attacking man, and placing him in considerable danger. Over a Dog unaccustomed to the encounter it is commonly conqueror; and its manner of inflicting injury is by biting the fore-legs of its foe: which it does with great severity. But some Dogs are invariably successful in encountering these desperate animals, without themselves suffering harm. A Dog had been severely bitten by a Badger, when by a lucky nip under the throat, a little above the breast, it at once deprived it of life; and ever after, in similar contests, it aimed at no part but this, which its experience had shewn to be so vulnerable. The success of its attack was so sure that it never failed to kill its enemy in a minute. Another Dog could as speedily dispatch a Badger by thrusting forward its neck to seize the foe, and throwing it into the air, his own body being at the same time kept cautiously back. As the Badger fell, the Dog sprung at its throat, and soon destroyed it.

With like discretion, but from a different motive, acts the Mur (a kind of Guillemot), when it has fallen in with a schûl of little fishes. I have watched with much interest the proceedings of this bird when capturing the stragglers of a school of young mullets (probably *Mugil chelo*) ; and the admirable skill with which their dispersion was prevented, until a full stomach had been secured. It is the nature of this bird, as well as of most of those birds which habitually dive to take their prey, to perform all their evolutions under water with the aid of their wings : but, instead of dashing at once into the midst of the terrified group of small fry, by which only a few would be captured, it passes round and round them, and so drives them into a heap ; and thus has an opportunity of snatching here one, and there another, as it finds it convenient to swallow them ; and if any one pushes out to escape, it falls the first prey of the devourer.

It was something like a soundly-reasoned conclusion in an Eagle, that the shell of a Tortoise, which resisted the efforts of his bill, would be broken by a fall from a great height ; and according to Pliny (l. X. c. 3.) the poet Æschylus suffered from this experimental philosophy: the bird dropping its prey on his bald head, in the belief that it was a stone. A similar stratagem has been practised by Crows when feeding on mussels: among whom it is not uncommon to see one of these birds bear its prey high in the air, let it fall on the stones, and then descend, to feed on it at leisure.

The Crow, which in shrewdness does not yield to any of its congeners, after carrying off a young duck from a pond, has been seen to lay it on the ground, and kill it by walking backward and forward over it: after which it was safely carried off to its nest. (Loudon's Mag. Nat. Hist., N. S. vol. ii. p. 512.) The manner in which this bird removes the egg of a gull or hen to some secure place to be devoured, when compared with that in which a like conveyance is made by the parent for the safety of its future progeny, affords a striking manifestation of the difference between appetite and affection. When influenced by affection, the brittle treasure is removed without flaw or fracture, and is replaced with tender care; but the plunderer at once plunges his bill into its substance, and carries it off on its point.

A few years since the Caterpillars of a neuropterous insect, popularly termed the Black Oak-fly, existed in unusual numbers, and were very injurious to the foliage of the oak, by devouring the young buds at their first appearing, by which means their aid in exciting the flow of the sap was lost, and the stripping of the bark was expensively delayed. Myriads of these caterpillars might be seen hanging

K

by threads of their own spinning from the branches, till they were fortunately discovered by a colony of Rooks, who resorted to the most ingenious, as well as the most effectual, methods of taking them: for, first, with their wings, they beat over the upper surface of the foliage, and then descended to the ground, to pick up the fallen fruit of their labour. I have known the Rook, too, to discover the presence of the caterpillar of the cockchaffer, at some depth beneath the soil, from the circumstance of a slight change in the tint of the grass leading that sagacious bird to infer that these worms were at the roots, which they were devouring; and the result was, that these destructive worms were extirpated.

In places frequented by the common Blackbird and Thrush, you may sometimes see a stone, which may be called the butcher's-block of these birds: to this they carry the Snails (*Helix aspersa*, *H. hortensis* and *nemoralis*) which they collect, and which they seem to know that their bills, without the aid of such a solid fulcrum, would find some difficulty in piercing. A still higher effort of reflection, and, it may be said, of invention, is related by Mr. Yarrell, (British Birds, vol. iii. p. 465) of a Gull, which, for the first time, had made a lark its prey, but had some difficulty in devouring it. After some ineffectual efforts to swallow it, he paused for a moment; and then, as if suddenly recollecting himself, he ran off full speed to a pan of water, shook the bird about in it until well soaked, and immediately gulped it down without further trouble. Since that time he invariably has recourse to the same expedient in similar

cases. It is amusing to observe the proceedings of
the Cormorant, Shag (*Pelecanus carbo* and *P. gra-
culus*), and the Looms (*Colymbi*), in dealing with
the refractory subjects which they sometimes fish up
in the course of their researches under water. If
the prize be a crab, it is taken to the surface, and,
fully aware of the danger of attempting to swallow
it whole, it is there dropped, and a smart peck of
the bill is made at the legs. These are either
knocked off by the blow, or the crab is induced to
throw them off, according to the known practice of
these creatures when injured. Each of these is then
seized and swallowed in succession; and the body,
by this time become a mere lump, is gulped down
last of all. A Launce or Shanny, if caught across
the mouth or held by the tail, is flung aloft, and
caught in a convenient posture as it falls. If the
prey be a Flounder or Plaice, it is thrown on the
surface, and pecked so violently as to break or dis-
locate the firm arrangement of transverse bones, and
thus deprive the muscles of their strong contractile
power, by which so rigid an obstruction was thrown
in the way of swallowing. It is then rolled up into
a cylinder, and easily disposed of. A close observer
of nature informed me, that his attention was directed to a Cormorant, which appeared to be much
distended about the neck and throat; but, while
watching its proceedings, the bird discovered his
presence, and endeavoured to escape, by which means
its attention became distracted, and an Eel started
from its jaws, and employed much active effort to
effect its retreat. Unwilling to lose so valuable a

morsel, the bird pursued it, and was again successful; but it was not now in haste to ingulph its prey.
Repeatedly and violently did it peck the fish through
the whole of its length, and then again it seized it
across its bill; but, still finding it capable of too
much activity, it continued to peck it, until the whole
of its powers of contortion were subdued, and there
was no further risk of its again effecting an escape
from its dungeon.

There was, within my knowledge, in the house of
my parentage, a small cupboard, in which were kept
milk, butter, and other requisites for the tea-table:
and the door was confined with a lock, which, from
age and frequent use, could be easily made to open.
To save trouble, the key was always kept in the lock,
in which it revolved on a very slight impulse. It
was often a subject of remark that the door of this
cupboard was found wide open, and the milk or
butter greatly diminished, without any imaginable
reason, and notwithstanding the persuasion that the
door had certainly been regularly locked; but it was
accident that led to the detection of the offender.
On watching carefully, the Cat was seen to seat
herself on the table; and, by repeated patting on the
side of the bow of the key, it was at last made to
turn, when a slight pull on the door caused it to
move on its hinges. It had proved a fortunate
discovery for Puss, for a long time before she was
taken in the fact.

CHAPTER XI.

INSTANCES were adduced in the last Chapter to illustrate the proposition,—that animals are capable of pursuing a process of reasoning from facts or principles recognized by themselves: that this process is not unfrequently of a refined and complicated description; and the possibility of our falling into a mistake on the subject, by a false interpretation of the phenomena, is obviated by the difficulty of supposing any other explanation of their actions than such as I have assigned to them. But this conclusion cannot be affirmed of all the instances of interpretation of animal conduct which we have noted; and even the Fox, cunning as he is in most of his proceedings, has received credit for a manifestation of wisdom, when his sagacity may be said to have sprung from an inferior source. When suddenly surprised by man, he has been known to assume the appearance of being dead, and has suffered himself to be handled, and even ill-treated, without betraying any signs of sensibility. This high degree of simulation and dissimulation has been ascribed to consummate wisdom, which, when a better means of escape did not offer itself, prompted him to the stratagem of feigning to be incapable of defence or flight until he had disarmed suspicion, and so escaped hostility.   Mr. Blyth (Loudon's Mag. Nat. Hist., N. S. vol. i. p. 5) says, "A Fox has been known to personate a defunct carcase, when surprised in a henhouse; and it has even suffered itself to be carried out by the brush, and thrown on a dungheap, whereupon it instantly rose and took to its heels, to the astounding dismay of its human dupe.   In like manner this animal has submitted to be carried for more than a mile, swung over the shoulder with its head hanging downward, till, at length, it has very speedily effected its release by suddenly biting."

Mr. Mudie, the writer of the article "*Fox*" in Partington's Cyclopædia, relates, from his own personal knowledge, the following particulars, illustrative of the facts now under consideration:—"One morning early a man in the North was going to his work through furze-bushes on a common, and came upon a Fox stretched out at length under the side of one of the bushes. The Fox was drawn out by the tail, and swung right and left, and then laid on the ground; but not a symptom of motion or life did he shew.   The man, never doubting that Reynard had gone the way of all Foxes, and nothing loth to add a foxskin cap to the list of his personal garniture, and the brush to the tail of peacock's feathers and other ornamental trophies over the little looking-glass that stood inclined from the wall of his cottage, took the animal by the tail, and swung it over the one shoulder, at the same time placing his mattock on the other, to keep up the balance; and having done so, onward he trudged to mend the high-road.—The animal had counterfeited death to admiration, and he did not mind being carried in the manner of a dead fox;—but he had no inclination to undergo that species of dissection which the point of the mattock was ever and anon giving his ribs: so, at last, he gave that decisive snap, which is the characteristic bite of foxes, on that portion of the labourer's rear which is supposed to be more sensitive to all manner of inflictions than any other region of the human body. The man felt that something was the matter, but knew not very well what: so, throwing the fox and mattock from him, he turned round to face the foe, whoever he might be, and in turning he espied his dead fox at the distance of full fifty yards, making for the brake with all imaginable speed.

" We shall mention one other anecdote, which came within the personal knowledge of the writer of this article, because it throws some light on the mode of action of the Fox, as well as confirms the truth of his counterfeiting death in all cases where there is a likelihood that it may ensue. The Parsonage of Kilmorac, in Inverness-shire, is situated in a highly-romantic spot, and the clergyman of Kilmorac was a man of great taste, and very hospitable; and he accordingly endeavoured to provide for his guests all the good things which his glebe-land would afford. A well-stocked poultry-yard is an essential requisite in such cases; but here foxes were so numerous, and their covers so near, that a poultry-yard was out of the question. A poultry-house was thus requisite, and the reverend Doctor prided himself not a little in having constructed one which was completely fox-proof; and for a good many years it had been impregnable. A friend of ours had spent a night in this romantic and hospitable abode; and while fresh salmon from the Beauly formed one article for the breakfast-table, new-laid eggs from the stronghold of the hens were, of course, to form another. The purveyor in these cases took the key and marched off, basket in hand, to bring the supply; but when she opened the door, a scene of the most direful havock presented itself: every perch and nest-hole was bedabbled with blood; dead hens lay in dozens on the floor, and in the middle was a full-sized Fox; stretched out at full length, and, apparently, a sharer of the common mortality. The maid never doubted the death of the Fox; but attributed it to a different cause—namely, that he had so gorged himself on the poultry, that he had burst. Here were three causes to rouse the mingled wrath and contempt of the servant; and after some exclamations she took him up by the tail, and swung him with all her might into the receptacle in which were accumulated the requisites for garden compost. The Fox fell safely, and rose again speedily, and scoured along until he gained the cover of the woods, leaving the servant in utter consternation."

It has been a matter of some surprise that, even when an entrance has been effected, it should be in the power of a fox to capture fowls, which are commonly perched in situations supposed to be inaccessible; and yet the wily creature never fails of obtaining as many of them as he pleases. And this object he secures with very little trouble: for, conscious of the terror his presence is sure to create, he has only to make a demonstration of an endeavour to reach them, and their fluttering is sure to bring them presently within his reach. The same fatal result frequently follows even when fowls are roosting on the branch of a tree, in which case it is only necessary for them to remain quiet, or move to a greater distance, to secure their safety.

The Opossum of North America (*Didelphis Virginiana*) is so famous for feigning death, that its name has become proverbial as an expression of this deceit. A like habit is common to the Land Rail (*Rallus crex*), the common Field or Sky Lark (*Alauda arvensis*), and to many Beetles. But in all these cases we may be permitted to doubt whether the cause assigned be the true one.

The character for subtlety which the Fox has had from the earliest ages is the main reason why his assumed or presumed inanimation when in danger has been ascribed to intention: for otherwise, some of the instances we have given, on this supposition, would not appear to be exceedingly well devised. In two instances which I have adduced, at least an effort at escape would have been the most judicious proceeding; and in his adventure with the countryman it seems surprising that this was not attempted. But a more probable explanation is, that the sudden-

K 3

ness of the encounter, at a time when the creature thought of no such thing, had the effect of stupefying his senses; so that an effort at escape was out of his power, and the appearance of death was not the fictitious contrivance of cunning, but the consequence of terror. And that this explanation is the true one appears, among other proofs, from the conduct of a bolder and more ferocious animal, the Wolf, under similar circumstances. If taken in a pitfall, it is said that it is so subdued by surprise, that a man may safely descend and bind and lead it away, or knock it on the head; and it is also said that, when it has wandered into a country to which it is a stranger, it loses much of its courage, and may be assailed almost with impunity. (Dr. Weissenborn, in Loudon's Mag. Nat. Hist., N. S. vol. ii. p. 124.)

A similar action to that of the Fox has been observed in a little animal, to which it is not common to ascribe more than an ordinary degree of cunning or confidence in its own resources. In a bookcase of wainscot, impervious to light, in which articles were kept which were more agreeable to the taste of mice than books, when, at midday, the doors were suddenly opened, a Mouse was seen on one of the shelves; and so rivetted was the little creature to the spot, that it shewed all the signs of death, not even moving a limb when taken into the hand. On another occasion, on opening a parlour-door, in broad daylight, a Mouse was seen fixed and motionless in the middle of the room; and, on advancing towards it, its appearance in no way

differed from that of a dead animal, excepting that
it had not fallen over on its side. Neither of these
creatures made an effort to escape, and were taken
up at leisure : nor had they received any hurt or
injury, for they soon displayed every mark of being
alive and well.

It would be as easy to catch a Weasel asleep
as off its guard; but it seems still more unlikely
that, in the disguise of death, it should suffer itself
to be cuffed, and pawed, and handled with impunity
by a Cat : yet it so happened that, while Puss was
reclining at ease, seemingly inattentive to all the
world around her, a Weasel came unexpectedly up,
was seized in a moment, and, dangling from her
teeth as if dead, was thus carried to the house,
at no great distance. The door being shut, Puss,
deceived by its apparent lifelessness, laid her victim
on the step, while she gave her usual mewing cry
for admittance. But by this time the active little
creature had recovered its recollection, and in a
moment struck its teeth into its enemy's nose. It
is probable that, besides the sudden surprise of the
capture, the firm grasp which the Cat had of it
round the body had prevented any earlier effort at
resistance from the Weasel : for in this manner our
smaller quadrupeds, which bite so fiercely, may be
held without injury; but the Weasel can hardly be
supposed to have been practising a deception all the
while it was in the Cat's mouth.

The influence of terror operates much in the same
manner on Birds. The little Goldcrest (*Regulus*

Cristatus) is a timid creature ; and yet it will sometimes approach so near to a man, as to appear indifferent to his presence ; but this absence of apprehension seems to proceed rather from the inability
of its organs or its imagination to comprehend such
a mass and mountain of being as a man while standing still : for if he put himself in motion, the bird
flies away in a fright at its utmost speed.   When
this pretty, diminutive bird is on the branch of a
tree, if you strike the body of the branch with a
stick or stone, though at some distance from the
twig on which it is perched, the shock brings it at
once to the ground, and it may be taken with the
hand ; when, if time be allowed it, the bird soon
revives, and may, if you are humanely disposed, be
again restored to liberty.

This misinterpretation of Motive—in ascribing to
subtlety what is due to a less calculating influence—
is traceable to the suddenness of the animal's recovery, at perhaps the most fitting moment for its
security.   It is easy to suppose that the apprehension
of danger, which first led to the suspension of its
powers of intelligence, may continue to operate, and
delay their return, some time after a sort of consciousness has been restored to it ; and the following
instance in point will shew that a long interval is
not necessary between the return to sense and the
display of its wonted activity :—A Water Rail was
found nearly dead from cold and hunger, and indeed so
benumbed, as to be taken up by the hand as it lay
on the snow.   Placed on a footstool before the fire,

the warmth very soon revived it; and the first signs
of returning animation were shewn in its opening
its eyes, and turning its head about very quickly.
Almost immediately afterwards it sprung off the
stool, without preliminary standing up, or stretching
its limbs, and ran swiftly about the room. (Zoologist,
vol. ii. p. 766.)

But if even the wisest of men have not always
been alive to their own safety, we may the less
wonder that the boasted cunning of the Fox has
occasionally yielded to the influence of luxury and
ease. To such, at least, rather than to dissimulation or terror, I would assign the explanation of
the want of vigilance it has sometimes displayed.
It was perhaps, after prowling about through the
night, with good success, that a Fox laid itself
down to rest, in broad daylight, in a place exposed
to ordinary observation: and in one instance its
sleep was so long and sound, that a messenger
was dispatched to procure a gun from the distance
of more than half a mile, and the fatal shot was
fired before it awoke.

In the month of December, at about five o'clock
in the morning, a coast guard's man chanced to
open the door of a chall in a farm yard, which
he knew to be empty of cattle; and his attention
was attracted to the sound of some creature that
appeared to be breathing loudly in its sleep. The
noise which the man made was not slight, and
it was increased by his striking a light with
flint and steel, and calling to his companion;

but the Fox, which lay stretched out on a heap
of straw, was only aroused by his exclamations
of surprise at the discovery. It could only have
entered the place through a window; and was
probably lulled into forgetfulness by the comfort of
the accommodation it met with.

CHAPTER XII.

It has been a theme of remark by Moralists as
well as Philosophers of all ages, that the living
body is never at a stay, but is continually hasten-
ing on to accomplish its cycle of change, until
the weary wheels of life can no longer act. But,
within the space of this greater circle of existence,
there are more circumscribed movements, in which
the living systems are destined to act in support
of life: in the course of which certain energies are
put forth, which, for limited periods, display peculiar
functions, all essential to the well-being of the creature, which afterwards cease to act, and are succeeded by other energies. The physiological action
of the human body is known to pass through a daily
round of more or less excited arterial and nervous
influence, by which sleep is rendered as necessary to
its health at one season, as wakefulness and activity
are at another. Another cycle is completed in about
the time of a month; and the annual influence of
the seasons produces effects on the whole animated
creation, of which all are witnesses. In our own
climate it is not only the lengthening days, the
returning influences of the Sun, or the increase of

stimulating food, though each and all of these contribute to the general effect by their action on the
susceptibility then awakening to external impressions; but it is also in the reviving susceptibility
itself, that we discover the chief cause of the striking
phenomena now about to be manifested. The bodily
organs appropriated to peculiar functions assume an
increase of magnitude and energy; and these again
return to the general system of life a new stimulus,
by which, in turn, others are led to a still higher
manifestation of energy. It is probably by such
means that the nervous influence is directed to the
production of a reflex action on some functions, in
preference to others; and thus some organs are
brought forward with a predominant influence, which
before appeared to be of no other consequence than
as mere minor portions of the general system. A
similar movement in Man, acting through the same
circle of reflected action of one portion of nervous
or vascular influence on another, and through them
on special secreting and muscular structures, at the
age of puberty causes the beard to grow; in the
Deer excites the growth of horns; and in Birds
produces a greater elegancy and brilliancy of plumage, combined with a desire to increase and multiply their species. In our migratory Birds we thus
discern the cause why some visit us in summer, and
others leave us, while others only change their more
limited range; and in all the feathered tribes this
change becomes a stimulus to the function of architectural construction, which, in its development
among them, displays itself in building a nest.

The nest of a bird is so interesting an object, so curiously and admirably contrived for an evident purpose, of materials apparently so little calculated for the formation of such a structure, and its form and position are so varied according to the aptitude for comfort of its inhabitants, combined with security from discovery and danger, that it has ever been contemplated as a surprising manifestation of skill and intelligence in the little beings engaged in its fabrication. Indeed, in no case are the mental faculties of animals so wisely and forcibly developed as in the contrivances by which they shew their care for their young; and a pleasing and instructive volume has been devoted to this subject alone. Our research, at present, lies within a more limited field of investigation, and relates rather to the natural excitements which set the little architects to work, and to the influences by which we may judge their designs to be modified and controlled. So powerful in birds is the force of this temporary disposition to fabrication, that, as we have already had occasion to mention, several of these elegant structures are built in succession, before the advance of a succeeding function sets them on a new task, and their proneness to action becomes diverted to another portion of the same natural round of duty. Under the influence of this propensity, it will happen that one of the parents, whose time is not wholly occupied in providing sustenance for the newly-excluded young, sets about the construction of another cradle, long before it can be required for the accommodation of another brood. This anticipated proceeding, however, is so far of use, that it renders it more easy for the parents to produce two, or even three broods of young in a season.

Paley has remarked on the absurdity of supposing that a young bird, in the first few days of its life, when the little care it is able to feel is concentrated in the desire of obtaining food, can be engaged in treasuring within the cells of its memory a plan for the construction of a nest: of the future want of which, on such a supposition, it must have begun to form an imagination, for the accommodation of anticipated descendants of its own.   Yet, at the next return of the season, this bird of the former year is not found wanting in the ability required; and, what is still more surprising, it is not less shewn by one which has been reared from the egg in the nest of another species.   The original tendency still appears, and the pattern is strictly and rigidly adhered to, in accord with the outline of that of the original race. It is, too, hardly less remarkable that there is in species connected by family affinities a close approach to the construction of a common type of nidulation: a circumstance which tends to prove that the formation of this procreant cradle is influenced by an instinctive impulse, of the precise nature of which, as regards the form and the nature of the materials, an attempt at explanation, in our present state of knowledge, must be exceedingly unsatisfactory.   This instinct, however, must be regarded as of a higher kind than those blind gropings and dim intelligences of creatures working, not in the light of nature, but in the dark, which we have been accustomed to associate with the term ; and as more nearly approaching, in its rank, to a class of phenomena, which, when displayed in man, has been ranked among the higher efforts of genius, as implying an adaptation of faculties to certain ends rather than others, and a proportionate skill in their application. It is a disposition in certain creatures to peculiar modes of proceeding, and the selection of certain materials to work with and work upon, equivalent to the natural bias in men for specific objects of study, and especially of the varieties of architecture. The limitation of range, in this faculty of construction, is in conformity with the universal law, that the faculties of the lower animal tribes shall be confined in their nature and extent, while in man there are no bounds set to his enlarging and still enlarging intelligence ; and that the aptitude displayed in particular excellencies is not only consistent with, but arises from, their deficiency in others. It is thus that the development of one organ—whether in the brain, by which a specific presiding power of the nervous system is secured, or in the motive power, by which a skilful execution is provided, and by the union of which a permanency of the faculty is propagated in the race—is necessarily attended with a sacrifice of the development of others, either of similar or contrary kinds. A sufficient number of instances will be brought forward to shew that, while the word INSTINCT has been employed to designate the fundamental influence in this proceeding of tasteful and useful architectural construction, there is also present a process of inductive reasoning, which is based on closeness of observation, and includes a comparison of causes and consequences, and a provision for such contingencies as may possibly arise.

The nests of birds vary in situation and material, according to the nature of the place in which they are built, or any other peculiarity of circumstance which may arise, but they still maintain the preference for the original model, which is never much departed from. Thus the Raven and Crow, in inland situations, build their nests in trees; and in so doing they select a place in which concealment is less regarded than inaccessibility to predatory animals or man. But near the coast, though trees may abound, they give the preference to chinks in some craggy cliff at no great height, and so approachable, as to be looked into without difficulty; but when an attempt is made to reach the nest, some obstacle is there which the bird had evidently calculated upon, and which renders closer approach exceedingly hazardous. Much more ingenious than Crow or Raven, the schoolboy, when he has made up his mind to attain anything, whether worthy or worthless, will soon find out the way or the implement by which he can reach it; and accordingly we have known the young of the Raven drawn from the nest—so inconveniently placed as to be thought, by the simple birds, too remote and inaccessible to be disturbed by boy or man—by means of a hook at the end of a long rod, when all actual contact of the cruel hand was found to be impossible.

We have already mentioned the skill shewn by the Magpie in making the most of any local advantage. Mr. Bewick has a humourous vignette, in illustration of this foresight, in which he shews that the bird has not only secured its own safety, but has laid a trap to plunge his assailant in the river; and the known character of this bird makes it probable that this result was not out of the reach of its calculation. Instances also are not uncommon where failure in bringing out their young in safety has led to such a variation of their proceedings as could only have originated in a determination to obviate in future the possibility of such contingencies. In a country void of trees, a Magpie has been known to construct its nest in a gooseberry-bush, close to the ground, but fenced so much the more about by an immense assemblage of interwoven thorns; and I have noticed in one hedge, at no greater distance from each other than a hundred yards, two nests of this species, one of which was not elevated a yard above the ground, but was unusually fenced with a thick structure of thorns, to give additional security to the formidable bush of the same in which it was constructed, and the other was placed more than twenty feet from the ground, on the top of a very slender and solitary elm—the expectation clearly being that no creature would venture to climb so fragile a column.

The situation of the nest of the Rook is, more than that of any of its natural family, a matter of taste; its position never being found wild in the woods, although the whole colony, in very stormy weather, will quit the ordinary roosting-trees, to resort thither for shelter. The association of these birds in the neighbourhood of a human habitation is clearly not, in the first place, for protection; for however quick the feathered races are to discern a friendly feeling in the human race, a cottage, though surrounded with trees, has no power to attract them; while an aristocratic mansion in the gothic style of building, is irresistible; and a Rook has been known to occupy a tree not higher than twenty feet from the ground, rather than remove to a distance from so dignified a neighbourhood: though there was no bond of attachment arising from long association of affection, for the building in its present condition is of no remote date.

The nest of the Swallow (*Hirundo rustica*) is with us sometimes built in the shaft of a chimney, at a depth down of two or three feet from the top; on the rafters in barns, or other untenanted buildings, where such a structure is freely accessible; and not unfrequently in crevices of caverns on the rocky coast. It is singular, when the latter situation is chosen, that, although the cavern is openly exposed to the observation of persons continually passing by it, and the birds shew no hesitation in flying in, however numerous the observers, yet the precise spot where the nest is is so well concealed as to be not easily found; and the bird will not enter it if an observer take his station within the secluded space, so as to be within view of it. Pliny has noted of the Martins, what we ourselves have seen in dry summers, that, as their nests are constructed of mortar strengthened with straws, if there be a deficiency of the plastic materials, they will make a substitute for it by sprinkling the dust with moisture from their plumage, and then mould it to use.

The Martin (*Hirundo urbica*) is a still more familiar bird ; and, in nest-building, manifests more confidence in man than any other of the feathered tribes. Their time for working in the erection of these clay tenements is in the early part of the day, so that the mortar may have the benefit of the drying influence of the sun, the afternoon being employed in hawking after food. But in a situation near the sea, which was covered by the tide at their usual time for labour, these birds have exercised so much reflection on the natural phenomena of the ebb and flow of the tide, as to employ the morning in collecting food, reserving their labour for the time when, they reasoned, their materials would be accessible to them. The mortar is conveyed in a pellet on the top of the bill ; and they are careful not to hasten the structure too fast, lest its own weight, while loaded with moisture, should bring it to the ground. An instance is remembered where, from some such cause of suspicion as to the stability of the edifice, a Martin had recourse to the wonderful expedient of working in a straw, as a binding beam along the curve of the structure ! The ends were, it seems, secured without difficulty, but the efforts of the little builder to bend down the arch formed by the rising of the middle were in vain : for, whenever the pressure was removed, it persisted in maintaining its elasticity. The baffled bird glanced about, as if in contemplation of the difficulty, and seemed ready to receive any suggestion which might be offered, till, tired of watching the invariable result of so many efforts made in vain, the observer walked on. Returning an hour or two afterwards, the little architect was observed to have resorted to the only plan which could be effectual : he had left the ends free, which thus projected a little from the mortar, and the structure was complete at last.

In spite of opposition from man, as if they could not believe it possible that he in whom they had so much trust could be their foe, they persevere in building nests in favourite situations, all hinderances thrown in their way notwithstanding. But they do not so readily endure the persecution of their feathered neighbours, of whom the Sparrow is the most bold and pertinacious. It is related of the Martin that, in one instance, when a pair of sparrows had forcibly expelled them from their nest, they collected a company of their kindred, who, one and all, working together, soon plastered up the entrance to their tenement, and left the intruders to lament with their lives this violation of the right of original possession. In another instance under observation, consciousness of their own illegality, and of the danger of being expelled from the seat of usurpation, led the Sparrows to new exertions in making the nest their own. They had begun their invasion of the right of property by casting the unfledged young to the ground ; and with such good will did they work, that, while the latter were yet alive, they had completed their own arrangement of materials within, having made the house their own by the alterations they had contrived in it, and the expense they had gone to in labour and materials. Under dread of these intruders, Martins will build their nests in a low place, in confidence that Man will protect them from the rapacity of their old enemies, and in the conviction that their foes will not follow them into such near neighbourhood to the human race.

The unusual and unnatural situations which birds sometimes select for their nests warrant the belief that the little builders have been exposed to some such annoyance, and have adopted this extreme measure to avoid a repetition of the injury. Mr. Yarrell (British Birds, vol. ii. pp. 218, 221) gives the figure of a Swallow's nest, which was built on the bough of a sycamore tree hanging low over a pond. Two series of eggs were laid in it; and the first brood were reared, but the second died unfledged. But perhaps the most extraordinary instance of this instinct is related in the Zoologist (vol. ii. p. 657):—" A small steamer, the Clarence, lies at Annan Waterfoot, and plies between it and Port Carlisle, in the way of tugging vessels. A pair of Swallows built their nest last year under the sponsons of one of the paddle-wheels, not more than three feet above the water, and succeeded in bringing forth their young. There they are this summer again. During neap-tides the Clarence plies every other day, and often every day. When she leaves the Waterfoot, the birds leave her, and keep on the Scotch side; and then,

L

when she returns and is nearing Annan, the Swallows invariably meet her, and accompany her to her berth."

I have known the nest affixed, in a Baronial mansion, to the door of a bedroom, to which they had obtained access through an aperture in a turret; and the young were consequently swung to and fro at each opening of the door. It is worthy of remark, (for it is perhaps a generic habit,) that, in constructing the nest, the Swallow tribe labour from the outside, and the form is made by judgment of the eye: whereas the habit of our smaller birds of other families is to work from within, and thus to adapt it in form and size to the model of their own bodies.

For its own resting-place, the Sparrow generally prefers a comfortable hole in a wall, from which it can watch the feeding of poultry, and, in the absence of danger, descend to snatch a share from them. To this retreat it conveys a large assortment of straws and feathers; but as this bird— the emblem of impudence and cunning—is no favourite with the farmer, an order is issued to the boys of the household to rob the nests as fast as the eggs are deposited. In a case of this sort, where three or four successive layings had been destroyed, the whole colony, as if by mutual agreement, quitted the place of their past disappointments, and settled themselves among the thickest foliage of some trees at a distance from the farm—a situation which, though common in some districts, neither they nor their ancestors had ever before occupied, and where their large and clumsy nests were objects of curiosity to their human neighbours.

It was perhaps from persecution of some sort, either of birds, or its worst enemies, the smaller quadrupeds, that a Thrush chose for its nesting-place the extraordinary situation of a depression in the ground in the middle of a field of turnips, from whose leaves it gained its own protection and shade. When found, the nest contained four eggs; and, curiously enough, the outer wall was formed of portions of turnip-leaves, while within it was lined with the usual coating of mortar.

The nest of the Holm Thrush (*Turdus visci-vorus*) is also sometimes modified according to circumstances, and evidently from a calculation of what the bulk and weight of the expected young ones may require. Its usual site for building is among the firmer branches of a tree, with little re-gard to concealment; where, trusting to the support which will be afforded by these diverging branches, it does not follow the example of its kindred species, in strengthening the edifice with a lining of plaster. On one occasion, however, an other-wise excellent situation in a pear-tree lay under the inconvenience of having too wide a space between two out of the four surrounding props; and this portion of the structure was accordingly the only part that was strengthened by the addition of a firm layer of clay.

There are few British birds which shew more knowledge than the Dipper or Water Ouzel (*Cinclus*

L 2 .

aquaticus) in adapting the form and position of the nest to the exigencies of situation : for, in its habits and haunts, it not only differs from the species to which in form it seems most nearly allied (*Turdi*, the Thrushes), but the sites among which it must make its selection compel it to adopt considerable variations. This bird keeps in the neighbourhood of rapid streams, and seeks its food at the bottom of their waters. It therefore dips and dives with great facility, as well for its subsistence, as to escape its enemies. Its nest is as large as the crown of a man's hat, though the cavity is less ; and in form it bears some resemblance to the nest of the Wren. Its shape is somewhat circular, its texture well-woven, and its roof sloping, with an orifice in the side, only large enough to admit the bird, and so placed as to be most concealed. The lining varies in various specimens ; and the site selected is the bank of the stream. As its favourite mode of escape when in danger is dropping into the water, and passing off to a distance beneath its surface, the only spot which could be selected within a given range, in the instance we have under notice, was not so well fitted for concealment as might have been desired ; and therefore its plan was, to mislead an observer, if any prominent part of it struck his attention. The nest was placed upon a stout stone, projecting from a promontory which overhung the deepest pool to be found in the course of the brook. And it is to be remarked that, though this species is of retired habits, in two instances I have known the nest to be laid at a short distance from a road, along which there was frequent passing of people. The front of the nest rose immediately from the face of the support, in such a manner that anything falling from it must drop into the stream. The material was moss, entwined with portions of a living bramble; and, to aid the deception, pieces of the stem of a dead bramble had been laid along the top, as if fallen there by accident: but they were so fastened to the structure as to make the whole look like a natural elevation of ground, rising from the overhanging stone to the level of the bank. The nest had no lining, and its bottom was the bare stone, on which the eggs and young rested; and here, in this snug, successful patch of deception the brood was reared. At the time when it was built the river was too deep and rapid to make it probable that any one would discover it on that side; and, as a combination of deceptive fabric and unsuspected situation, a better instance will rarely be found of the art of thrusting a thing forward to the sight, with the utmost confidence in the choice of arrangement and colour to secure it from detection.

In another instance of craft in the same species, a similar plan was adopted, with even a greater display of skill. Some brambles protruding from the bank of the river at Lerryn, in bending downward to dip their extremities in the stream, had collected a large mass of grass and leaves, which the winter-floods had floated with the current. The water had so far subsided, that this accumu-

lation hung suspended at the height of a few
inches above the stream; and in this pendent
cradle a Water Ouzel thought fit to build her
nest, the orifice being directed inwards, or toward
the bank: so that, concealed by the overhanging
growth of shrubs and herbage, and suspended
close to a good depth of water, the bird was able
to enter and leave her home with almost perfect
security from observation. And this well-contrived
arrangement would have escaped the notice of
all observers, if a net had not been thrown in
to take some fish which had swarmed there;
which alarmed the bird, and drove her from her
nest, and so betrayed the place. So much respect,
however, was shown to this manifestation of art,
that no injury was permitted to be inflicted upon
the ingenious creature.

Few birds show more care and ingenuity in
concealing their nest than the common Furze Chat
(*Sylvia rubicola*): so that, though it is one of the commonest birds on our sea-coasts, and on downs covered
with furze, its eggs are not often found. It builds
on or near the ground, in short clumps of furze;
and if the nest is placed on one side of a bush,
the entrance to the covered passage is usually at
a good distance, and on the opposite side.

Instances of unusual foresight in the mode of
constructing a nest, or in the choice of its situation, are related in most books on Natural History, and they might be much multiplied; but
the following, taken from Loudon's Magazine,
and Mr. Yarrell's History of British Birds, are

sufficient to show how decidedly *mind* presides over the proceeding :—" The piece of water called Old Pond, about one mile from Godalming, on the London road, is a most attractive spot to water-fowl; and an island in its centre is the resort of some of them in the breeding season, and also a variety of other birds, which find it a safe and unmolested place for the same purpose. One day, having pushed off from the shore, and moored the little shallop to some of the osiers which surrounded the island, I began my accustomed examination. The first object that attracted my attention was a lot of dry rushes, flags, reeds, &c. enough to fill a couple of bushel-baskets. This mass was lodged about twenty feet from the ground, in a spruce-fir tree, and looked for all the world as if it had been pitched there with a hayfork. I mounted instantly, thinking of herons, eagles, and a variety of other wonders. Just as my head reached the nest, ' Flap ! flap !' out came a Moorhen ; and, dropping to the water, made off in a direct line along its surface, and was soon lost in the rushes of a distant bank. The nest contained seven eggs, warm as a toast. The situation was a very odd one for a Moorhen's nest ; but there was a reason for it : the rising of the water in the pond frequently flooded the banks of the island, and, as I had before witnessed, had destroyed several broods by immersion."

At the time that the young of such water-fowl as occasionally form their nests in trees or other elevated situations are about to quit their station their wings are very little developed, and there might, in consequence, be much danger in their too rapid descent to the ground; but there is proof that the foresight of the parent has already calculated on overcoming this difficulty: the Goosander, Guillemot, and more than one species of Duck, are known to have taken the labour of carrying their brood from a distance to the water. The Cormorant also must accomplish this, probably by suspension from the bill, when the nest is in such an inaccessible situation, that, if the young were precipitated, it would be on the rocks below, to their own destruction. There is probable proof, too, that the Woodcock is in the habit of conveying its young ones to a remote feeding-place before they are able to fly; and, there is reason to believe, in the same manner.

Mr. Yarrell, quoting Mr. Selby, from the proceedings of the Berwickshire Naturalists' Club, says, " During the early part of the summer of 1835, a pair of Waterhens built their nest by the margin of the ornamental pond at Bell's Hill, a piece of water of considerable extent, and ordinarily fed by a spring from the height above, but into which the contents of another large pond can occasionally be admitted. This was done while the female was sitting; and as the nest had been built when the water-level stood low, the sudden influx of this large body of water from the second pond caused a rise of several inches, so as to threaten the speedy immersion and consequent destruction of the eggs. This the birds seem to have been aware of, and immediately took precautions against so imminent a danger: for, when the gardener, upon whose veracity I can safely rely, seeing the sudden rise of the water, went to look after the nest, expecting to find it covered, and the eggs destroyed, or at least forsaken by the hen, he observed, while at a distance, both birds busily engaged about the brink where the nest was placed; and when near enough, he clearly perceived that they were adding, with all possible dispatch, fresh materials, to raise the fabric beyond the level of the increased contents of the pond, and that the eggs had, by some means, been removed from the nest by the birds, and were then deposited upon the grass, about a foot or more from the margin of the water. He watched them for some time, and saw the nest rapidly increase in height; but I regret to add that he did not remain long enough, fearing he might create alarm, to witness the interesting act of replacing the eggs, which must have been effected shortly afterwards: for, upon his return, in less than an hour, he found the hen quietly sitting upon them in the newly-raised nest. In a few days afterwards the young were hatched ; and, as usual, soon quitted the nest, and took to the water with their parents. The nest was shown to me *in situ*, very soon afterwards; and I could then plainly discern the formation of the new with the older part of the fabric."

A similar instance is recorded in the History of the Mute or domesticated Swan, vol. iii. p. 117:— " This Swan was eighteen or nineteen years old, had brought up many broods, and was highly valued by the neighbours. She exhibited, some eight or nine

years past, one of the most remarkable instances of
the powers of instinct ever recorded. She was sitting on four or five eggs, and was observed to be
very busy in collecting weeds, grasses, &c. to raise
her nest: a farming-man was ordered to take down
half a load of haulm, with which she most industri-
ously raised her nest and the eggs two feet and a
half: that very night there came down a tremendous
fall of rain, which flooded all the malt-shops, and
did great damage. Man made no preparation, the
bird did; and instinct prevailed over reason. Her
eggs were above, and only just above, the water."

Yet this occurrence in the history of the Swan,
remarkable as it appears, is not novel, according to
Mr. Waterton:—" There is a peculiarity in the nidi-
fication of the domestic Swan, too singular to be
passed over without notice. At the time that it
lays its first egg, the nest which it has prepared is
of a very moderate size; but as incubation proceeds,
we see it increase vastly in height and breadth. Every
soft material, such as pieces of grass and fragments
of sedges, are laid hold of by the sitting Swan, as
they float within her reach, and are added to the
nest. This work of accumulation is performed by
her during the entire period of incubation, be the
weather wet or dry, settled or unsettled; and it is
perfectly astonishing to see with what assiduity she
plies her work of aggrandizement to a nest already
sufficient in strength and size to answer every end.
My swans generally form their nest on an island,
quite above the reach of a flood; and still the sitting bird never appears satisfied with the quantity

of materials which are provided for her nest. I once gave her two huge bundles of oaten straw, and she performed her work of apparent supererogation by applying the whole of it to her nest, already very large, and not exposed to destruction, had the weather become ever so rainy." (Essays, 2d Series.)

It is probable that this disposition to accumulation, in its general bearing, has reference to heat rather than the flood; but that the Wild Swan has a foresight regarding danger, and a quick perception as to the means of securing safety, appears from an instance mentioned by Captain Parry, in his Northern Voyage. Where everything was deeply involved in ice, the voyagers were obliged to pay much attention to discover whether they were travelling over water or land: but some birds, which formed their nest at no great distance from the ships, were under no mistake in so important a matter; and when the thaw took place, it was seen that the nest was situated on an island in the lake. It was built of mosspeat, and measured five feet ten inches in length, four feet nine inches in width, the cavity two feet deep and fifteen inches wide—an edifice of no small magnitude for a country so badly furnished with materials.

A philosopher judged with admiration of the mathematical talent of a plain countryman, when he saw the way in which he arranged the sticks which made up a faggot: why, then, should we refrain from admiration of the skill of a little bird, when, in addition to the mechanical perfection of the structure, it distributes its materials in such a manner as

will best attain the end in view? The foundation of
a Goldfinch's nest is laid with small leaves, moss, or
fibrous lichens; and then so much wool is thinly and
regularly drawn throughout, as shall form a tissue of
felt, which by its contraction binds all firmly together. I have known the latter article fetched from
a great distance; which shews how important is this
web, in the bird's own mind, to maintain the stability of the edifice, when distended with the weight of
an increasing family within. The rudest portions of
the materials are placed on that side where there is the
least support, with an evident view to the construction of a regularly-formed, as well as safe and comfortable cradle. Within and above this the work
shews the skill and care of an artist, whose own body
was the measure of the final dimensions. As it was
found that lichen was too rigid for the interior, the
finer fibres of a kind of grass were minutely in-
woven with it; and with these were included a thick
coating of the down of the thistle, which the parent
had the sagacity to perceive was preferable to wool
for the lining. That the rim might be firm enough
to confine and sustain the cavity, it was formed of a
doubling-over of the finest entwined fibres of grass,
which likewise supported the sides; and the strength
with which the whole was worked together may be
judged from the little injury it had sustained during
the long residence of the young within it.

The nest of a Yellowhammer offers less variety of
materials, and shews less calculation in their arrangement; but if this be a defect in our eyes, it is compen-
sated by the skill and scrupulous care with which

the moss, of which the walls are chiefly formed, is interwoven by the persevering labour of the builder. The lining, chiefly of hair or feathers, is slighter than that of the Goldfinch; but, no doubt, the warmth of these linings is fitted to the peculiarity of constitution of its young, and to the faculty they have of eliciting heat, and of subsisting with more or less degrees of it.

It is common for both parents to collect the materials for building, but the business of construction is the especial work of the female. I have watched a couple of Wrens (*Sylvia troglodytes*) engaged in bringing what they could obtain from the neighbouring hedges, and lodging it close by the selected nook, with all the industry imaginable. When enough of the coarser stuff has been accumulated, the male departs to discover where the softer materials may be obtained when they shall be wanted; while the female takes on herself the task of arranging and working up the structure of the edifice. It is plain that they understand each other's intentions, and that there is a general agreement as to the specific object of the work, to render it secure. Care is taken to conceal it, by fitting the outward aspect to the colour and nature of the things with which it is surrounded. I have known it formed of the pale, decaying leaves of a tree, when placed in contact with an earthen wall; and it has been constructed of the fibres of hay, when affixed to a rick of that material: though in either case the labour of forming it thus in conformity to circumstances must have been greater than that of seeking farther for more manageable materials.

When a bird has made no more than the first advances in building a nest, a little interruption of its work is sufficient to drive it away; and it is said that the Great Bustard (*Otis tarda*) will forsake her nest, if only once driven from it by apprehension of danger; but when the eggs are laid, and still more when the young are produced, it is only repeated meddling with them which will induce the parents to forsake them. This strength of attachment is most powerful at an early period of the season; and though some birds will go on in the process of rearing a brood until autumn is well advanced, and some even resume it after the moulting is ended, (and a Kestrel, *Falco tinnunculus*, has been seen sitting on eggs in the middle of October,) yet, at so late a date, they are more easily led to leave them to perish. It is supposed that, in such late broods, there is commonly an unusual proportion of hen-birds.

It is at this time of incubation and rearing that the play of natural affection is discovered: of the force of which a human mother is well qualified to judge, when she observes it urging the timid Hen, and much smaller creatures, to combat such formidable adversaries as the Hawk, Crow, Rat, and Dog; or when it alarms her to agony at the sight of a brood of Ducks, which she has hatched for her own, adventuring into an element which, to her apprehension, is one of danger. I have been informed of an instance in which even a Rabbit has been known to assail a Weasel, at the sight of which on ordinary occasions its strength is prostrated through terror; and this it did with such success by means of its fore-feet, that it succeeded in compelling it to retreat. The impression itself is instinctive, though guided and vindicated by the conclusions of reason; and not less in the human than in the animal parent. Though this feeling be of shorter duration in animals than in man, it does not affect the principle on which it depends; and its more transitory existence is a wise provision of creative Wisdom, which has connected it with an organism, whose energy is periodically excited, and which, in some races, does not influence every individual, even for many successive seasons: but its force, when called into exercise, is so powerful as to produce a revolution in the prevalent feelings and habits of a wild animal, of a more extraordinary influence than even in man himself. In obedience to its dictates, the bird, whose delight it has been to enjoy unbounded freedom in the expanse of air, will confine itself to a solitary spot, shut in with a few leaves, for weeks together; and consent to endure, all this time, not only the irksome dulness of confinement, but the strong craving of hunger, while abundance is near at hand to supply its wants. In spite of its natural timidity, an intruder is suffered to approach very close, before it will betray the situation of its treasure by an unseasonable effort at escape. Restrained by this influence, the Stormy Petrel (*Procellaria pelagica*), to whose habits the expanse of ocean is a

home, and the greatest distance from shore the most
welcome, clings for a time to the land, and there
immures itself in a hole in the ground: the Swift
and Swallow cease to fly and scream; and even the
most ravenous winged creatures deny their own
appetite, that they may indulge the greater pleasure
of supplying the cravings of their young.

I was once witness to a curious instance of the
yearning for progeny in a diminutive Bantam hen.
She had been bred in the house, and was accustomed to perch on the bar of a chair, or on a
fender by the fire; and at night would retire to
a bird-cage, for protection against Cats and Rats.
When under the impulse of laying, she made
several attempts to introduce herself into the small
compartments or pigeon-holes of a bookcase: failing in this, she next took to the bedrooms;
and it was only by vigilance that she was prevented from depositing her eggs on the soft cover-
lets of the beds. The laying was suspended for
some days, in consequence of her indignation at
being driven from these selected spots; but at
last the eggs were deposited, in the regular course,
and the nest robbed of all that it contained. There
was, at this time, a nest of the common Hen in a
secluded part of the garden; and the parent had
been sitting on its eggs, till, compelled by hunger,
she left them for a short time. This absence
was fatal: for the Bantam had in the mean time
found its situation, in a covered recess in the
hedge; and I saw her creep into it, with all the
triumph of the discoverer of a treasure. The

real mother soon returned, and great was her
agony at finding an intruder in her nest. The
expression of her eye and the attitude of her head
were emphatic of surprise at the impudence of the
proceeding ! But, after many attempts to recover
possession, she was compelled to resign her rights, for
the Bantam was too resolute to be contended with ;
and though its body was not big enough to cover
the whole of the eggs, and thus some of them were
not hatched, yet in due season the pride of this
audacious stepmother was gratified by strutting at
the head of a company of robust chickens, which
she passed off upon the feathered public as a brood
of her own.

It is a remarkable fact that more than one pair
of birds will sometimes unite in occupying one nest,
and either rear their broods in common, or one of
them will perhaps surrender the future care of them
to the other. A Thrush had built its nest in a low
tree in a garden ; and on the second day after it was
finished it was observed that four eggs had been
deposited in it. Through the attention thus excited, it was ascertained that two mothers were
engaged in supplying the number, which at last
amounted to ten, and from which nine living young
ones were produced. These eggs were certainly sat
on by one parent only.

This is, also, the easiest mode of accounting
for the very large number of eggs and young sometimes found in one nest. A Partridge has been
the ostensible parent of twenty-two young ones ;
and, as if conscious that so large a family could

not have all the attention they required from the mother alone, the male also has gathered them under his wings, the pair of parents sitting side by side, but with their heads and tails reversed. I have been credibly informed that as many as thirty-one Partridge eggs have been found in one nest. Mr. Yarrell mentions the association of Landrails with Partridges under the care of one parent. A Guinea-fowl has been known to lay her eggs in a Partridge's nest; and on board ship, so many young Mice were discovered nestled together as could not possibly have belonged to one mother.

CHAPTER XIII.

THE demands of young birds on the care and lovingkindness of their parents we must suppose in some measure akin to the powerful feeling which sways the breast of the higher animals in the same relationship with each other. But it sometimes extends beyond the more immediate connection of kindred; and instances are not uncommon where it has excited sympathy even in creatures of another species, and that too in cases where, from the absence of the breeding impulse, this affection must be sought rather in compassion than in a mere instinctive disposition. That the Cuckoo should be fed by a foster-parent might be expected, since, as in the like instance of Ducks hatched by a Hen, she believes the bantling to be her own, and may have learnt to regard the unusual bulk of the solitary inmate of her nest as an evidence of the success of her motherly care. But there are proofs of the fact that, when a young Cuckoo has been placed in a cage, birds which could never have seen such a fledgeling before have set about feeding it with loving zeal

and untiring perseverance. In one case some
Canaries, who were at large in a room, were seen
to cling to the cage in which the young Cuckoo
was confined; and on being permitted to enter,
they supplied the orphan so regularly with food,
that in a little time it refused to receive its sustenance from any other hands.

A like loving feeling has also been shown to
other little neglected ones by birds of a different
race to their own; and the proceeding has been
conducted in such a manner as to show that, while
sometimes it has originated in mere involuntary
compassion, at other times it has sprung from a
deliberate affectionate disposition of the mind of
these little creatures. Its particular direction may,
at times, be excited by that expression of want,
which is part of the language common to kindred
families in the early portion of their life, as was
the case in the following instance. A gentleman
of my acquaintance, an observer and lover of the
instincts of Nature, placed a couple of fledgeling
Greenfinches (*Fringilla chloris*) in the same cage with
two Canaries, who immediately took them under their
care and assumed the office of parents; and though,
at first, they found some difficulty in inducing the
young to receive food from them, they continued
their assiduities, till kindness at last prevailed, and
they were allowed to feed them regularly. I have
also learned the following curious facts from a
competent observer:—The nests of a Missel-Thrush
and Chaffinch (*Fringilla cœlebs*) were near each
other in the same tree, the former having young

and the latter only eggs. When the former bird approached to feed its brood, the Chaffinch quitted her nest, and prevailed on the Missel-Thrush to resign the food to her; and with it she proceeded to supply the young ones. A number of the young of the Longtailed Tit (*Parus caudatus*), which had acquired the habit of taking their own food, on being placed in a cage with other birds won the regard of an old Meadow Pipit (*Anthus pratensis*), which manifested an anxiety to feed them. (Loudon's Mag. Nat. Hist., N. S. vol. i.)

The two following instances are also from the same work (vol. vii.) : " At the bottom of the walk between the house and our garden, in winter runs a brook, but in summer there is only still water, which is inhabited by Waterhens, &c. The Waterhens have become quite tame, from persons constantly passing and repassing. This year, in the spring, a pair of them hatched some young ones; and, as soon as they were feathered, made another nest, and hatched some more. The young ones of the second hatch left the old birds, and have been adopted by the young ones of the first hatch, who have each taken one, and seem to take as much care of them as the old ones could have done : they feed them, and never leave them. Only one young one has remained with the old hen."

" I discovered the nest of a pair of Redstarts (*Phœnicura ruticilla*), called here Firetails, in a hole in a wall in my garden, from the male bird's constantly sitting on a particular tree near the place where the nest was, and from his continually uttering his plaintive and garrulous note while any object to excite alarm was in sight. I mention this, because from his attention to his mate I was particularly interested in the pair, and watched them with great care. In about two or three days after I had discovered them (the hen was then sitting), the male bird, while on his usual station, was, to my great grief, killed by a stone which his familiarity had tempted an idle boy to throw. I saw him killed myself. On my going by the place the next day, I was excessively surprised to see a male Redstart sitting on the very same tree from which, the day before, the other bird had been knocked down. On my going near the nest, it flew away with evident tokens of alarm; and on my putting my hand to the nest, the hen bird flew off. All I need say in addition is, that the eggs were hatched, and the foster-father (for such he certainly was) assisted, as cock-birds usually do, the hen in bringing up the young brood. The circumstance has puzzled me extremely, both then and since. How could the Redstart be possibly made acquainted that the hen was without a mate? She could not have been off the nest long: for if the eggs had once got cold, they could never have been hatched; and the Redstart is a solitary bird, and by no means common here."

In reference to the latter portion of this paragraph it should be observed, that in almost every season there are some among our common native birds, and probably some also of the immigrants, in which the procreative impulse is not excited or continued, or not till late in the season; and that this is the

main reason why some species do not greatly
increase and multiply, although individuals among
them may rear a numerous brood. Among these
it is not difficult at any time to find a disengaged
mate ; or it is possible that a separation of a former
union may have taken place, by the prevailing influence of pity for the bereaved young.

In connection with this subject, we may mention
the instinct of cleanliness, to which most wild animals
are attentive, and which forms a curious chapter in
their history. Many birds will carefully remove the
mutings of the young from the neighbourhood of
their nest ; and as this is especially necessary, as
regards the comfort of the nest in the earliest stage
of their existence, it is a visible ordering of creative
Providence, that the first discharges should be en-
veloped in a membranous film formed by a secretion
of the intestine, by whose means it is carried away
without difficulty. But the care thus shown is a
proof that a secondary intention, and one significant
of much prudent foresight, exists in the minds of the
parents : for while we find that birds which make no
secret of their nesting-places are careless in such
matters, the Woodpecker (*Picus viridis*), and the
Marsh Tit (*Parus palustris*), in particular, are at
pains to remove even the chips which are made in
excavating the cavities where the nests are placed,
and which might lead an observer to the sacred
spot.

CHAPTER XIV.

AMONG the remarkable examples, in which a combination of instinct with a skill only to be derived from reasoning founded on observation has been shown by animals in the protection of their young, may be reckoned the arts employed by some birds to allure an intruder from the neighbourhood of their nests. The art of the Partridge is familiar to the sportsman, and excites admiration in all the lovers of Nature. At the signal of silence and retreat, the infant young may be seen to run to the shelter of the nearest cover, while the parent seems seized with a sudden lameness and inability to fly. She flutters along the ground, with drooping wings, in an opposite direction to that which the brood has taken; and not until she has successfully misled the observer does she resume her powers, and wing away to a greater distance.

But this stratagem is not confined to the Partridge. A friend was passing along a lane, in search of objects of natural history, when he saw a female Cirl Bunting (*Emberiza cirlus*) spring from the hedge, and drop to the ground, along which she fluttered, as if unable to fly. She was soon joined by her mate, who from a short distance had observed her motions; and, like her, fluttered along the ground, as if he also could not fly. His suspicions being excited, he began to look about for a reason for all this art; and soon discovered the nest with eggs in the place from which the female had made her first appearance.

" The Lapwing," says Mr. Conway, " will fly round and round, tumbling and tossing in the air, and at the same time making the country resound with the echoes of its endless ' Peewit !' and thus lead the intruder farther and farther from its nest. The Grouse, if disturbed from her nest, will shuffle through the heath in a very awkward manner, and will not take wing until she has proceeded a considerable distance. I once found a Skylark do the same. Having been informed of the nest, in a corn-field, I proceeded thither to see the eggs, and finding the bird on the nest, having my butterfly-net in my hand, I easily captured her. When I took the bird into my hand, she feigned death, and allowed herself to be handled for a considerable time, and that rather roughly; and when I threw her from me, in the expectation that she would take wing, she fell to the ground like a stone, and there she lay for me to push her about with my foot, until I at last thought that I had injured her in the capture, and that she was absolutely dead. Remaining quiet, however, for a very short period, the bird began moving; and with one wing trailing along the ground, and shuffling along as if one of her legs had been broken, she proceeded for a considerable distance, and then took

M

wing.—In pursuing an azure-blue Butterfly, I was diverted from my object by the melodies of a Nightingale almost close at my side. The singing was in one continuous and uninterrupted melody: there were none of those frequent breaks, which are so characteristic of the song of the Nightingale when heard at a little distance : it was one incessant warble. I can hardly call it a warble either : it was an unceasing effort : so much so that I stood perfectly astonished, and at a loss to conceive how it was possible for so small a creature to exert herself so mightily. I began, however, to think that the nest of the melodist could not be far off; and as I had never yet seen the nest of this bird, I determined to watch her closely, in order to discover it. But I was nearly giving up the search as useless : for as soon as I entered the copse, no matter at what part I made my entrance, there was the Nightingale close at my side, delighting me with her melody, and hopping from spray to spray and from bush to bush, and thus leading me the round of the wood at her pleasure. When, however, all hope of finding the nest had nearly vanished, I fell in with it by pure accident ; and I then discovered that the singing of the bird had always led me in a direction from the nest."

I will here venture to express my conviction that, in the case of the Lark just mentioned, no settled plan of deception was attempted, and the little terrified prisoner was perfectly sincere in the exhibition she made of the suspension of her faculties. Her case is rather one of those on which we have remarked in a former Chapter, and which has been described as one of mere pretension of death; but the instance related above has been reserved to this place, that it might be associated with the stratagems employed by the Partridge and Lapwing: in which also it may be questioned whether the lameness and fluttering were not as much the paralysing affections of fear as of cunning. Instances are also known in which the Black-headed Bunting (*Emberiza schœniclus*), Ring Plover (*Charadrius hiaticula*), as well as the Eider and other Ducks, have had recourse to a similar stratagem, although it is not common to these races.

But it is not every species that has recourse to the art of allurement to effect this object; and besides the Hawk tribe, the Missel Thrush is a familiar case, in which threatening is employed to drive away an intruder. While the hen-bird is sitting on the eggs, all is secresy and silence; but as soon as the young are excluded, the nature of the parents appears to have undergone a change. On approaching within a dozen feet of the nest, the clamour of the birds is loud and incessant, and resembles the winding up of an enormous jack. A nearer advance is met by the mother, who flies past within reach of the hand, as if she would inflict vengeance on the enemy; and the noise is uttered with such suddenness as might well terrify a dog or cat, or even a child. A similar disposition has been noticed in a kindred species, the Fieldfare (*Turdus pilaris*), which in England is a shy bird, and, unless tamed by severe

M 2

cold and want, not to be approached easily; but within a fortnight after it had been seen in England, it was met with in Norway by Mr. Wayne, so bold and fearless, when engaged with its nest, as to approach and settle in bushes above his head, and scold with violence. (Zoologist, vol. ii. p. 724.)

The following incident, though apparently trivial, is an example of the exercise of memory of no recent date, and of the carrying out of a resolution which was undoubtedly the result of remote experience. A Brown Owl (*Strix aluco*) had long been in the occupation of a convenient hole in a hollow tree; and in it for several years had rejoiced over its progeny, with hope of the pleasure to be enjoyed in excursions of hunting in their company: but, through the persecutions of some persons on the farm, who had watched the bird's proceedings, this hope had been repeatedly disappointed, by the plunder of the nest at the time when the young ones were ready for flight. On the last occasion, an individual was ascending to their retreat, to repeat the robbery, when the parent bird, aware of the danger, grasped her only young one in her claws, and bore it away; and never more was the nest placed in the same situation.

In many of the higher order of animals the attachment of the parents, and especially of the mother, to the young, rises even to fury: so that the Tiger and Lioness, and even some of the wild animals of our own country, will seek their prey with more reckless ardour, at greater distances,

and with less of personal consideration, than at
any other time in their lives; and in case of
danger, as when pressed by the pursuit of hunters,
they will encounter much risk, before they can be
induced to surrender an object so dear to them.
It is worthy of notice, too, that on such occasions
the young permit themselves to be carried along
in the chase, suspended from the mouth of the
parent by the loose integument of the neck or
back, without displaying uneasiness: on the contrary, they seem perfectly aware of the object in
view. The Fox has done this repeatedly; and it
is a common practice for the Cat to remove her
young when they are too much visited by the
prying hands of the members of the family. The
nest of a little grass Mouse (*Mus messorius*) was
discovered in a garden, as it was supported a little
above the ground on the stalks of grass, the weeds
having been cut down by which it had been shel-
tered; and when it was examined, and found to
contain seven young ones not yet able to see,
the whole was replaced as much as possible in the
same situation, the only difference being that it
was more exposed to observation than before. In
a very short time the parent revisited her nest,
but presently retired; and she was observed to
nibble blades of grass, and run off with them
under the weeds which still remained standing.
Though closely watched in this proceeding, her
precise object was not immediately perceived :
but at last, being detected in conveying away a
young one, the nest was re-examined ; when the

discovery was made that all of them had been removed, the whole transaction having taken place in the space of five minutes.

On the same subject, I may quote here the remarkable relation made by Pliny of the touching conduct of a Panther when her young were in circumstances of great peril. "Demetrius, a physician, relates a remarkable account of a Panther, which had stretched itself in the public way, as if waiting for the approach of some man. The father of Philinus, who appears to be the original authority for the truth of the narrative, and who was himself a student of Philosophy, was proceeding in that direction ; but at sight of the danger, his fears prompted a retreat. But the creature adopted such significant, though awkward, means of allaying his apprehension, by rolling itself about, and fawning upon him, that his attention became attracted to the grief with which the animal was evidently afflicted. When his apprehensions had thus become calmed, she led him by the garment to a pit at some considerable distance, into which her young ones had fallen, beyond her reach to extricate them. Having accomplished her evident wishes, both the dam and her whelps accompanied him back to the frequented district, with such signs of joyful gratitude as would do honour to man." (Lib. 8. cap. 17.)

There is no good reason for discrediting this account : for the Cow and the Sheep, among our domestic animals, in similar circumstances have acted in like manner. But the belief of this at

other times untamable creature, that Man was
able to accomplish a task in which itself had
failed, is less extraordinary than the hope, in
which it could have had no ground of expectation
from experience, that he possessed so much of the
spirit of kindness as to be willing to make the
attempt. It is only one of many instances I have
noticed, in which, either in love, or in awe and
fear, homage to Man is more willingly bestowed by
animals, even of the wildest race, than they ever
show to any other race, however powerful, or
however gentle; and this ·reverential regard might
be turned to the benefit of humanity in many
respects.

Whatever share Instinct might have had in
prompting the little creature to make the effort,
the following anecdote is a proof that much ingenuity of reasoning had been exerted in rendering effectual the stratagem resorted to by a
Starling to recover its young one from captivity.
The Rev. Mr. Sladen, in the Zoologist, vol. ii.
p. 761, says, " A Starling had a nest and reared
young ones under the eaves of the roof, within the
basin of a drain-pipe which receives and carries off
the water from the gutters. Here I used to see
the mother coming to feed her young ones, which
she did frequently. They were very voracious, and
as they got stronger they pushed forward so eagerly
to obtain the first supply of food, that they fell
out of the basin one after another. Three, I
know, fell out, one of which was killed. The
others were taken up unhurt; and I had them

placed in a basket, covered over with netting,
which was hung up near the nest, in expectation
that the mother-bird would not fail to supply
them. This was done overnight, and next morning I found to my surprise that one bird had
disappeared; so I watched to see what would
become of the remaining one. It made a great
crying to arrest its parent's attention, and the
parent was not unmindful of it: I saw her fly
near the basket with food in her bill. She settled
on the roof and gutter within sight of the basket,
but went away without trying to feed the prisoner.
This was done several times, and at last I discovered her object: for the young bird's hunger becoming more and more pressing, it continued struggling
to reach the food, and contrived to get out through
the netting, when it fell to the ground without
injury. Though unable to fly, it was strong upon
its feet, and it ran upon the lawn. The parent now
came down to it with food as before, but not yet
to feed it: she flew on a little way from it, and so
enticed it into the corner of a shrubbery under a
wall, where I discovered the missing young one also,
and where she constantly fed them throughout the
day."

CHAPTER XV.

I⊤ is the opinion of Naturalists, that, however powerfully the feeling of love to their offspring, and the mixture of reason with instinct in the development of it, is diffused among animals of the land, nothing of the kind exists among fishes; and that the utmost extent of the care bestowed by them in increasing and multiplying their kind consists, as in the familiar instance of the Salmon, in covering over the spawn at the bottom of the river, in a furrow of the soil which itself has made; or in depositing it in some situation which shall expose it to the influences of light and air.

The ancient naturalists, Oppian and Aristotle, were however of a different opinion; and the latter, more particularly, asserts, probably on the authority of fishermen, that some fishes are in the habit of forming nests, in which they deposit and watch over their spawn. But this supposition of the father of systematic Natural History has been slighted, as without foundation, by more modern Naturalists; and it is only recently that a claim has been re-advanced in favour of this instinct in

M 3

fishes. It is not a little extraordinary that the
species for which this claim has been made are
those with which we might have been most familiarly acquainted ; and our ignorance of their
habits therefore can only have proceeded from
inattention.

The first minutely-recorded observation of this
habit is found in a little Magazine, " The Youth's
Instructor," for the year 1834 ; and though the
writer is clearly unacquainted with Natural History
as a science, his observations bear much of the
character of truth, and may be easily either
corroborated or set aside as untrue by those who
are more favourably placed for observation. " The
Pricklefish," he says, (which I suppose to be the
common Stickleback, *Gasterosteus trachurus*,) " in
a large dock for shipping on the river Thames,
thousands of these fish were bred some years
ago ; and I have often amused myself for hours
by observing them. While multitudes have been
enjoying themselves near the shore, in the warm
sunshine, others have been busily engaged in making their nests, if a nest it may be called. It
consisted of the very minutest pieces of straw, or
sticks, the exact colour of the ground at the bottom of the water, on which it was laid : so that
it was next to an impossibility for any one to
discover the nest, unless they saw the fish at
work, or observed the eggs. The nest is somewhat larger than a shilling, and has a top or
cover, with a hole in the centre, about the size of
a very small nut, in which are deposited the eggs,

or spawn. This opening is frequently concealed by drawing small fragments over it; but this is not always the case. Many times have I taken up the nest, and thrown the eggs to the multitude around, which they instantly devoured with the greatest voracity. These eggs are about the size of poppy-seeds, and of a bright yellow colour; but I have at times seen them almost black, which I suppose is an indication that they are approaching to life. In making the nest, I observed that the fish used an unusual degree of force when conveying the material to its destination. When the fish was about an inch from the nest, it suddenly darted at the spot, and left the tiny fragment in its place; after which it would be engaged for half a minute in adjusting it. The nest, when taken up, did not separate, but hung together like a piece of wool. This fish is about two inches long; the back is of a dull green colour; the throat and belly are of a silvery white.

" There is also to be found amongst them a beautiful fish, about the same length, but very slender. The body is of a bright green colour, somewhat duller on the sides; the throat and belly are a bright red; and they have a large and beautiful eye. These I have more than once taken; but they are very seldom to be met with. I have seen shoals of the former, consisting of many hundreds, if not thousands; but I have seldom seen one of the latter. This beautiful little fish will live in a glass, but not for a very great length of time.

" The place chosen by these fishes for their nests is where the ground forms an inclined plane, and in about six inches of water. This fish may be taken by fastening a small worm to a very fine string. The fish will hang to the worm, and suffer itself to be drawn out of the water, before it will quit its hold. I think they breed early in the month of August.—T. CROOKENDEN, *Lewisham.*"

From the unobtrusive nature of the publication in which this communication appeared, and in some degree also from the observer not being a man of scientific knowledge, Naturalists remained as ignorant as ever of the fact which it communicated : subsequent observers of a similar habit are therefore not the less entitled to the credit of original discovery.

The following extract from a Communication to the Royal Institution of Cornwall, republished in the Zoologist, will further establish the fact, and describe some of the particulars of this habit among fishes. " During the summers of 1842 and 1843, while searching for the naked mollusks of the county, I occasionally discovered portions of seaweed and the common Coralline (*Corallina officinalis*) hanging from the rocks in pear-shaped masses, variously intermingled with each other. On one occasion, having observed that the mass was very curiously bound together by a slender silken-looking thread, it was torn open, and the centre was found to be occupied by a mass of transparent amber-coloured ova, each being about the tenth of an inch in diameter. Though examined on the spot with a lens, nothing could be discovered to indicate their character. They were however kept in a basin, and daily supplied with sea-water, and eventually proved to be the young of some fish. The nest varies a great deal in size, but rarely exceeds six inches in length, or four inches in breadth. It is pear-shaped, and composed of seaweed, or the common Coralline, as they hang suspended from the rock. They are brought together, without being detached from their places of growth, by a delicate opaque white thread. This thread is highly elastic, and very much resembles silk, both in appearance and texture : this is brought round the plants, and tightly binds them together, plant after plant, till the ova, which are deposited early, are completely hidden from view. This silk-like thread is passed in all directions through and around the mass, in a very complicated manner. At first the thread is semifluid, but by exposure it solidifies ; and hence contracts and binds the substances forming the nest so closely together, that it is able to withstand the violence of the sea, and may be thrown carelessly about without derangement. In the centre are deposited the ova, very similar to the masses of frogspawn in ditches."

The account goes on to say, " It is not necessary to enter into minute particulars of the development of the young any further than to add, that they were the subject of observation till they became excluded from the egg, and that they belonged to the Fifteen-spined Stickleback

(*Gasterosteus spinachia*). Some of these nests are
formed in pools, and are consequently always in
water : others are frequently to be found between
tide-marks, in situations where they hang dry for
several hours in the day ; but whether in the
water, or liable to hang dry, they are always carefully watched by the adult animal. On one occasion, I repeatedly visited one every day for three
weeks, and invariably found it guarded. The old
fish would examine it on all sides, and then retire
for a short time, but soon returned to renew the
examination. On several occasions I laid the eggs
bare, by removing a portion of the nest ; but
when this was discovered, great exertions were
instantly made to re-cover them. By the mouth
of the fish the edges of the opening were again
drawn together, and other portions torn from their
attachments, and brought over the orifice, till the
ova were again hid from view. And as great
force was sometimes necessary to effect this, the
fish would thrust its snout into the nest as far as
the eyes, and then jerk backwards till the object
was effected. While thus engaged it would suffer
itself to be taken in the hand, but repelled any
attack made on the nest, and quitted not its post
so long as I remained ; and to those nests that
were left dry between tide-marks, the guardian
fish always returned with the returning tide, nor
did they quit the post to any great distance till
again carried away by the receding tide.

"The next nest with which my rambles have
brought me acquainted is of a different character,

shewing considerably less skill in the fabrication, but more perseverance and continued energy. In the last-mentioned case the nest was formed indiscriminately of various kinds of seaweed, or the common coralline, whichever happened to grow on the spot selected. In the present case it is invariably formed of the common coralline, forced into some cavity or crevice of a rock; and is maintained there by no other bond than that of compression. As the coralline of which it is composed is sometimes not to be found within one or two hundred feet, it must be gradually gathered and brought from a distance; and as the quantity is large, it shews an intelligence and perseverance truly remarkable. But the most extraordinary part of it is to conceive how the materials can be so closely compacted by the force of any fish. The ova are small, being about the fifteenth of an inch in diameter, and of a semitransparent yellow colour. They are not contained in a cavity, like those of the Stickleback, but are deposited irregularly throughout the mass, sometimes in clumps, and at others placed irregularly on the coralline. From the compact character of the nest, and the ova being found in all parts of its structure, it is evident that the eggs must be deposited while the nest is in progress of formation.

" Having preserved the ova till the young had effected their escape, to detect the species of fish to which they belonged, judging from their shape and spotted appearance they seemed to be the young of the Rockling (*Motella vulgaris*). On this point, however, there is no certainty, as, from the inaccessible places in which the nests are placed, they cannot be conveniently watched after the tide has flowed sufficiently to cover them: for they are always left dry, for a longer or shorter period, during the rise and fall of the tide.

" The next to which I shall refer differs from both the preceding; and it may perhaps be doubted whether the term *nest* is strictly applicable to it, as the fish merely makes use of a natural cavity in the rock, in which the ova are deposited, and remain adherent: but as it shews a deviation from what has been considered as the usual mode of spawning in fish, it may be briefly noticed. The cavities selected are almost always nearer the low than high water mark: they have generally rather narrow openings, and the roofs are smooth, or are at least not much broken by fissures. On the roofs and sides of such cavities the ova are deposited, and thickly arranged, looking as if they were vaulted with a pavement of round stones. As the ova are of a beautiful and bright amber colour, with a highly-polished surface, they have a very brilliant appearance as the light falls upon them in their dark recess. They are semicircular in form, and about one-tenth of an inch in diameter. Having succeeded in hatching them, they prove to belong to the common Shanny (*Blennius pholis*). This opinion of their character has been repeatedly confirmed, as it is the habit of this fish to retire beneath stones, or to crevices of the rock, during the recess of the tide, where they remain dry until the sea returns. By enlarging the openings of the cavities, I have generally succeeded in capturing the adult animal at the farthest part of the chamber, and on one occasion found it depositing the ova."

Of the truth of a large part of the foregoing particulars I am myself a witness: but further observation on the nest first mentioned renders necessary a correction that will somewhat modify our views; and while it leaves the subject of instinctive care of their progeny in fishes uncontradicted, deprives the species to which the structure has been ascribed of its present claims to parental affection. In the month of May, 1845, I obtained a nest formed of seaweeds, and in all respects like those which have already been described; and when it was discovered hanging from the rock, two individuals of the Fifteen-spined Stickleback were in close attendance on it. As, on examination, some of the ova were seen to be springing into life, much attention was paid in watching their development, which was gradual, and occupied several days, proceeding as if the ova in different portions of the mass had been deposited at small intervals of time. As the young moved about the vessel with much activity, they coveted the shelter of some floating weed; but descended eagerly to assail and tear such of their brethren as died and fell to the bottom. Being from the first impressed with the conviction that they were the young of the Fifteen-spined Stickleback, I was much surprised to notice the great difference of their shape from that of their supposed parent, more especially in the parts before the eyes, which, instead of being elongated and slender, were short and round. In consequence of this they were closely examined with glasses, and drawn with the aid of a microscope of low power; and though I failed to detect satisfactorily the ventral fins of that fish, (chiefly perhaps from their slender form and transparency,) yet, from the declivity of the head, protuberance of the belly, the pectoral fin, and the length of the dorsal and anal fins, which in some specimens were continuous with the caudal, and in others separated by a slight notch, I had no hesitation in referring them to the common Shanny (*Blennius pholis*).

It is scarcely a contradiction to the statement we have just made to adduce the other mode of deposit ascribed to that fish at the conclusion of the foregoing paper, of the accuracy of which I have no doubt, and of the newly-liberated young from which I had, at the time, an opportunity of making an examination. But the simplest instinct will vary its proceedings according to circumstances; and the smallest glimmering of reason will direct it to modify these proceedings according to situation, and as they may best lead to the desired result. In many creatures of the land this variation is of common occurrence, and is not only directed according to a change of circumstances, but sometimes seems to be under no better influence than caprice. The Daubers, a genus of North American Wasps (Zoologist, vol. ii. p. 582), to save themselves the labour of building a cell, have been known to make use of a small bottle, closing the orifice with clay; and the Mason Bees (*Osmiæ*), which usually deposit their eggs in holes dug by themselves in walls or sandbanks, will embrace the opportunity of saving themselves labour, by employing for the same purpose the empty shell of a snail. But whatever obscurity may hang over this interesting proceeding in fishes, I believe we have fallen into error in ascribing the zealous and persevering attendance of the Stickleback to the force of parental affection. Further examination, especially by dissection, will probably shew that the love displayed bears a nearer resemblance to that of a glutton for his good things.

It is seldom that we have an opportunity of extending our observations to the deeper recesses of the ocean; but better occasions will probably show that an habitual care for the safety of the young is not rare among the inhabitants of the deep; and among these the following deserves our notice. The beautiful pale yellow purses, as they are termed, of the Roughhound (*Scyllium catulus*), can scarcely fail to attract the attention of an observer, who will conclude that the lengthened and twisted tendrils which adorn the four corners must be designed to answer some important end. When taken from the body of the fish, and dipped in water, they begin to twist themselves round, and to contract their length, so as to form a close attachment about any substance in the neighbourhood. From an examination of numerous specimens it appears that, when about to deposit the egg, this fish begins by moving round the tuft of coral, or the stone, to the stability of which it means to commit the safety of the precious deposit; and thus the first-protruded tendrils are secured in their attachment. The ovum follows; and then the fish takes a wider range, and fastens together, as a covering, the outer branches of the tuft, by means of the tendrils which are last excluded. The species of Zoophytes to which I have seen these ova attached (and rarely more than one at a time) are the *Sertulariæ* and *Gorgonia verrucosa;* and as the branches of these are flexible, the contraction and twisting of the tendrils have the effect of binding them so closely together, as to secure, and even conceal, the ovum lodged within.

An extract from Kohl's " Russia" will serve to shew that observation only is wanted to make us acquainted with similar habits in a much more extensive range. " One of the most remarkable of the fish of the Black Sea is called by the Russians *Bitshki,* which always produces fever in those who eat it, and which builds for its young a nest like a bird. The male and female unite their cares in its construction, gathering reeds and soft seaweeds, and depositing them in small holes on the shore. In this the female not only lays her eggs, but watches them carefully like a hen; and when the little ones are hatched, they remain near the mother till they are sufficiently grown to venture alone into the world of waters."

To secure their young from danger, some creatures have been said to adopt modes of defence which have been received with doubt and even disbelief by eminent Naturalists, but which deserve mention in this place, because they have been affirmed as facts, after long observation, and are countenanced by the belief in them of so good an observer as Gilbert White (Nat. Hist. of Selborne, Letter 17.)

The habit referred to is the alleged practice by some creatures of receiving their young, in case of alarm, not only into the mouth, but into the stomach, from which they again emerge when the danger is over. This fact will require the clearest proof to satisfy those who know the fallacy that often attends the observation of even a scientific inquirer: for it has been pronounced impossible by men whose names, in matters of philosophical importance, would decide a question. On the other hand, its truth is affirmed by many curious observers of nature, far apart in time and place, as a thing which they have personally seen for themselves; and it must be borne in mind that the unprejudiced observation of a plain inquirer has in the end been sometimes shewn to be nearer the truth than the speculations of the more able theorist. It is to be regretted that these statements do not admit of being decided by experiment: for the creatures to whom such habits are ascribed lose many of their instincts when in captivity, and the occurrence of the phenomenon is more likely to fall under the notice of the ignorant or incurious, than of the philosophic spectator. The opinion that this is a habit of the Blue Shark (*Squalus glaucus*) is as ancient as the time of the poet Oppian. (Book I.)

> Others, when aught disturbs the ravaged seas,
> And trembling young their conscious fears express,
> Extend their jaws, and shew the safer way:
> The frighted stragglers soon the call obey,
> Within the conscious roof uninjured rest,
> Safe as the chirper in his mossy nest.

Thus the Blue Sharks, secure from chasing foes,
Within their widen'd mouths their young enclose :
They near their fondlings, like some careful nurse,
Observe their motions, and restrain their course,
Eye every wave, and shew the doubtful way,
Teach where to hunt, and where to find the prey.
When big with secret guilt the waters heave,
They in their mouths their shelter'd young receive;
But when the waves at their own leisure roll,
And no fierce robber drives the scatter'd shoal,
Again the parents' pointed jaws comprest
By force compel them from their pleasing rest.

Ælian also delivers the popular belief of his day, in ascribing a high degree of parental love to this fish; although it must be confessed that the supposed fact is rendered doubtful when he ascribes this feeling to the father, who, at least among Sharks, may well be supposed ignorant of his own offspring.—" What an excellent father," he says, " do we witness in the Blue Shark ! He diligently watches over his partner's offspring, and guards them from snares and injury. Whilst they swim along with the buoyancy and carelessness of youth, his anxiety continues ; and sometimes he bears them on his back, sometimes moves them from one side to the other. If one of these little ones should be seized with fear, he opens his mouth to receive it ; and he does not disgorge it until the danger is clearly passed."

Mr. Darwin, in the Journal of his Voyage (Chap. 1.), gives some reasons for believing that imprisonment in a Shark's stomach is not necessarily fatal ; and states that a species of Diodon has been known to eat its way from thence into liberty. I have also been informed by a gentleman, that he saw a White Shark cut open on board a ship; when some young ones were found in its stomach still alive and active.

A habit similar to this is also affirmed of the Adder (*Vipera communis*), of which remarkable instances have been reported by intelligent persons, who could have no wish to deceive; and the latest of these was by a gentleman well informed on such subjects, and alive to the scientific importance of the circumstance. From him we learn that, having fallen in with a little family party of adders, he saw the young ones take refuge in the mouth of the parent, which she extended for that purpose; and that, on destroying her, the young were found there enclosed, and were ungrateful enough to hiss at him when he delivered them literally from the jaws of death.

CHAPTER XVI.

IT is not necessary to pursue further the subject which occupied our attention in the last Chapter; but, whether we regard the developments of Instinct in their intensity, or in their variety, there are none which so frequently press on our observation as those connected with the affection of animals for their young, and the unwearying watchfulness with which they protect and preserve them.

Though we find this influence almost universal among animals, so much so as to be a primary law of their being, there are exceptions to this law, and especially in a bird with which we are familiar—the Cuckoo—who shews a remarkable deficiency in this love of its kind. The Cow Bunting, a native bird of America, is said to be similarly wanting in parental love; but we have better opportunities of knowing the habits of the common Cuckoo (*Cuculus canorus*) of our own country. It had long been known that the Cuckoo did not build for itself, but that its egg was dropped into the nest of some smaller bird, by which the young Cuckoo was tended till it was capable of caring and catering for itself; but the minor facts and minuter details of this strange proceeding were uncertain and discredited, and what could be believed was mixed up with suppositions which were very apocryphal, till the philosophic spirit of Dr. Jenner applied itself to the development of the truth. He succeeded in proving the correctness of the popular opinion, that the Cuckoo does not pair, or build a nest: that, in most cases, a single egg only is deposited in the nest of some one of the smaller insectivorous birds, without much preference of species: that there is probably a considerable interval between the times of its laying its several eggs; and in one case, which he witnessed, where two eggs of the Cuckoo were found in one nest, there was reason to believe that they were the produce of two parents. As finding a nest just fitted to receive the intruding egg must be a matter of uncertainty, it is said that the Cuckoo not only possesses the power common to most birds of retaining its egg for a time, till everything is in readiness for its reception; but also that, when the nest it has selected is difficult of access, it will first lay its burden on the ground, and then convey it somehow to its destination. Instances are not uncommon where this power of conveying away the precious egg, to avoid danger to it, has been practised by the Partridge and Lark; and this offers the most easy explanation of the fact, that the egg of the Cuckoo has been found in situations

N

to which so large a bird could not otherwise have gained access.

The Cuckoo's egg is hatched at the same time with those of the foster-parent, where the latter have not been injured: for there is reason to believe that the eggs of smaller birds are a favourite diet with the Cuckoo; and that its prying habits, in the early part of the season, are chiefly directed to their discovery. A gentleman who is curious in outdoor observation of Nature assured me that on visiting some nests of Linnets, which he knew were in a particular thicket, his advance scared away a Cuckoo from among them; and on examining these nests, he found all the eggs broken and destroyed.

As soon as the young Cuckoo emerges from the egg, his utmost efforts are directed to expel his foster-brothers from the nest, with any eggs which may remain unhatched; and as the form of its body, from a depression between the shoulders, and its superior strength, make it powerful to play the tyrant over the hapless young ones beside it, it is always successful, and they perish one and all: for " he will bear no brother near the throne." The foster-parents have nothing else to do, then, but to feed the young intruder; and as its appetite is great, it tasks their utmost industry to provide enough for its cravings. It is requisite also that this waiting upon it should continue longer than would have sufficed for their own young: for the Cuckoo does not readily acquire the habit of feeding itself, much less of seeking its own food; and it looks not a little ridiculous to see so unwieldy a bird taking its nourishment from creatures whom it is big enough to swallow with the morsels they bring. The parent Cuckoos have left this country long before the time that their young have become capable of taking the same journey: so that no creature is so entirely deprived of the instruction or influence of its race; and yet the habits of the bird are strictly maintained, as soon as its powers are developed by age.

The student of Nature has, in his researches, to encounter anomalies, which he is unable to reconcile with the laws that seem to govern the otherwise regular course of Creation; and in all that relates to the instincts and habits of animals it is scarcely possible to find a species in which there are so many and such great anomalies as in the Cuckoo. And this exception to the rule, too, is the more remarkable, as this bird is the only one of its genus in which, as far as is known, any such deviation is found. But a closer examination of natural laws has sometimes taught the philosopher that an apparent anomaly is only an exception to his theory, and not to the truth of Nature itself; and so far from offering an inexplicable difficulty or contradiction, it may become useful in illustration of the actual law, which could not be made clear without it. The absence of a particular organ in a species or class, a modification of its form, or a casual exception occurring in an individual case, has enabled the physiologist to estimate

N 2

its use in those where it occurs, and the affinities, or the modifications of other organs, in those in which it does not. The like advantage may also be looked for, in considering the principle of the vital actions, by an examination of the variations displayed in the habits of the Cuckoo and Cow Bunting.

We may observe, too, that, in what appears to be an anomaly of habit or structure, though our attention is chiefly drawn to their most prominent display, there are no instances to be found where these stand out so singly and apart as to have no gradations, by which they may be known to be allied to the more ordinary forms ; and it is by examining these that we come at a correct knowledge of things, of which, if these were neglected, we should know little or nothing : for these are the keys to knowledge. Instances illustrative of this principle may be seen among the commonest of our birds : in which, while the impulse to increase prevails in some individuals, in others it does not exist at all ; and where the development of an egg is not the primary excitement, there is no disposition to that allied influence which urges them to build, or to those further habits which make up the series of the procreative organism, of which intense affection for their offspring and undaunted courage in their defence are admirable parts of the display. Accordingly, in every season, there are individual birds, which, like the Cuckoo, show no disposition to attach themselves to a mate.

In gallinaceous birds again, for the most part, the male feels no powerful impulse urging him to do more than his natural duty, and works not with the female in building the nest ;—nor will he sit on the eggs, or assist her in supplying the young with food. And in both sexes of some other species, though all the subsequent offices are attended to, no constructive instinct is developed. the eggs are simply laid on the naked ground, or on the hard surface of a rock. In a species among which it is usual to form a nest, here and there an individual pair will be found, who perform the business of incubation without it : so says Mr. Yarrell of the Yellowhammer (*Emberiza citrinella*), a bird which is in general careful in this particular. The Kingfisher (*Alcedo ispida*) sometimes constructs a nest, and at other times deposits its eggs on the bare earth, or at the extremity of a long dark passage. The Goatsucker (*Caprimulgus Europæus*) and various Tringæ, are mostly contented with a mere depression in the ground. The Ostrich is even less attentive than the Cuckoo to the well-being of its brood : for in the warmer regions of Africa she leaves her eggs to the fostering influence of the sun, and the heat-hatched young neither know nor need a mother's care.

We have already taken occasion to adduce individual instances, where certain birds so far depart from the habit of their species as to place their eggs in the nest of another individual of their own kind, and even of another kind ; as is

the case with the Guinea-fowl. But the Cuckoo
invariably does what in these is only an occasional habit, and so far it is an important difference. But while these instances show that portions of the chain of this affection are sometimes
varied or interrupted without disturbing the last
result, an example still more remarkable, because
more invariable, and more allied to the habit of
the common Cuckoo in its prominent particulars,
occurs in the Carolina Cuckoo (*Coccyzus Ameri-
canus*), a bird which has been taken, though not
often, in our own country.

Mr. Yarrell (British Birds, vol. ii.), quoting from
Mr. Audubon, says, " Its appearance in the state
of New York seldom takes place before the beginning of May, and at Green Bay not until the
middle of that month. Unlike our English Cuckoo,
this American species builds a nest, and rears its
young with great assiduity : but it sometimes robs
smaller birds of their eggs ; and its own egg, which
is not easily mistaken, from its particular colour,
is occasionally found in another bird's nest.—A
nest, which was placed near the centre of a tree
of moderate size, was reached by a son of the gentleman on whose ground we were. One of the old
birds, which was sitting upon it, left its situation
only when within a few inches of the climber's hand,
and silently glided off to another tree close by. Two
young Cuckoos, nearly able to fly, scrambled off from
their tenement among the branches of the tree, and
were caught by us after a while. The nest was taken,
and carefully handed to me. It still contained three

young Cuckoos, all of different sizes, the smallest apparently just hatched; the next in size probably several days old; while the largest, covered with pen-feathers, would have been able to leave the nest in about a week. There were also in the nest two eggs, one containing a chick, the other fresh or lately laid. The two young birds which escaped from the nest clung so firmly to the branches by their feet, that our attempts to dislodge them were of no avail, and we were obliged to reach them with the hand. On now looking at all these young birds, our surprise was indeed great, as no two of them were of the same size; which clearly shewed that they had been hatched at different periods, and I should suppose the largest to have been fully three weeks older than any of the rest. Mr. Rhett assured us that he had observed the same in another nest placed in a tree within a few paces of his house, and which he also shewed to us. He stated that eleven young Cuckoos had been successively hatched and reared in it, by the same pair of old birds, in one season, and that young birds and eggs were to be seen in it at the same time for many weeks in succession. On thinking since of this strange fact, I have felt most anxious to discover how many eggs the Cuckoo of Europe drops in one season. If it, as I suspect, produces, as our bird does, not less than eight or ten, or what may be called the amount of two broods in a season, this circumstance would connect the two species in a still more intimate manner than theoretical writers have supposed them to be allied. Having mentioned these circumstances to my friend Dr. J. M. Brewer, and requested him to pay particular

attention to these birds while breeding, he has sent
me the following note :—' The fact you intimated to
me last July, I have myself observed. The female
evidently commences incubation immediately after
laying her first egg. Thus I have found in the nest
of both species of our Cuckoos (the other is the Black-
billed American Cuckoo) one egg quite fresh, while in
the other the chick will be just bursting the shell ;
and again, I have found an egg just about to be
hatched, while others are already so, and some of the
young even about to fly. These species are not uncommon in Massachusetts, where both breed, and
both are much more numerous some years than
others.' "

CHAPTER XVII.

We have already found occasion to admire the beautiful structures which the feathered tribes are accustomed to build for the seclusion and protection of their young; and, in selecting the few instances of this sort which have been adduced, preference has been given to the birds of our own country, because they fall more frequently within our view, and are more likely to make an impression on our attention. We might easily have referred our readers to instances of Instinct still more curious, but occurring in remote countries, where difference of circumstances, of materials, and of enemies, (among which the inquisitive Monkey and the gliding and insidious Snake are especially to be noted, against whose intrusion no preparations for defence can be deemed too great,) added to differences in the natural families of the birds themselves, could not fail to produce many traits of character in such birds, which would have been novel in themselves, and greatly illustrative of the general argument. But, for the most part, in such instances, too little attention

N 3

has been paid to the more minute, but characteristic particulars ; an omission which must lessen
the value of these relations. To derive as much
benefit as we can from the more remarkable instances of Instinct related by travellers, where
they are confirmed and explained by examples
within our own reach, it is recommended to the
reader, in visiting public museums, to examine
carefully the specimens there collected with reference
to the proofs thus obtained of skill and intention.
The nests of the Tailorbird and Pensile Grosbeak
shew such complexity of structure and admirable
arrangement of materials, that we can give no
other interpretation to such skill than that it is the
result of a well-conducted process of reasoning,
founded on shrewd observation, implying a knowledge of the nature of the dangers which beset
them, and the best means of avoiding them.

The next consideration is, to show that there
are structures of no ordinary labour and complication, which owe their existence to other motives
than the powerful one of care and comfort of the
progeny ; and this I will endeavour to demonstrate,
by referring to the habits of some of our commonest
wild animals, and to some less-known habits of animals in foreign lands.

The burrowing animals of our own country are
the Fox, Badger, Rabbit, the several species of
Shrews, and pre-eminently the Mole; together with,
in a less degree, Rats and Mice : which, with the
Otter, Polecat, Weasel and Stoat, may rather be
said to accommodate to their use the conveniences

of this sort which they find already prepared, than to form any for themselves.

The first-named of these animals, indeed, however desirous of possessing, are not always inclined to be at the labour of excavating, a retreat for themselves: for it is an instance of the variation of their intelligence according to circumstances, that they are ready to adopt any expedient which saves them from irksome toil. The Fox especially, having no consciousness of moral honesty, and a high opinion of his own activity and cunning, will expel the Badger from his burrow, if it appears fitted to his own purposes of concealment; and in these cases it is not so much the secresy of the retreat, as the difficulty of an enemy approaching it when it is discovered, and penetrating to its recesses, which is its principal recommendation. It is on this account that, when he harbours near the sea, he selects a situation which neither man nor dog can enter but at a disadvantage. He also takes the benefit of such stones and roots of trees as may retard the advance of the enemy, and expose him to his own formidable bite.

The Badger, whose presence in a district would not be recognised by any mischief he does, is even more choice in his care for the safety and comfort of his dwelling, though a quiet and secluded spot is of more consequence to him than concealment.

But the proceedings of the Mole are so much more within our observation, and have been so little examined in detail, that I shall select it for

particular description; and as Mr. Bell alone, of
all our Naturalists, has entered into the history
of this animal with a feeling of interest, and many
of that gentleman's deductions are drawn from its
manners in level and little-enclosed portions of
land, or from foreign sources, my remarks will
have the advantage of being made under some
variety of circumstances.

The habits of the Mole will vary with the soil,
and particularly with the structure of the ground,
as it is rich and deep, or shallow, level, rocky,
uneven, or intersected with raised mounds, or
hedges of earth five or six feet high, and of
the same thickness, such as divide fields in the
West of England. The presence of this animal is known by the heaps of fine earth, or
hills, thrown up during its subterraneous operations: in deep ground little of its labours can be
traced, except when thus marked: but in a thin
soil, or in hard ground, a ridge is often driven
along, which is distinctly raised above the ordinary level of the surface; and the mole-hill is
only elevated where the earth is so fine and fri-
able, that the removal of some part of it is necessary, to give the creature a clear course in
its runs backward and forward. The creep or
run is in a zigzag direction; and when the neighbourhood is very productive of its prey, exceedingly so, as if the animal was unwilling to pass
out of so fertile a district. But for the most part
it takes a straightforward course; and in the
open space of a down, it passes through more

than fifty paces of distance without lifting a heap, with a progress amounting to two or three human paces in a day, and the whole run is two hundred feet in length. In the course of this passage, advantage is taken of any obstructions which occur, as if conscious of the probability of pursuit; and the run is made to pass among the roots of dwarf furze, and even under a large stone, while, at irregular distances, openings are made, to allow of excursions on the surface, and the free admission of air. There are many lateral branches from the principal passage; but none of them extend to any great distance : for it seems wisely to avoid forming such a labyrinth as might confound itself in its daily course, or in its efforts to escape from an enemy, to whose depredations it is exposed even in its retreat. Its time of labour is chiefly at an early hour in the morning; but if every thing be still, it may be seen at work at other seasons. The slightest sound or movement of an approaching foot stops the work; and no further lifting of the earth will be attempted that day. These runs are mostly made towards the end of autumn; are this creature's hunting-grounds for food; are abandoned when the soil has been thoroughly searched through and through; and though they are formed with so much toil as to make it desirable not to desert it while there is anything to be done there, yet in a month or two the animal quits it for new ground, perhaps at a great distance, where the hunting promises better success.

A favourite spot for its winter-quarters, and one
it prefers at other seasons, is in enclosed fields,
under the shelter of a hedge of high-piled earth,
along the middle of whose base the run is carried, and in whose mass of mould it finds security from cold and from its natural enemies. The
heaps it throws up are cast on the sides, and at
intervals a lateral passage is driven into the field,
to which, when the inducement is powerful, it
transfers its principal operations; and there en-
counters its greatest hazards from the traps of
the mole-catcher, and the pursuit of the Weasel
and the Rat, with whom it fights furiously, but
without success. When undisturbed, the Mole
often shifts its quarters; and in making a new
selection, its choice seems to be much influenced
by caprice. It makes these changes especially in
the months of July and August; but I have known
it to take excursions of removal to such distances,
that no mark of its presence could be detected,
in the month of January, if an open and moist
season. A large part of such a journey must be
along the surface; and it is probable that at all
times this is its mode of emigration to distant
places. In summer much of its time is thus
passed in migrations from one field to another,
because the hardness of the ground renders it
difficult to throw up the soil, and follow up the
worms, which have sunk deeper down into the
soil: it shews the same love of change in moist
weather, when the ground is more workable; and
the practice indeed seems a periodical variation of

habit, common to it with the Shrews (*Sorex*), which also are inhabitants of burrows, and to all which species it seems essential to health. A fatality consequent on the emerging of the latter little creatures has excited the curiosity of Naturalists. They are often found dead in the paths, with no mark of injury about them to account for their death, which we have no doubt is to be attributed to their having been pounced upon by an Owl; who kills them by a nip of the beak without breaking the skin, and then rejects them, as meat for their masters, perhaps, but not for them, who have a taste for the daintier sort of delicacies. Limited in their powers of sight, they are also surprised by Cats, who immediately throw them away, as not liking them. Their deaths may be thus accounted for.

If not to its mind, the Mole repeatedly changes its quarters; and though shut up in darkness, it reluctantly continues on the northern declivity of a hill, where it has little light, and less heat, unless its other advantages are unusually great. Its migration from one district to another exposes it to great danger, as it is slow to escape, and little prepared to defend itself. The opening of a new track is often concealed in a heap of the soil which has been brought up from the interior; and at times it is firmly blocked up from within, but I have seen it left carelessly open. It is by these entrances that the Weasel, the Rat, and the larger Vole (*Arvicola amphibia*) sometimes enter, and are themselves taken in the trap.

The run is differently formed in spring, in consequence of a difference of object. Where fields are
not large, the hedge is still the selected spot; on
which account its nest is not often discovered. Mr.
Bell has given a sketch of the skilful arrangements
made for its safety at this time; but in districts where
the hedge is chosen for defence, no other departure
from its usual form is made than an enlargement of
the space, and a more comfortable lining. Fourteen
young ones have been discovered in one nest; but,
though the Mole is not a social animal, it is hard to
believe that they could have been littered by one
mother.

The Mole may sleep more in winter than in
other seasons, but it is not its habit to become
torpid at this time. In frost and snow, fine earth
is often seen freshly turned up as evidence of its
activity; but, as it is a creature of great voracity,
and cannot endure long-fasting, like many wild animals of that character, it is not easy to say how its
wants are at this time supplied. A dead or living
bird, numbed with the cold, is always a welcome
morsel; but its track has not been seen in the snow
in pursuit of it. It perceives the earliest approach
of a thaw; and, after long seclusion, a heap may be
seen protruding through the thin covering of snow
as evidence of its sensibility to change of temperature: a circumstance more easily understood when
we recollect that it is the radiation of heat from the
inner parts of the earth which exercises the first
influence in the change; and that it is because the
air abstracts this heat more rapidly than the earth

supplies it, that frost and snow are produced and continued. When, from changes in the atmosphere, this rapid abstraction ceases, the heat below becomes more sensibly felt; and this is first visible at the surface of the soil.

A good supply of drink is essential to the Mole's existence; and its healthy condition is marked by a softness and moisture about the snout, where its most perfect organ of sensation is placed. The flexibility of that organ, and its command over it, are indeed exquisite; but it is not used in the operations of excavation and lifting. This is the work of the feet, neck, and the hinder part of the shoulder; and in these parts the Mole is perhaps the strongest quadruped in existence, in proportion to its size. The heaps it throws up are not made simply by lifting: for the superfluous earth is collected at easy distances, and thrust along, until so much is accumulated as compels it to convey it out of the way, and then its work in tunnelling goes on again.

The Mole has more enemies than it is supposed to have: for though its disappearance from a district is sometimes due to emigration, there must be other causes at work to account for their extirpation in particular localities. They may destroy each other in their burrows, for they are exceedingly quarrelsome; the Fox and Weasel too are formidable foes; but the ceaseless war waged against them by man, the least excusable enemy they have, is the most destructive. Admitting that moleheaps, and loosening of the soil by the runs made through a field, are inconveniences, and even injurious; and that it is unsightly to see a gentleman's lawn disfigured with these tumuli : but such annoyances may be either removed or turned to advantage ; and it must not be forgotten that their destruction of more injurious creatures is considerable. If it is desirable to expel them from their haunts, it may be done effectually without destroying them : for their extirpation is sure to be followed by a fresh invasion. Evelyn says they may be driven away by placing garlick in their runs ; and perhaps assafœtida would be still more potent, if they must be drugged.

" The most unnatural of all persecutions," says that close observer, James Hogg, the Ettrick shepherd, " that ever was raised in a country is that against the Mole : that innocent and blessed pioneer, who enriches our pastures with the first top-dressing, dug with great pains and labour from the fattest of the soil beneath. The advantages of this top-dressing are so apparent and so manifest to the eye of every unprejudiced person, that it is really amazing how our countrymen should have persisted in endeavours to exterminate the moles from the face of the earth. If a hundred men and horses were employed on a common-sized pasture-farm, of from 1500 to 2000 acres, in raising and conveying manure for a top-dressing, they would not do it so effectually, so neatly, or so equally, as the natural number of Moles on that farm would do of themselves. It has been observed in Selkirkshire, that, where the Moles have been nearly extirpated upon the Duke of Buccleuch's pasture-farms, Slugs have increased to such a degree, as to render it probable that they really consume a great proportion of the herbage. On the pasture-land of other proprietors, where the Moles are not destroyed, the Slugs are certainly not so numerous. . . . . Now, it is well known, whatever may be the reason, and no other can be thought of, that the grounds upon which the Moles are destroyed do not keep so many sheep as formerly, when the Moles were not destroyed." (Loudon's Mag. of Nat. Hist., vol. viii. p. 227.) It may be observed further, that where no efforts have been made to destroy them, they do not increase beyond a given number, which varies according to the soil; and that their frequent destruction, by encouraging the increase of the creatures which are their food, aids indirectly in augmenting their numbers.

The following remarkable instance of ingenious contrivance in concealment and defence, in the absence of natural advantages, is reported of the *Conilurus constructor*, or native Rabbit of Australia, a smaller animal than the English Rabbit, and differing still more in being furnished with a long tail. The account is derived from observations made by Major Mitchell, as given in the eighteenth volume of the Transactions of the Linnean Society. " We had frequently, during the course of our travels, remarked large piles of dry sticks and brushwood, each of them big enough to make two or three good cart-loads, collected and heaped together in different situations, and evidently designed for some particular purpose. For a long time we imagined them to be the work of the natives, who are in the habit of communicating the intelligence of any strange or uncommon event to distant tribes by raising dense columns of smoke in different directions over the face of the country; and we fancied that these were their rude telegraphs, kept ready for immediate use, when an occasion occurred to require it. A more minute examination, however, soon convinced us of our error: we found, in fact, that the materials were not thrown promiscuously together, as would naturally have been the case had they been collected by the natives for the purpose of burning; but that each stick and fragment was so curiously intertwined and woven with the rest, that the whole formed a solid, compact mass, so firmly bound together, that it was absolutely impossible to remove a part without at the same time moving the whole fabric. Our Kangaroo dogs also drew our attention more particularly to the examination of these curious structures, by the constant ardour which they displayed in barking and scratching whenever we fell in with them, thus manifestly intimating that they expected to find something inside. At length we broke several of them open, a work of no small difficulty from the solidity of their structure, and were not a little surprised to find in the interior a small nest, occupied by an animal something between a Rabbit and a Rat, which had constructed this formidable and massive stronghold to protect itself against the attacks of the native Dog. For this purpose the little animal chooses some small bush or shrub, as a fixed *point d'appui*, to commence its operations; and by working round this, and interlacing the materials of its fortalice, first of all with the growing branches of the centre bush, and afterwards with one another, *gradually* extends it to the enormous dimensions already specified, and enjoys the reward of its perseverance and ingenuity in subsequent security and repose."

Though a different cause has been assigned for this peculiarity in another creature, I am inclined to ascribe it to the simple art of removing suspicion by misleading the attention, that the Baya bird suspends the flying glowworm to its nest: " These birds," says Dr. Buchanan, " that build hanging nests are at Cape Comorin numerous. At night each of their little habitations is lighted up by a firefly stuck on the top with a bit of clay. The nest consists of two rooms: sometimes there are three or four flies, and their blaze in the little cell dazzles the eyes of the bats, which often kill the young of these birds."

In our own country I have seen the conspicuous feathers of a Turkey fixed erect on the upper edge of the nest of a small bird, where, one would think, they would rather draw attention to it than divert it: at least they had that effect with me; but I am persuaded that the original intention was to give an accidental air to the artful structure, and thus escape suspicion.

Mr. Gould, in his History of the Birds of New South Wales, has described the proceedings of several species as exceedingly singular in their manner of hatching and protecting their young; but we will merely mention one in this place, as its peculiar construction cannot be ascribed to the ordinary motives which influence animals, but seems the result of something like a sentimental feeling of pleasurable indulgence. The bird alluded to constructs a bower and alley or run of two short parallel hedges, composed of twigs interlaced so artfully, that the inner face of each hedge is smooth, offering no impediment to the passage of the birds; while the outside is rough with the projecting ends and bifurcations of the twigs. The floor of this run or avenue is laid with sticks strewn with shells and bones, and the bower itself is ornamented with the brilliant feathers of various Parakeets. Here the birds play, and sportively pursue each other, perpetually traversing the avenue. This, however, is not the nest, which is concealed so artfully, that it has not been discovered even by the sharp-eyed natives.

CHAPTER XVIII.

In connexion with their habitations, we may class those arrangements which certain animals make in providing a refuge during the season of Torpidity: a condition which, in their wild state, entire classes of creatures assume as winter approaches; and of the expectation of which they show many signs long before the time arrives.

The condition of Torpidity has been supposed to be the same with that of sleep ; but modern examination into its physiology shows that it differs greatly. And that the creatures subject to both these influences are aware of the difference between them, appears from the variation in their preparations, according as they look for one or the other. An important deviation in the influence of these conditions on the animal economy is, that while sleep is the result of long wakefulness and much fatigue, and effects a restoration of their wasted powers, such alternations of activity and quietude do not supersede the necessity of the season of Torpidity in these creatures ; but if it be prevented, as it may be by abundance of food and a warm and equable temperature, although the animal may seem to have enjoyed itself the more for this omission of insensibility, the interruption is sure to accelerate its death in the end.

Torpidity has also been said to bear some analogy with the condition brought upon some kinds of animals, and in a remarkable manner upon man himself, by the power of intense cold, which benumbs the faculties, by rendering the nervous system insensible to its natural impressions, and in this manner suspends the action of the heart. The opinion that there was a close connexion in the nature of these influences appeared the more probable from the knowledge, that creatures liable to become torpid in the winter season might be thrown into a state of insensibility at any time, by the rapid abstraction of heat artificially. When under the influence of intense cold, we can follow the progress of the feeling of inertness, until the sense of pain is lost in obtuseness of the capacity to sustain it, and the propensity to drowsiness is too powerful to be resisted. But, however close the similarity, and though sleep may form a part of the phenomenon of Torpidity, as it often does of the condition of death, the essential difference is too great to admit of their being mistaken for one another; and there are circumstances in the latter which show it to be an instinctive proceeding, in subordination to propensities congenial with the natural functions, and influenced by inclination, rather than a compulsory yielding to irresistible impulse.

Long before the period of hibernation, and while the degree of temperature, and the abundance of subsistence, occupation and amusement, one would suppose, would postpone the anticipation of such a state, creatures ordinarily subject to it are found entering upon a series of labours, which, to the eye of reason, are as clearly indications of pro-spective intention, as the building of a nest for incubation, or the storing of food for a time of scarcity. In some parts of the Russian dominions, as early as the month of August, while summer is in its glory, and everything invites to enjoyment of the present rather than care for the future, the Rat-Hare (*Lagomys*) sets about collecting the herbs which are to form its winter-bed, and spreads them out to dry in the sun. In September these dried vegetables are gathered into heaps, which are sometimes the fruit of the labours of a single individual, and at others the united efforts of a company. The Hampster in the Alps, and in our own country the Dormouse, the Shrew, and, in a less degree, the Hedgehog, have the same habits: in all their proceedings making a marked distinc-tion between their ordinary summer residences, or the receptacles for their young, and those in which they are to pass the, time of insensibility. After accomplishing these preparations, a long time is suffered to pass before these animals finally retire to their winter retreats; and then they wrap themselves up in the accumulated materials, with a care and skill that indicate how well they are aware of the danger of exposure. The Dormouse and Harvest-Mouse, whose summer nests have been placed on elevated stalks of grass, or in the branches of a furze-bush, now wrap themselves up in a ball, so closely woven together as to admit of being rolled about without disturbing its slumbering inhabitant, and stow themselves away in some crevice or recess among the entangled roots of a tree beneath the soil.

The faculty of sleep is but little under human influence. Like one of Glendower's spirits, it will not come when we call upon it ; and perhaps chiefly from the resemblance there is between it and torpidity, it seems never to have been thought probable that the final action in this chain of proceedings—the actual assumption of this insensible condition—could be as much under the influence of the creature's will, as the actions which preceded it. But as it is of advantage to employ the animal structure and physiology, and even their irregular action and organization, to throw light upon those of man, in this instance we may be allowed to reverse the inquiry, and obtain an explanation from some remarkable instances of what appears a kindred faculty in human individuals.

Augustine says of Restitutus, a Presbyter, that he could at pleasure deprive himself of all sense, and would do it as often as he was asked, which many did, who were desirous of witnessing so wonderful a power. On hearing certain doleful sounds uttered in the tone of the hired mourners at funerals, he would lie as one that was dead, and altogether senseless ; and when pulled about roughly, or when his flesh was punctured, and even when burnt with fire, he had no feeling of it till he revived, and the wounds became painful. In these trances, he did not appear to breathe; but he said that he heard the voices of his friends, if they spoke louder than ordinary, the sound seeming as if it were at a great distance.

Hieronymus Cardanus informs us, too, that he was able to pass, as often as he pleased, into the same condition, so that he had no more than a vague impression of the words spoken to him, without understanding their meaning. He was not conscious of being pulled or pinched; nor did he feel the pain of the gout, though that disorder was on him at the time. He was sensible of the coming on of this condition as commencing in the head, and diffusing itself downwards from the brain along the spine. There was also a kind of fluttering sensation of separation at the heart, as if the soul were departing; and this was communicated to the whole body in a manner which he describes as if a door opened.

But the most extraordinary instance of this power of voluntarily suspending the animal faculties is related by Dr. Cheyne of Colonel Townshend. " Some time ago," says the Doctor, " Dr. Baynard and I were called in to Colonel Townshend, a gentleman of honour and integrity, who was seized with violent vomitings. We attended him twice a day; but his vomitings continuing obstinate against all remedies, we despaired of his

recovery. While he was in this condition he sent
for us one morning ; and waiting on him, with
Mr. Shrine, his apothecary, we found his senses
clear, his mind calm, and his nurse and several
servants about him. He told us he had sent for
us to give some account of an odd sensation he
had for some time observed in himself ; which
was that, composing himself, he could die or expire
when he pleased, and yet somehow come to life
again. We could hardly believe the fact, much
less give any account of it, unless he should make
the experiment before us. He continued to talk
above a quarter of an hour about this surprising
sensation, and insisted on our seeing the trial made.
We all three felt his pulse first. It was distinct,
though small, and his heart had its usual beating.
He composed himself on his back, and lay in a still
posture for some time : while I held his right hand,
Dr. Baynard laid his hand on his heart; and Mr.
Shrine held a clean looking-glass to his mouth. I
found his pulse sink gradually, till at last I could not
feel any : Dr. Baynard could not feel the least motion
in his heart; nor Mr. Shrine see the least soil of breath
on the mirror. Then each of us by turns examined
his arm, heart, and breath, but could not discover the
least symptom of life. Finding that he still continued
in that condition, we began to conclude that he had
carried the experiment too far, and was actually
dead. This continued about half an hour. As we
were going away we observed some motion about
the body, and upon examination found his pulse

and the motion of his heart gradually returning :
he began to breathe gently, and speak softly. We
were all astonished to the last degree, and, after
some further conversation with him, went away
fully satisfied, but confounded and puzzled, and
unable to form any rational scheme that might
account for it."

CHAPTER XIX.

WE have already had occasion to refer to the habit of migration, as periodically observed in every quarter of the globe by numerous kinds of birds ; and we have endeavoured to trace the causes to which it may be ascribed : but there is a less obvious migration, at uncertain seasons, among some kinds of Quadrupeds, which has scarcely come under the notice of Naturalists ; and which requires to be spoken of here, as a manifestation of the working of an instinct, although the influencing cause and minuter particulars are as yet unascertained.

The narrative given by Wormius and others, of the assembling, in such immense numbers, of the Lemmings of Lapland (*Mus lemmus*, Lin.), who forget for a season their shy and retiring habits, in the stronger impulse that urges them forward ; and the story of their descending at irregular intervals from their native mountains, to the destruction of everything vegetable and eatable in their progress, may be exaggerated. But the irregularity of this migration, in respect to time, and the total suspension of their usual love of solitude, when taken in connexion with the fact that the country is thinly peopled with other living beings, (so that the instigation can hardly be a compulsion from without, or a deficiency of food,) and the appearance of combination in the assembling of such a multitude, when that very assembling is a proof of a novel impulse ; added to these facts, the natural affinity of the species to races which migrate in like manner in other lands, but in less numbers :—all these things together combine in demanding inquiry into this department of Natural History—neglected too much—the occasional variety in the instinct of animals.

The change of quarters, in a similar way, which takes place annually among the smaller animals of Britain is a movement involving no great risks, no great departure from their usual haunts and habits : it ceases as soon as they have found fresh fields for their operations ; and being performed by night, is attended with much secrecy : but so far as regards species, my inquiries have led me to include in this list of migrants the Badger, the Rat, the domestic Mouse, at least one species of field-Mouse, the Polecat, the Stoat, the Weasel, and the Hare. In some of these cases, and especially in the Hare, though simultaneous in the species, the journey is made singly, as if each individual had received the impulse at the same time, and acted on it for itself, without communication of any kind with the rest. The field-Mice (*Mus sylvaticus*) have, however, been seen moving in vast numbers ; and no one could say from whence they came, or by what impulse they had been guided.

Badgers, which are ordinarily solitary animals, have been known to assemble in a troop, and, under the guidance of an apparent leader, proceed on a tour of emigration. A country labourer, attended by his sheep-dog, at midnight found himself encompassed by half-a-dozen of these animals, whom he took to be parents with their young, proceeding to some distant spot. On discovering him, they did not wait for the attack, but began it; and though he soon wrenched a stake from a hedge at hand, and was well assisted by his dog, both dog and man were compelled to beat a retreat.

In another case of falling in with these wanderers by night, my informant judged the party to be nine or ten in number, as well as he could count them in the dark. They grunted and gathered about him, and followed him up closely through a field, till he passed through the gate, and then they left him. Another person counted twenty-one in a company; and the smallest of these were placed in the middle of the escort, preceded and followed by the larger. That at these times they will attack any one who comes in their way is the opinion of the few persons I have known who have had opportunities of observing these animals. In one case, where a man was attacked, he was compelled to fly to a heap of stones for defence, and fling them at his assailants with all his might.

A similar habit of migration in bands is reported of Polecats; and, in one case, of Stoats by daylight. In a dark night a wayfaring man encountered a large number of these creatures; and, directed by the sounds they uttered, rather than by sight, when they encompassed him about, he succeeded in killing seven, mostly young ones. On another occasion three were killed *.

* The habit of Weasels, of travelling and hunting in companies by night, gave rise to a superstitious belief in the West of England, which is hardly yet extinct. It was once a common opinion in that quarter of the country that there were a set of diminutive creatures, of the Elfin family, vulgarly called Dandy Dogs, who went hunting the Hare by night under the direction of one or more ghostly huntsmen; and it is within memory that individuals have affirmed that they have not only heard the full cry of these hunters, but have risen from their beds and accompanied the unearthly pack, but at a fearful, respectful distance; and that these imps of hounds have followed the chace with lively yelpings, and all the motions of their bigger brethren who love " the hunting of the Hare." It may be in connexion with this superstition that country people commonly call the Weasel a fairy.

We have already had occasion to notice another superstition, attended with more ridiculous results, which had its origin in the cunning shown by the Hare in managing to escape from the Hounds, and the suddenness with which the pursuers have been baffled, and found themselves at fault. According to the philosophy of these wise men of the West, this can only be accounted for by a reference to the powers of magic, and worse, by which what seemed a timid Hare was in truth a Witch, wandering abroad in this disguise for some wicked ends of her own, who had suffered herself for a while to be surprised by her enemies till she recollected herself, and, calling on the infernal powers for aid, was saved. This has been proved beyond doubt by the sudden discovery on the same spot of some decrepit old woman; who, when the hounds and their enraged masters came up to her, was found quaking with consternation that could only be supposed to arise from her guiltiness, so hard run, and nearly punished. This belief in the occasional

o 3

A large flock of Rats was met, late in the evening, in the street of a small town; and the interruption to their expedition being as unexpected by them as by the man who met them, they were driven like a flock of sheep before him into a house, where they took refuge under chairs and anything affording shelter, and seemed bewildered with fear; but they were soon expelled, and continued their journey. On another occasion, and at the same hour at night, another party of these migrants was met, and diverted from their way, but in this case they were not driven into a house. At the same time of night, in the end of the month of June, a company of common domestic Mice was seen proceeding along a street, as if migrating; and though people were occasionally passing, being unmolested, they held on their way without deviation.

Numerous and unaccountable assemblages of such wild animals as are by habit solitary have been seen and recorded from the remotest ages, when their coming became a public calamity, and they were supposed to be intimations of divine displeasure, or auguries of approaching evils. Pliny quotes Theophrastus as saying, that such multitudes of Mice prevailed in the Grecian island

change of the human into the animal form has been widely spread, both in ancient and modern times. Apuleius found it prevalent in Thrace, and made it the amusing foundation of his philosophical romance, the Golden Ass; and at this day it is believed in Abyssinia, that there is a family connexion between Man and the Hyæna, not at all to the credit of the gentleman who affects not to acknowledge the other gentleman as descended from Adam.

Gyarus, that they compelled the inhabitants to leave the place; and Plutarch says the same of the country of the Troad. It was a received opinion that these assemblages of creatures usually so solitary were the effect of divine anger: and the more so as their disappearance was as sudden and inexplicable as their coming, no trace of them being left behind, not even in the presence of a straggler, or one of their dead. Apollo obtained the name of Smintheus from being supposed to have delivered a city of that name from such a visitation of Mice; and records of similar occurrences are to be found in the history of Europe in the middle ages, though obscured by a pardonable mixture of superstition.

The history of Hatto, surnamed Bonosus, Duke of Franconia and Archbishop of Mentz, is one of these; and though probably much exaggerated, it may be true in its chief particulars. His conduct was severe to the poor; and in a time of great scarcity, under pretence of feeding them, he is said to have got great numbers into barns, and there to have burnt them, saying that he was thus consuming the Rats which were devouring the fruits of the land. Not long after this there appeared immense numbers of Rats, although no one could tell whence they came; and they followed him wherever he retreated, entering his chambers by the windows, and penetrating through every crevice; and his men which were appointed to the service were not able to drive them away. The prelate sought shelter in an island of the Rhine, retreating into a tower near the little city Bingen; but the Rats swam across, scaled the tower, and actually gnawed him alive : a circumstance which has happened to others besides him, without any imputation of peculiar guilt. His own fears probably contributed to his fate ; and if the public pronounced this great assemblage of predacious animals a divine judgment, it is no wonder if his conscience, by joining in the accusation, prevented him from protecting himself.

Olaus Wormius gives the form of exorcism used by ecclesiastics on these occasions. The Roman Naturalist notices, as worthy of remark, that these armies of field-Mice will not permit strangers from another district to join company, but persecute them until they are destroyed.

I find the following account of the migration of Porcupines in the Baron de Bode's Travels in Lauristan and Arabistan (Persia). " On visiting the subterraneous passages which branch in various directions under the ruins of Persepolis, I found a great number of Porcupine bristles, and the dry manure of that animal, heaped in the long and narrow corridors. In answer to my inquiries, why no living Porcupine was to be seen, I was informed that these animals occupy the cool cells of the now-deserted palace of Jemshid during the heats of summer only, and migrate to the south in thousands as soon as the cold weather commences ; about the same time, and nearly in the same direction as the Nomads, who drive their flocks of Sheep and Goats to the warmer pastures of Jaum, and Láristán, towards the Persian gulf. It is not scarcity of food which prompts the Porcupines to quit their royal abode ; because the plain of Nerdasht has numerous villages, and the fields are always stocked with some sort of grain : it is the cold which drives them away, while instinct directs them to the more genial climate of the South. I was assured that they travel in considerable bodies, and pick out the shortest way, traversing hill and dale. Not one Porcupine remains behind ; but with the return of spring and warm weather they resume their wonted quarters under the walls of Persepolis."

CHAPTER XX.

We may look through the mighty accumulations of ancient and modern literature, sacred and profane, and nowhere shall we find a more beautiful piece of pastoral poetry than the 104th Psalm. Among other reasons for praise of the great Creator of all things, the sublime Psalmist glorifies God that he has so separated day and night, so divided light and darkness, that while man has the day assigned to him for his labour and pleasure, the lower animals, and especially the destructive kinds, have the night appointed for their time of activity. We may discern and admire the providential arrangement thus made; but the natural cause is less obvious to observation, and is therefore a proper subject of inquiry.

The creatures which make night their day for prey, or other purposes of activity, are of various species; and those which are of our own country may be arranged under the following divisions:—

1. Those to whom the presence of light is irksome, from the natural organization of some por-

tion of their structure. This especially regards
the eye, to the proper action of which a powerful
glare of light is injurious. The ears of such creatures also are easily impressed with minute sounds
almost inaudible to man, which direct them in
the dark, in the absence of more perfect powers
of vision; and, for the same reason, the louder
noises of the day are distracting to them, and
they avoid them by flying to the most solitary,
silent retreats. In some Bats, the external ear
is more developed than in any other class of creatures; and, if you watch them narrowly, you will
see the long-eared Bat (*Plecotus auritus*) of our
own country, when on the wing, erect and direct
its ears in a variety of ways, and even corrugate
its margin into segments, so as to show the com-
pletest voluntary power imaginable in using these
instruments to collect the minutest impulses and
movements of other creatures in every direction.
The curious leaf-like structure of the nostril, in
one division of this family (*Rhinolophus*), is equally
under the power of the will, and contributes to
the same ends. The minute size of the eye in
these creatures is not inconsistent with acute vision,
though it does not allow of a wide range of sight; but
the remarkable promptitude with which the muscular motions answer to the sudden impulses of
the will in these nocturnal animals is not the
least wonderful part of their economy. They cannot discern injurious objects at a great distance;
and therefore it becomes the more imperative that
they should possess the power of instantly turning

the direction of their flight, to avoid dangers lying in their way.

But this capacity for suddenness and celerity of action, though highly conspicuous in these smaller animals, is by no means confined to them, or only to the connexion of muscular motion with volition; but it is also seen in, and is probably dependant on the greater or less celerity of transmission of the perceptive influence through the course of all the nerves. This appears in a remarkable manner in the great difference experienced by individuals in the rapidity with which the sensations of external objects or events are conveyed to the mind by the senses of sight or hearing: so that in watching the occurrence of minute actions, or such as require extreme accuracy of perception, as in the use of astronomical instruments, certain persons are able to seize on the instant of their occurrence with more readiness than others. This quickness of perception is still more discernible in the sense of hearing than in seeing: so that an appreciable difference of time is often to be distinguished between the first vibration of sound on the drum of the ear, and its intelligent delivery on the sensorium. On these accounts many persons are more prompt in connecting muscular action with perception than others; and in this acuteness some animals greatly excel mankind, though, it appears, with some exceptions as to race, as in the Lemurs, whose actions and perceptions are characterized by being slow and deliberate.

I possess a series of comparative sketches of

the eyes and ears of birds; and find from observation, that, while the expansion of the latter organ has no necessary connexion with the musical capacity of these interesting creatures, it has an evident relation to their nocturnal habits. Seaborn or sea-going birds, and especially such as manifest crepuscular habits, have small orifices to their ears, well guarded with feathers, so that not a drop of water can penetrate through them in diving; and acuteness in discerning minute sounds must be the less necessary to them, as the roaring of the ocean, to which they are continually exposed, must shut out every advantage they might derive from this source: but in land animals of nocturnal habits, the enlargement of the tube or expansion of the ear is only found in the timid animals which have to fly for their lives—as in the Hare and Rabbit; while the Feline race (the Cat and the Lion), who have little to fear, and whose search is predaceous, are less able to detect every passing sound.

The faculty of giving forth brilliant light from the eyes is common in the Cat, and has been seen in several other members of that family. Fishermen have informed me that they have observed this also in the Blue Shark (*Squalus glaucus.*) In the domestic Cat it is only seen when the creature is under excitement; and, at the first glance, we might suppose that a power so appalling to the timid would be more likely to alarm and repel their prey, than serve them in securing it, which is the case: for its effect is to arrest the attention of the little animal; and though nothing but a pair of shining globes glares upon them, the fascination of stupor or curiosity prevents them from resorting to their only means of safety—flight. I will mention here the case of a couple of schoolfellows of mine, who, from want of eyebrows, were so sensitive to ordinary light, as to be incapable of pursuing their avocations of study or play in the common glare of day, and were thus compelled to be crepuscular; but at night their activity was striking, and in strong contrast to the timid movements which they made in the day.

A kindred class of nocturnal animals to those which we have named above are such as are influenced by a liking for the moisture and freshness of the dewy air, which those among my readers who have been exposed to it will remember as exciting sensations differing greatly from any which the day affords. Certain sensitive conditions of the human constitution will make us all alive to these atmospheric influences; and this fact affords us another and a probable explanation of the phenomena of Moles and Shrews in the dry weather of summer emerging from their safer haunts and holes to enjoy the dew on the grass, as refreshing after long dryness of the ground in which they are burrowing all the rest of the day.

A third division, who are nocturnal only through fear of their natural enemies, and especially of man, would be active by day, if they could be so with impunity. The Fox is foremost among these wary ones, who will put no trust either in man or dog. He chooses the obscurest nights, when clouds rest on the earth, and the eye can scarcely penetrate the gloom, for his excursions to places of danger, which old experience had made him remember, as demanding the most careful application of all his powers of cunning. This is the time, too, when many of our smaller wild animals unbend themselves in gambols in which they could not indulge by day. Cats and Rats might say with the poet,

'Tis only daylight that makes sin :

for their felonious movements by day are made under the restraint of caution : but the pleasures of their night are unrestrained, and according to their then unbiassed instincts; and they are often social, and joyous in their way of amusing themselves. Even the poor Ass, condemned to slavery while light continues, finds time to amuse itself with its kind, and enters on any sport which is started by its fellows with an activity of gratification, in strong contrast with the compulsory, sluggish motions it shews in its ordinary employment. In pursuit of a favourite object by night, it has been known to ascend to situations, and overcome difficulties, which no driving could induce it to attempt by day. Man also is a nocturnal animal in the hotter parts of Africa and South America, in the same manner as he is a subterraneous animal in the winter of some part of the Russian dominions.

We may sum up this chapter by saying, that wild animals could not maintain their existence in populous countries, unless they resorted to such means of safety and security as we have been describing; and that their movements by day as well as by night are kept up with such short intervals of sleep as they can contrive to indulge when no enemy disturbs them in their haunts and hiding-places.

CHAPTER XXI.

An animal may be said to be in a wild condition when it is surrounded and influenced by creatures and by circumstances as wild and unmodified as itself, and when its actions are governed by the joint operation of instinctive propensity and natural understanding, the latter having been educated, if we may use the term, by perception, memory, and reflection. Common observation shews us that many kinds of animals cannot long exist in a country where those conditions are not permitted to them; and as the most constant and most powerful interference with animal habits is the animosity of man, his existence in a civilized state is incompatible with their existence; and thus the animals who cannot or will not give up themselves to his service, and submit themselves to be the slaves of his interest, must soon become extinct. But, to fulfil the former condition to any great extent, docility and teachableness are essential requisites; and these combined with some power of reasoning must be the results of long training, and shew that these creatures have laid down some of their passions—have lost especially their

terror of man, as their master, and submit themselves to his will.   When these requisites have
been secured, the further progress of the work
of domestication will depend on the skill with
which their instincts are developed ; and this consists in the exercise of propensities which, in truth,
have existed in them from the beginning, but
have not been till now worked upon, and brought
into effective operation.   Domestication is a consummation of the art of taming a wild animal,
and in its nature amounts to this: that by kind
and appropriate treatment the creature is persuaded to submit itself to such conditions, that,
when external circumstances, unknown to it in
its wild state, are presented to its notice, its
instincts, manifest or occult, readily assume the
new direction, which soon becomes no longer
strange, but natural.

There are numerous examples to shew that the
operation of these new influences and habits have
a reflex action ; and that as the primary impulses
are excited and directed by the structure, as well
of the individual organs as of the brain and
nerves or sentient system, so, in return, the force
of the newly-acquired train of feeling, thought,
and action exerts a strongly-modifying impulse on
the organs and systems through which the operation has been conveyed.   Some individuals and
races are more easily subjected to this permanency of modified habit than others ; and the
more so in proportion to the range within which
these habits are made to revolve : but the remark

is of general application,—that the races of domesticated animals are now born with this modified constitution of structure and habit ; and that
it requires less attention to keep up this condition, and make it permanent, than was necessary
in their free condition, when the education of the
wild races began, and their organization had not
been assimilated to its action.

But, as the continued presence of the general
conditions of the domesticated state is necessary
to render it natural, and permanent, in such
creatures as have been brought under its influence, it will not be surprising if instances occur,
in which the old Nature re-asserts her powers,
and the propensities of the untamed condition
become too strong for voluntary restraint. Such
things are no more unaccountable than the re-ap-
pearance of likeness to some ancestor of a family
in an individual member of it, where all beside
have a different cast of features ; or where a
child manifests a complexion or a mental habit
differing from a large family of brothers and sis-
ters, but resembling that of some remote relation—
a case of no uncommon occurrence. In our own
country the most familiar examples of this return
to a wild condition are to be found in the Cat
and Dog : in the former, this being the result of its
wandering, rather by accident than design, from
the house to the wood, to prey on birds, at all
times a favourite morsel, and, in the nesting season,
to be taken in every bush. To be useful in a

house, Puss must be kept on a low diet, which will intensify and make keen her appetite for

Rats and mice, and such small deer.

Hard experience has taught her not to covet the vocal delicacy which she sees suspended high up out of her reach in a cage ; but in the seclusion of a wood, she can pick her bird and prey with impunity, and if not disturbed, and hunted down, in a generation or two the land would be overrun with these predatory creatures, which at one time must have been very destructive.

But this relapsing to the wild condition from the lessons and habits of domestication, though less common, is more formidable, in the Dog ; and there are circumstances in its case which lead us to consider it with closer attention, as it is a greater departure from the trustworthy habits of the animal, its indulgence is attended with more subtilty and caution, and it exercises its propensity upon the most valuable portion of man's property. Perhaps too, as in most instances of the outbreaking of contradictions to accustomed good habits, the mental struggle against temptation has ended in a victory of the appetite ; and thus it indicates a degree of madness never effectually to be removed.

" A Dog," observes the Author of " The Origin and Prospects of Man," a book extravagant enough in many respects, but correct in this remark, " who, when taking possession of a piece of meat, has experienced a pleasant taste, will, when he again sees a piece of meat, connect, with the idea of taking possession of that meat, the image of a pleasant taste, expect such a taste, and be tempted to take the meat. When, after taking it he has been whipped, he will, with the idea of the prior pleasure resulting from the act, connect the idea of a later pain, following that pleasure, and with the idea of a future pleasure resulting from the future similar act also connect the idea of a future similar pain. If the idea of the pain preponderates over that of the pleasure, he will resist the temptation, and leave the meat untouched. Thus arise, from sensations and recollections of prior actions, beliefs, expectations, from these consequent impulses to produce or to avoid such actions in future."

This influence acts more powerfully on brutes, as they want what we are blest with—moral sense; but as instinct is to their animal nature what conscience is to our moral nature—a restraint, preventing them from what is injurious to their well-being, it follows that when this force of self-restraint is violated, the whole of the natural influences run wild, and even opposition to their depraved habits is a stimulus to their exertion. But, however the revived ferocious propensity is exercised, it is with many of the accompaniments characterizing the creature in its wild condition among its congeners. When instigated by a craving for blood, the Dog rarely hunts its prey near home : it seems to know that it can

indulge it more safely at a distance, where it is
unknown. A Dog in my own neighbourhood, with
this propensity, would pass by its own master's
flock, of which it was the guardian, and go a
mile or two away, to gratify its craving by slaugh-
tering a lamb in the field of a stranger. When
successful, it has dragged its victim over many
obstructions to the very neighbourhood of its own
home, where it might have helped itself with what
to ordinary cunning might seem security. The
sense of shame shewn by a Dog on the discovery
of its evil doings is as strong as its expression of
pleasure on winning a word of encouragement ;
and the reproachful looks and words by which its
disgrace is expressed humble him so much, that
he cannot lift up his head, and look his monitor in
the face.

Nor is it only among ferocious animals, and
where sensual appetites are the moving cause,
that a return to the wild habits of Nature is
observed. The common Pigeon (*Columba livia*)
quits its comfortable dove-cot, where all its wants
are supplied, and where it is as little under restraint as if it had no master, and at risks, to
which it is not long insensible, takes refuge in
nooks of rock on the sea-coast, and endures all
the penalties of the wild condition, in the necessity of perpetual vigilance, and laborious exertions
of flight, which alone can save it from a host of
enemies, and this for no other object than to have
its own wild will, and be at liberty.

Where these natural propensities, whether casual or permanent, are less brought down to the tamed condition, and they are revived by the excitement of a new feeling, it is not uncommon for the creatures so changed to fall into a morbid habit, which, however monstrous, is only a vitiation of strong natural passion. Under this impulse the Cat will devour her own offspring; the domesticated Rabbit its little ones if they are at all interfered with; the newly-taken Hedgehog will kill and eat her young; and the little Canary her own eggs. In a state of captivity, when perhaps wanting its natural sustenance, the Brazilian Coata (*Ursus lotor*) will gnaw and devour its own tail—the last substitute to which we should think it would have recourse.

There may be particular periods in the lives of animals when these propensities are most liable to revive. The impulse to a departure from domestic habits, as in the case of the Pigeons, may be most powerful at the time of nesting, when a longing for quiet is especially felt; and as those who have once shunned the haunts of man are not likely to return to them, the young have the further motive of local attachment, to lead them to continue in their rocky homes. Most of the wild Rock Pigeons in England are probably descendants of families who have thrown off the domestic state. This return to perfect freedom will also recur at the season of moulting, when a great revolution takes place in the feelings and habits of most birds. It is then that birds who have been instructed in artificial melody forget their acquirements; and a movement towards the wild condition is sometimes seen in Geese, which, on the recovery of their wing-feathers, forsake the farm-yard in a body, and fly off to the sea-side.

That the disuse of a habit, or of the ordinary function of an organ, will induce failure in the structure of that organ or in the course of that habit, which will become a permanent alteration, is confirmed by Dr. Prichard (Natural History of Man, p. 35) from certain facts communicated by Mr. Ronlin, referring to the Cows of Columbia. In Europe, we know that the udders and teats of Cows grow to a great size, and that the milk is given from them without difficulty: but in that country, though the race was originally European, the practice of milking the Cows having been omitted through several generations, the udders and teats have decreased in size; and now that they have returned to the old habit, they find it hard to recover the advantage they have lost: the flow of milk continues only in the presence of the Calf; and if the Calf dies, the milk ceases altogether.

The wild Oxen and Horses which now range in freedom over the uncultivated plains of South America are descendants of the races of Europe, removed to those new regions at no more re-mote date than the time of the subjugation of the country by the Spaniards; have all the wildness and instincts of the earliest untamed animals; and even their colour has partaken in the change. It is not a little surprising to discover that, in an earlier condition of that continent, the Horse was a native of it : for its bones are now found fossilized, in company with those of other creatures which have ceased to exist. The influences, whatever they were, which operated to the extinction of the race, must have been as transitory as they were universal and powerful, and do not affect the imported animals : for they find the climate and circumstances highly congenial to their nature.

No portion of the human race is more completely in a condition of unreclaimed nature than the natives of Australia ; and the length of time which this wildness has endured has been sufficient to impress their organization so forcibly as to render it hereditary. Archbishop Polding, in his evidence before a select committee of the legislative council of the colony of New South Wales (1845) remarks, that "acuteness of the senses in discovering and obtaining food is propagated in the offspring : so that the latter, independent of instruction, are found to possess these qualifications in a far higher degree than the colonists. A love of wandering and change is also impressed on their character, which makes any continued labour irksome to these tribes, who are always in motion without cause : in this respect resembling the Gypsies of our own country, who are ever moving from one district to another, not by a gradual progress, but by sudden starts from a distance ; and in them also the disposition is not to be eradicated by education."

The natives of Australia are not influenced by

savage ferocity, or subject to any furious passions: for though they devour their children when they die of illness, they are warmly attached to them while they are alive; and according to the evidence of Mr. McArthur, in disposition they are rather a mild and merry race: a character which, though usually averse from restraint, is ready to be satisfied with the security and abundance supplied by civilization. They also possess some of the higher principles of understanding: such as a strong sense of justice; which is really the prevailing impression where, at the first view, their conduct appears to be the contrary. They are accused of proneness to shed blood, and to steal the sheep of the colonists; but in *their* estimation, the settlers have invaded their lands, and, by exterminating the Kangaroo and Opossum, have rendered themselves public enemies. If the settler hunts their Kangaroo, they cannot believe it wrong to do the same by his Sheep; and the question of ownership between a wild and domesticated animal is too refined for a savage comprehension. Many of the infant children of this race have been adopted by the people of the colony, and brought up in the lessons and practices of civilized life, with sedulous attention to their mental and religious instruction; and that deficiency of mental capacity is not the hindrance to their profiting by these advantages is proved in the fact, that these children learn their school-lessons with rapidity, and in many cases outstrip their competitors of the European race. Yet, in spite of these influences, it has been found that, at the critical period of life when youth starts into the adult condition, the instinctive forces have re-asserted their powers; and these pupils of civilization, who have hitherto suffered their nature to be moulded into new forms, have suddenly thrown off all restraint, and rushed into the Bush, to join their naked countrymen in the pursuit of a precarious subsistence, exposed to all the inconveniences of hardship and want. Many reasons are assigned for this reviving of a natural propensity : among the most plausible of which is, their strong sexual impulses, and the difficulty they find in obtaining a suitable alliance anywhere but among the savage tribes.

But this can have but a limited influence : for the endeavours to reclaim this people have not been confined to one sex; and consequently fit companions might have been more readily found in the city than the wild. If, through motives of attachment, an individual is led to quit familiar habits, the passage would seem more easy from the wildness of destitution to quiet and abundance, than the reverse. Educated females also of this race show as strongly the wandering disposition; and the change is effected with the less difficulty, because, as is asserted by an observer, they are entirely wanting in the feeling of gratitude : a virtue which, even in civilized communities, is less lasting than any other.

Another reason assigned as a hindrance to the permanency of this people in civilization is, that they cannot be made to discern the present or prospective benefits of the superior knowledge of the higher races of men, as many animals are wise

enough to do, and the power which their owners
have to afford them protection and supply their
wants. The natives of Australia think themselves
superior to the whites: which perhaps proceeds from
the obvious inferiority of the latter in some qualifications highly valued among themselves; and hence
they are reluctant to learn anything from them, or
to suffer their children to do so. And that pride has
also a share in this feeling may be inferred from the
fact, that they shew equal repugnance to mix with
the natives of a remote district of their own land.
But this must be of still less force than the former
motive in inducing them to plunge again into savage
habits: for the children thus removed from their
parents must have been taught to discern and feel
what their parents will not learn—the comforts of
their new situation; and the modes of thinking of
their tribe must have become altogether strange to
them. It is the innate disposition only, then, which
in the great change of their animal constitution can
so powerfully influence them, and compel them to
throw off all the restraints learned in the long course
of instruction, so as to have become their second
nature.

No animal is capable of enduring so much change,
and of manifesting still such variety of instinct, as
the Dog; and it is this which has made it the
most completely domesticated of creatures. But
place it once more where the attaching influences
of domestication are at an end, and its old good
habits are exchanged for new and bad ones, which
show the civilized condition to have operated on

such parts of its character as we should have thought little likely to be affected. Even the barking of a Dog is a language learned in domestication. A really wild Dog does not bark, but howl; and in countries where the Dog returns to a savage condition, he forgets to bark, and learns again to howl. It is remarkable too, and will perhaps explain why barking should ever have become the natural language of a Dog, that the wild sounds of some of the kindred species, as the Wolf, Fox, and Jackal, resemble the Dog's in its domesticated state.

The object of man in taming animals is his own advantage, with no more regard to benefiting these creatures than is consistent with his own selfish ends; and the result is to deprive them of some of their best and most characteristic qualities. Their natural skill, strength, vigilance, and swiftness are by turns counteracted or fostered, or made unnecessary, by the care he takes to anticipate their wants, and supersede their own exertions in those employments in which creatures in their wild condition attain the highest excellency. Domestication, therefore, is a state of luxury, in which animals, so far as their original nature is concerned, exchange the perfection of their existence for a provision of the comforts of sensual ease and safety. But we cannot truly compare this constrained condition, even in its perfection, with that which seems to corre-spond with it—the civilization and domestication of the human race—as some philosophers have done, injuriously comparing it with what is called

p 3

the natural, but which is more properly the savage, condition of our kind.

It is as contrary to reason as to revelation, to believe that man was created in anything short of a highly-civilized condition. If created an infant, he must have perished for want of extraneous help; and if we may suppose the frame of his body perfect in all its parts when he awoke from the hands of his Maker, we must suppose his mental powers and accomplishments as perfect also. The condition of the savage, as he is seen in our days, is a retrogression, but not to the starting-point of his existence : we may see this in many remains of customs and feelings of a higher and purer state both of simple piety and polity, still lingering among the wild races of men. And many of their unintelligible practices may be explained by referring them to a former condition of civilization.

The great distinction between the civilization of men and the taming and domestication of animals lies in this—that the refinements of men are not the work of compulsion, and the teaching and training of others, as of mothers their infants, but are the work of his own will—the voluntary efforts of his own energies; and will be retained, and the ground he has won will be maintained, no longer than he continues to put forth the same or more active powers of body and mind with which he commenced the conflict.

The necessities of man are the originators of his inventions; and his inventive genius will be kept at work as long as there is a craving void

or want to be supplied. Nor does this remark
apply to his mere sensual wants only, but to
those higher objects yet to be attained, in the
unexhausted worlds of science and imagination,
and the nobler acquirements of the invisible world.
The refinements of civilized men would indeed be
a misfortune, if it assimilated them to the domesticated animal, so well satisfied with the comforts he receives at the hands of others as to
look for no more, and no better ; and if it rendered them unwilling to risk these for the attain-
ment of a greater good. When the desire to add
to his advantages is not thought worth the pain
it would cost him and the risk of the attempt, it
would be no hardship to him that a greater power
stood between him and his desires, saying, " Thus
far shalt thou go, and no farther ;" and the end
would be that the governor and the governed would
sink together.

CHAPTER XXII.

In the earliest stages of Science the importance of Anatomy to the successful practice of Medicine and Surgery must have been evident; but it was not till the laws of Physiology had become a severe study, that a knowledge of the structure and development of the lower animals was found to be essential to a right understanding of their economy. The importance of this inquiry was first appreciated in our times by the illustrious John Hunter, a man so much in advance of the attainments of the age in which he lived, that his advocacy of this study subjected him to the sneers of men whose names are now remembered only as bywords of reproach and shame.

Carrying into practice the principles he enounced, he was the chief light by which the Science of Nature has been illustrated in this country; and if that more profound portion of it, Psychology, or the Science of Intellect, has advanced less, and is still less understood than the laws of simple Animation, the neglect lies with those students who have shown an unworthy reluctance to employ

Comparative Metaphysics, in union with Physiology, in their researches. The day is gone by when the students of Mind should waste their time in abstract disquisitions and reasonings *à priori* on the Nature of Spirit, and in laying down its law of derivation, subsistence, or action: for it is undeniable that such profound inquiries have ended in very shallow and unsatisfactory results; and that Physical Science has advanced only in proportion as it has shaken off the encumbering trammels of such an absurd system of study. That confidence which the search for truth ought ever to inspire should make the seekers after it bold in following such guides as Hunter and Cuvier, and men of kindred minds, and superior to the fear of degrading the human mind, of which they may be accused, in seeking an explanation of its phænomena in the mental propensities and capacities of inferior creatures.

In the youth of his existence, Man can only acquire his first ideas of the world about him through his sensations; and, as we have already shown, it is probable that the physiological manner in which these impressions are received and conveyed by the organs of sense is the fundamental cause of the specific Identity of Man, as a Genus and an Individual; and will account for the vast variety of human character in all the varying nations of the world, and in every stage of man's existence. This will include the multiplicity of inclinations and talents with which Man is endowed: from mere simple human com-

prehension of the plainest and poorest things that
lie about his feet in his every-day path, to the
high-reaching thoughts and loftiest contemplations
of things above him, things past, and things to
come,

> Till old Experience do attain
> To something like prophetic strain.

Indeed, learned Jews were of opinion, that there
was a peculiarity of nature—a congeniality, a
fitness, a necessary preparation, as well as a higher
moral excellence—essential to the man made for
prophetic communications.

It is this original impression of character which,
while it leaves the race a single species standing
apart in the scale of Nature, is the reason why
Man should also form a Genus of himself; and
it was the pressure of this great truth on his
mind which led Linnæus to depart, for once, from
his usual method of defining a creature by the
distinctive marks of its external organization, and
to dwell rather upon the nobler gifts and attributes still to be discerned in man, however inferior
to his brother man, however remote in situation,
degraded in habits, or despised for his colour.
It is internal consciousness that marks the genus
of Mankind. Making this the grand distinction
in our classification, we may arrange all humankind in species, making the entire race a multiplied assemblage of distinctions equivalent to the
various ranks in the lower animals scattered over
the world; and every human congeries may be
as well defined by its mental qualities, which are

variations of the common type, as other creatures are by variations in their organic development. It will not, then, be by texture or colour of skin, by the formation or mal-formation of the head, but by his capacities, and the direction which they take for good or for evil, that the species of Men will be characterized.

Examples have already been given to show, what indeed is obvious to daily observation, that the instincts, feelings, thoughts, and aspirations of men and animals vary according to the conditions of youth and age, and to other constantly occurring and recurring influences; and as the events of life necessarily increase our knowledge, and make up what is commonly called our experience, the usual mode of accounting for the changes to which all habits are liable is by referring them to these influences. This may be correct in part, but it is not universally so; and even where its operation is unquestionable, there is still another principle at work, to which experience itself is indebted for the wisdom it attains. This is the intimate dependance of the bias or impulse of the mind, and its capacity for intricate inquiry and clear conclusion, upon the condition, and especially upon the firmness, of the mental organ.

Intenseness of study disorders the functions of the brain, and injures the general health. Great abstraction of thought will bring on catalepsy, or a temporary suspension of the whole thinking power, and will impair the brain for life. To some men, not otherwise deficient in mental grasp, certain subjects also are dangerous ground. I have known a student who could not read Butler's Analogy of Religion without suffering such a disturbance of the functions of the brain as warned him to desist in time. In early life, the brain is too lax in its structure and limited in its powers of action, to permit safely the study of some of the profounder parts of knowledge, which the injudicious anxiety of parents often forces upon young minds; or indeed long-continued study of any sort. Rash is the attempt in early life to enter on the study of Algebra or Geometry, or whatever else demands sedulous exercise of the powers of reasoning, in preference to the lighter labours of memory. The accumulation of facts; the learning of languages; and the investigations of natural history, are safer subjects for youthful study, which build up the mental powers, and do not break them down. The obscurity in after-life of many of the young men who have won the highest honours in our Universities too plainly shews us that their labour was beyond their strength, and could not be sustained; and as such unnatural efforts are sure to be followed by exhaustion and inaction, this strong endeavour after eminency defeats itself: for it is by steadily-sustained labour only, and not by violent efforts, that great results will be secured. Even the best-prepared minds can pursue the favourite study only at certain seasons: the inspiration must be waited for in its visitation till it comes, and the organs must be disposed to action, or the exercise will be as useless as it is irksome.

It is not uncommon to meet with individuals

possessed of the sounder faculties of adult or advanced age while young in years, of which Augustus Cæsar and William Pitt are illustrious examples; and such men cannot fail to stand high above the men of their age. We also meet with men who show the feelings and habits of boyhood at an advanced age. An arrest in the development of some faculties, while others have advanced to maturity, is also of ordinary occurrence; and imbecility is one of the results of these suspended developments. The following case of this kind possesses characters of very uncommon occurrence.

The child is seven years of age, but has all the appearance of a child of from two to three years old. Take it as at that time of life, and its stature is stout, its look natural, though rather dull, its lips pouting, and its temper sullen, but not greatly so. The teeth were developed pretty early; but she did not learn to walk till three years old: from which time no further developments, bodily or mental, were apparent; but the whole were arrested entirely, and at once. The forehead is low, and the elevation rounded as in infancy; the integument in the middle of the forehead resembling a pad: the fontanel is widely open; and the occiput remarkably protuberant. The utterance of words is slow, but intelligent, like a child three years old; and she plays in the same manner, with the same toys, and prefers to associate with playmates of this age, rather than with children of her own. For four years she has made no advance in intelligence or knowledge of any kind; nor in stature, nor in the development of any bodily organs: so that an observer would suppose her to be a healthy child, of three years old, and no more.

A Jewish Rabbi of the fifteenth century, in his " Book of Principles," gives the fortieth year of the age of Man as the highest point and apex of his capacity for wisdom; after which period his progress in knowledge and his decline are associated with the healthy or unhealthy condition of his material organization. It is melancholy to mark the gradual disappearance of the energies, and lastly of the existence, of the mental powers, till they end

In second childishness, and mere oblivion;

and Man becomes as merely vegetative as when he first began to be. Yet even in old men we sometimes see their decline so slow, that, when they are fast advancing to the age of fourscore and ten, little loss of strength has perceptibly taken place in their powers of thought; so that the delay of decline in these old men is equivalent to the arrest of development in children of early years. As want of memory for present things is a remarkable defect in the later condition of a long life, the latest manifestation is distinguished by a dreaming, delirious connexion of the senses with the events and persons of its early stage; and it is consoling to an observer to believe that gratification thus becomes the inward state of that condition which to a hasty observer seems one of humiliation.

But there is another irregular condition in the
law of organic development which bears no more
than a remote analogy to the former, the consideration of which, as it is of common occurrence
in animals, will give us a clearer insight into many
of their faculties. A deficiency in the multiplicity
or energy of influential parts is sometimes accompanied by an increase in the number or violence
of others; and a like effect of additional development sometimes follows upon the mere tendency to
increase of action, as though the redundancy was
excited by superabundance of the general action.
It was therefore remarked by the Jewish writer
whom we have just quoted, that the most violent
and insane occasional propensities, passions, and
vices of the human race are the natural dispositions of some one or other of the animal creation.
We must bear in mind however that the latter
word, as implying moral guilt, is not strictly applicable to them, but simply designates a condition
in which the sensual energies natural to them are
suffered to act without restraint: a state which
in Man would be criminal, because it would be
attended with that which does not exist in brutes
—consciousness, and the knowledge that he is
doing evil. Their instinct is no more than a
spontaneous power of guarding against injury to
their present well-being, and of grasping what is
advantageous, independent of the necessity of
balancing probabilities. What in Man, then, would
be a vice, as repugnant to his inward consciousness and rectitude, to the outward commands

of his Maker, and to the authority of the laws natural and moral made for his guidance, in an animal may be, and often is, the impulse which leads it to safety and enjoyment, with no drawback, foreboding future ill consequences.

It may help us to an understanding of that obscure and disputed subject—the primary intention of the creation of animals—to suppose that they were made to manifest certain conditions of *being*, which should be strictly temporal, without aspirations after or capacity for intellectual improvement, and the dread of future evil. It is a condition plainly unprepared to enter into and enjoy a higher state ; and by this want of moral responsibility animals are saved from falling lower than they are. The limit to the degradation of the brute is the line strongly drawn by Nature, beyond which it cannot pass—that a violation of instinct will be productive of pain, from which its nature turns away. The degradation of a brute can never be so low as moral guilt and baseness can reduce the pride of Man ; and this the degraded man too surely feels is the additional bitterness in the cup which *he* must drain whom sensuality has degraded.

It is only by a study of the psychological nature of Animals, as shown in their actions, and by comparing them with those of Man, that the distinction between the simple condition of political justice and the higher moral condition can be drawn ; and this may be taken as one instance out of many of the intrinsic nature of many brutal excellencies, as distinguished from that highest excellency in Man which is called virtue.

It is in correspondence with these principles of a partial development of the higher prerogatives of mental excellency, that we discern in animal actions methods of proceeding which it is hard not to regard as of a moral or intellectual character, but which, on investigation, seem to be merely politic. We witness among Birds the execution of justice on such culprits as offend against the principles and regulations of their community. The Rook offers a familiar example of this in refusing to build its nest in privacy, or anywhere but in the neighbourhood of some dignified mansion; and as the nests of this bird require repair in spring, it often happens that the new materials are not to be obtained near at hand, and they are compelled to search for twigs at a distance, or else to break them off nearer home while in a growing condition, which is a work of much labour. To the younger members of the community, not learned in the laws of *meum* and *tuum*, this is an irksome task; and they are not long in coming to the conclusion that much trouble may be saved by watching their opportunity, and helping themselves from the growing structures of older builders around them in their absence, little imagining, we dare say, that their proprietors will detect the loss of here one and there another of the twigs inserted in the walls of their edifices. The discovering that they have been robbed is, indeed, no small proof of observation and reasoning: for the actual carrying off of their goods is never or but rarely seen by the owners, as the rogues take care not to be caught in the fact; and we know that an egg may be taken away, and the parent bird be none the wiser. Birds are more alive to the least change in the external look of the nest than to the eggs within. But the rascals among Rooks have little calculated on the power of observation of their older neighbours, and how well they, from experience, can compare the work done, and compute the time it ought to have taken if they had worked honestly, and found their own materials. The wrong-doers being discovered, the punishment is appropriate to the offence: by the destruction of their dishonest work they are taught that they who build must find their own bricks or sticks, not their neighbours'; and that if they wish to live in the enjoyment of the advantages of the social condition, they must endeavour to conform their actions to the principles of the Rookery of which they have been made members.

It is not known what enormities led to the institution of another tribunal of the same kind called the Crow Court; but, according to Dr. Edmonson, in his View of the Shetland Islands, its proceedings are as authoritative and regular; and it is remarkable as occurring in a species (*Corvus cornix*) so near akin to the Rook. The Crow Court is a sort of general assembly of birds who, in their usual habits, are accustomed to live in pairs, scattered at great distances from each other; and when they visit the South or West of England, as they do in severe winters, they are commonly solitary. In their summer haunts in the Shetland Islands, numbers meet together from different points, on a particular hill or field; and on these occasions the assembly is not complete, and does not begin its business, for a day or two, till, all the deputies having arrived, a general clamour and croaking ensue, and the whole of the court—judges, barristers, ushers, audience and all, fall upon the two or three prisoners at the bar, and beat them till they kill them. When this is accomplished, the court breaks up, and quietly disperses.

While we are recording these transactions we will make mention of another which falls, indeed, far below them in gravity, as the bird is of a less dignified demeanour, but it seems to resemble the higher tribunals in its nature. There are few dwellers in the country, or in the more secluded parts of the town, who have not seen and heard the sudden and noisy persecution with which a company of Sparrows will visit some unfortunate individual of their race who has fallen under their displeasure. It begins without preparation, and is of short continuance; but it is unanimous, and is carried on with a clamour which seems to express the most violent vituperation of the Sparrow who has committed himself. When he has been thus severely reprimanded, however, he seems to be as well received by the community as before.

A great number of cases, having a similar impress of the exercise of a sense of justice, might be adduced

from long observation of many kinds of animals, which
would forcibly illustrate the views which some philosophers have taken of the nature of morals, according
to whom the virtue or righteousness of an action in the
individual consists almost wholly in its utility to the
community of which he forms a part, as distinguished
from that which in motive and purity is moral and
universal.   This simply utilitarian virtue in some animals, in other races, and still more in the human
race, would become the worst of vice, of badness,
and madness ; and destroy the only true distinction
between what is most to be commended as good, and
what is most to be detested as vile.

INDEX.

Q

Q 2

A SELECT CATALOGUE

OF

WORKS ON NATURAL HISTORY, ETC.

PUBLISHED BY

JOHN VAN VOORST, 1, PATERNOSTER ROW.

THE NATURAL HISTORY OF GREAT BRITAIN. *This Series of Works is illustrated by many hundred Engravings ; every species has been Drawn and Engraved under the immediate inspection of the Authors ; the best artists have been employed, and no care or expense has been spared.*

A HISTORY OF BRITISH QUADRUPEDS, INCLUDING THE CETACEA. By THOMAS BELL, F.R.S. F.L.S. Professor of Zoology in King's College, London. This Volume is illustrated by nearly Two Hundred Engravings, comprising Portraits of the animals and Vignette Tailpieces. 8vo. Price 28s.

" Mr. Bell's very beautiful book ought to be in the library of every English gentleman who is interested in the natural history of his country. The wood-cuts are beautiful, and the name of the writer is a guarantee for the excellence of the descriptions," &c.—*British Magazine.*

THE BIRDS BY MR. YARRELL. Second Edition, 3 vols. 8vo. 4*l.* 14*s.* 6*d.*

COLOURED ILLUSTRATIONS OF THE EGGS OF BIRDS BY MR. HEWITSON. 2 vols. 4*l.* 10*s.*

THE REPTILES BY PROFESSOR BELL. 8*s.* 6*d.*

THE FISHES BY MR. YARRELL. Second Edition, 2 vols. 3*l.*

THE CRUSTACEA BY PROFESSOR BELL. Now in course of Publication, in Parts at 2*s.* 6*d.*

THE STARFISHES BY PROFESSOR EDWARD FORBES. 15*s.*

THE ZOOPHYTES BY DR. JOHNSTON. Second Edition, 2 vols. 2*l.* 2*s.*

THE FOREST-TREES BY MR. SELBY. 28*s.*

THE FERNS AND ALLIED PLANTS BY MR. NEWMAN. 25*s.*

THE FOSSIL MAMMALS AND BIRDS BY PROFESSOR OWEN. 1*l.* 11*s.* 6*d.*

A few copies of each have been printed on large paper.

THE ANCIENT WORLD; or, Picturesque Sketches of Creation. By D. T. ANSTED, M.A., F.R.S., F.G.S., Professor of Geology in King's College, London, &c. &c. Post 8vo., with 149 Illustrations, price 12s.

"This is a very instructive and interesting book."—*Examiner*, June 19.

THE BIRDS OF JAMAICA. By P. H. GOSSE, Author of the " Canadian Naturalist," &c. Post 8vo., price 10s.

"The result is a very attractive and original volume, valuable to the naturalist for its information, and acceptable to the general reader for its life-like descriptions of the habits of the birds and the landscapes in which they are found, as well as for incidental glimpses of colonial manners and character."— *Spectator*, May 15.

OBSERVATIONS IN NATURAL HISTORY; with a Calendar of Periodic Phenomena. By the Rev. LEONARD JENYNS, M.A., F.L.S. Post 8vo, 10s. 6d.

" At the same time scientific and popular, the work cannot fail to please even the most careless general reader. Every page teems with interesting notes on the habits and manners of quadrupeds, birds, fishes, insects, &c.; many we would gladly quote, but must content ourselves with advising our readers to purchase the book itself, promising them a rich treat from the perusal."— *Westminster Review*.

FIRST STEPS TO ANATOMY. By JAMES L. DRUMMOND, M.D., Professor of Anatomy and Physiology in the Royal Belfast Institution, Author of " First Steps to Botany," &c. With 12 illustrative plates, 12mo., 5s.

" This is a very able publication ; the work of a master throwing off the results of his own knowledge, not the compilation of a man sitting down to teach that he may learn. The little book will be an acquisition to any one, as containing an account, at once clear, popular, and scientific, of the general principles of vegetable and animal life, as well as the substances by which animal life is set up and sustained."—*Spectator*.

A MANUAL OF BRITISH BOTANY; containing the Flowering Plants and Ferns, arranged according to the Natural Orders. By CHARLES C. BABINGTON, M.A., F.L.S., F.Z.S., &c. Second Edition, 12mo., 10s.

" We have no hesitation in recommending Mr. Babington's ' Manual' as the best guide to the students of practical botany in this country."—*Annals of Natural History*, July.

OUTLINES OF STRUCTURAL AND PHYSIOLOGICAL BO-
TANY. By ARTHUR HENFREY, F.L.S., Lecturer on Botany at
the Middlesex Hospital; late Botanist to the Geological Survey of
the United Kingdom. With 18 Plates, Foolscap 8vo., 10s. 6d.

" It is not a mere compilation, but a careful digest, evidently prepared by
one who is thoroughly conversant with his subject; the topics are admirably
arranged, and the results succinctly and for the most part very clearly stated.
* * * We may unhesitatingly recommend this little treatise to the general, and
especially to the medical student. Compendious as it is, we know of no work
in the English language which gives so much information upon Vegetable
Anatomy in such small compass, or so well exhibits the present state of
knowledge and opinion upon this class of subjects."—PROFESSOR GRAY, in
' Silliman's Journal.'

HERALDRY OF FISH. By THOMAS MOULE. Nearly 600 fami-
lies are noticed in this work, and besides the several descriptions of
fish, fishing-nets, and boats, are included also mermaids, tritons,
and shell-fish. Nearly 70 ancient seals are described, and upwards
of 20 subjects in stained glass. The engravings (205) are from
stained glass, tombs, sculpture, and carving, medals and coins,
rolls of arms, and pedigrees. 8vo. price 21s., a few on large paper
(royal 8vo.) for colouring, price 2l. 2s.

" The heraldic memoranda scattered throughout are singularly attractive.
Mr. Moule is learned in his subject, and draws in an endless variety of illustrative matter from other sciences, and from history and biography."—Atlas.

THE VICAR OF WAKEFIELD. With 32 Illustrations by WM.
MULREADY, R.A.; engraved by JOHN THOMPSON. 1l. 1s. square
8vo., or 36s. in morocco.

" And there are some designs in the volume in which art may justly boast
of having added something to even the exquisite fancy of Goldsmith."—Examiner.

A MANUAL OF GOTHIC ARCHITECTURE. By F. A. PALEY,
M.A. With a full Account of Monumental Brasses and Ecclesiastical Costume. Foolscap 8vo., with 70 Illustrations, 6s. 6d.

" To the student of the architecture of old English churches this beautiful
little volume will prove a most acceptable manual. The two chapters on * * *
form an epitome of the whole subject, so lucid, concise, and complete, that it
may be regarded as a model of succinct and clear exposition. Both in description
and analysis, Mr. Paley is remarkable for neatness and perspicuity; his style is
terse and precise, yet withal easy and elegant. The examples, engraved by
Thurston Thompson, are the perfection of wood engraving, as applied to architecture: exact in detail, picturesque in effect, and cut with equal firmness and
delicacy."—The Spectator.

BAPTISMAL FONTS. A Series of One Hundred and Twenty-five Engravings, examples of the different periods, accompanied with descriptions by THOMAS COMBE, and with an Introductory Essay by F. A. PALEY, M.A. 8vo., price One Guinea.

" These Illustrations make a handsome volume. The volume contains about one hundred and twenty-four specimens of the various transformations which Fonts have undergone from the twelfth to the sixteenth centuries, engraved on wood with a rare combination of architectural precision and picturesque effect. The details of the cuts are sufficiently explicit, and the engravings, though small, may serve as models for practical application by the ecclesastical architect who seeks ancient examples. Mr. Paley has furnished some general and apposite introductory observations."—*Athenæum.*

Works in preparation, now first announced.

AN HISTORICAL GUIDE TO ELY CATHEDRAL. By the REV. D. J. STEWART, M.A. Minor Canon. With numerous Illustrations: being the first of a Series of Cathedral Histories.

A HISTORY OF BRITISH MOLLUSCOUS ANIMALS. By Professor EDWARD FORBES, and SYLVANUS HANLEY, B.A. In monthly parts at 2s. 6d.

An Edition of WATTS'S DIVINE AND MORAL SONGS. With 32 Illustrations by C. W. COPE, A.R.A. Uniform with Mulready's Vicar of Wakefield.

A HISTORY OF THE ISLE OF MAN. By the REV. J. G. CUMMING, M. A. F.G.S. Vice-Principal of King William's College.

London, June, 1848.

BOOKS PUBLISHED BY MR. VAN VOORST.

The Illustrations to the Works enumerated in this Catalogue have been designed or drawn and engraved expressly for the Works they respectively embellish, and they are never used for other Works.

Illustrated Reprints.

WATTS' DIVINE AND MORAL SONGS. With 30 Illustrations by C. W. COPE, A.R.A.; engraved by JOHN THOMPSON. Square 8vo., 7s. 6d. or 21s. in morocco.

Uniform with the above,

THE VICAR OF WAKEFIELD. With 32 Illustrations by WILLIAM MULREADY, R.A.: engraved by JOHN THOMPSON. 1l. 1s. square 8vo, or 36s. in morocco.

Also of Uniform size,

SHAKSPEARE'S SEVEN AGES OF MAN. Illustrated by WILLIAM MULREADY, R.A.; J. CONSTABLE, R.A.; SIR DAVID WILKIE, R.A.; W. COLLINS, R.A.; A. E. CHALON, R.A. ; A. COOPER, R.A.; SIR A. W. CALLCOTT, R.A.; EDWIN LANDSEER, R.A.; W. HILTON, R.A. 6s. A few copies of the First Edition in 4to. remain for sale.

THE FARMER'S BOY AND OTHER RURAL TALES AND POEMS. By ROBERT BLOOMFIELD. With Thirteen Illustrations by SIDNEY COOPER, R.A., HORSLEY, FREDERICK TAYLER, and THOMAS WEBSTER, R.A. A few copies on large paper, of a size to correspond with the above, price 15s. (Small Paper copies, 7s. 6d.)

GRAY'S ELEGY IN A COUNTRY CHURCH-YARD. Each stanza Illustrated with an Engraving, from 33 original drawings by the most eminent Artists. Post 8vo., price 9s. cloth. A Polyglot Edition of this Volume, with inter-paged Translations in the Greek, Latin, German, Italian, and French Languages. Price 12s. And of uniform size.

THE BARD. By GRAY. With Illustrations by the HON. Mrs. JOHN TALBOT. Post 8vo. 7s.

A CABINET EDITION OF THE HOLY BIBLE ; The Authorized Version. With 24 highly-finished Steel Engravings. In embossed binding, 10s. 6d. And uniform,

THE BOOK OF COMMON PRAYER. With 10 Engravings. In embossed binding, 4s.

A CABINET EDITION OF THE ECONOMY OF HUMAN LIFE. In Twelve Books. By R. DODSLEY. With 12 Plates engraved on steel, from original designs, 18mo. 5s.

AIKIN'S CALENDAR OF NATURE ; or, Natural History of each Month of the Year. With additions, by a Fellow of the Linnæan and Zoological Societies, and 18 designs by Cattermole. Small 8vo., 2s. 6d.

Architecture.

ARCHITECTURAL PARALLELS; or, The Progress of Ecclesiastical Architecture in England, through the Twelfth and Thirteenth Centuries, exhibited in a Series of Parallel Examples selected from Abbey Churches. By EDMUND SHARPE, M.A. 121 Plates in tinted outline, each 18 in. by 12 in., half mor. 13l. 13s., or large paper, 16l. 10s.

INSTRUMENTA ECCLESIASTICA: a Series of Seventy-two designs for the Furniture, Fittings, and Decorations of Churches and their Precincts. Edited by the Ecclesiological, late Cambridge Camden Society. 4to. 1l. 11s. 6d.

A MANUAL OF GOTHIC MOLDINGS. A Practical Treatise on their Formation, Gradual Development, Combinations, and Varieties; with full Directions for copying them, and for determining their Dates. By F. A. PALEY, M.A. Second Edition, Illustrated by nearly 600 Examples. 8vo. 7s. 6d.

Other Works by MR. PALEY.

THE CHURCH RESTORERS; A Tale, Treating of Ancient and Modern Architecture and Church Decorations. With a Frontispiece. Foolscap 8vo. 4s. 6d.

A MANUAL OF GOTHIC ARCHITECTURE. With a full Account of Monumental Brasses and Ecclesiastical Costume. Foolscap 8vo., with 70 Illustrations, 6s. 6d.

BAPTISMAL FONTS. A Series of 125 Engravings, Examples of the different Periods, accompanied with Descriptions; and with an Introductory Essay. In 8vo. 1l. 1s.

DECORATED WINDOWS. By EDMUND SHARPE, M.A., Architect. Each Part, price 2s. 6d., will contain Eight Examples selected from the Parish Churches of England, engraved on Steel, with accompanying Descriptions; the concluding part will be Introductory, and Illustrated by Woodcuts, &c.

PERRAN-ZABULOE; with an Account of the Past and Present State of the Oratory of St. Piran-in-the-Sands, and Remarks on its Antiquity. By the REV. WM. HASLAM, B.A., Resident Curate. Foolscap 8vo., with several Illustrations, 4s. 6d.

HERALDRY OF FISH. By THOMAS MOULE. The Engravings, 205 in number, are from Stained Glass, Tombs, Sculpture, and Carving, Medals and Coins, Rolls of Arms, and Pedigrees. 8vo., price 21s. A few on large paper (royal 8vo.) for colouring, price 2l. 2s.

Natural History.

THE ISLE OF MAN; its History, Physical, Ecclesiastical, Civil, and Legendary. By the REV. J. G. CUMMING, M.A., F.G.S., Vice-Principal of King William's College, Castletown. Post 8vo., with Illustrations, 12s. 6d.

PROFESSOR OWEN ON THE ARCHETYPE AND HOMOLOGIES OF THE VERTEBRATE SKELETON. 8vo. 10s.

A SYSTEMATIC CATALOGUE OF THE EGGS OF BRITISH BIRDS, arranged with a View to supersede the use of Labels for Eggs. By the Rev. S. C. MALAN, M.A., M.A.S. On writing-paper. 8vo. 8s. 6d.

RARE AND REMARKABLE ANIMALS OF SCOTLAND, Represented from Living Subjects: with Practical Observations on their Nature. By SIR JOHN GRAHAM DALYELL, BART. Vol. First, 53 Coloured Plates, 4to., 3l. 3s.

JOHN VAN VOORST, 1, PATERNOSTER ROW.

A FAMILIAR INTRODUCTION TO THE STUDY OF POLARIZED LIGHT; with a Description of, and Instructions for Using, the Table and Hydro-Oxygen Polariscope and Microscope. By CHARLES WOODWARD F.R.S. 8vo., Illustrated, 3s.

ANATOMICAL MANIPULATION; or, The Methods of pursuing Practical Investigations in Comparative Anatomy and Physiology. Also an Introduction to the Use of the Microscope, &c. By ALFRED TULK, M.R.C.S., M.E.S. and ARTHUR HENFREY, F.L.S., M.Mic.S. With Illustrated Diagrams Foolscap 8vo., 9s.

———

THE NATURAL HISTORY OF GREAT BRITAIN. This Series of Works is Illustrated by many Hundred Engravings; every Species has been Drawn and Engraved under the immediate inspection of the Authors; the best Artists have been employed, and no care or expense has been spared. A few copies on larger paper, royal 8vo.

THE QUADRUPEDS, by PROFESSOR BELL. 1l. 8s.

THE BIRDS, By MR. YARRELL. Second Ed., 3 vols. 4l. 14s. 6d.

COLOURED ILLUSTRATIONS OF THE EGGS OF BIRDS, By MR. HEWITSON. 2 vols. 4l. 10s.

THE REPTILES, By PROFESSOR BELL. Second Edition, shortly.

THE FISHES, By MR. YARRELL. Second Edition, 2 vols. 3l.*

THE CRUSTACEA, By PROFESSOR BELL. Now in Course of Publication, in Parts at 2s. 6d.

THE STARFISHES, By PROFESSOR EDWARD FORBES. 15s.

THE ZOOPHYTES, By DR. JOHNSTON. Second Ed., 2 vols., 2l. 2s.

THE MOLLUSCOUS ANIMALS AND THEIR SHELLS, By PROFESSOR ED. FORBES, and MR. HANLEY. Now in Course of Publication, in Parts at 2s. 6d.; or Large Paper, with the Plates Coloured, 5s.

THE FOREST-TREES, By MR. SELBY. 28s.

THE FERNS AND ALLIED PLANTS, By MR. NEWMAN. 25s.

THE FOSSIL MAMMALS AND BIRDS, By PROFESSOR OWEN. 1l. 11s. 6d.

A GENERAL OUTLINE OF THE ANIMAL KINGDOM, By PROFESSOR T. RYMER JONES. 8vo. 1l. 18s.

———

* " This book ought to be largely circulated, not only on account of its scientific merits, b because it is popularly written throughout, and therefore likely to excite general attention to a subject which ought to be held as one of primary importance. Everyone is interested about fishes—the political economist, the epicure, the merchant, the man of science, the angler, the poor, the rich. We hail the appearance of this book as the dawn of a new era the Natural History of England."—*Quarterly Review*, No. 116.

———

JOHN VAN VOORST, 1, PATERNOSTER ROW.

CPSIA information can be obtained
at www.ICGtesting.com
Printed in the USA
BVHW091455210219
540835BV00021B/466/P